Singapore's Dunkirk

By the same author

Alarm Starboard!

Singapore's Dunkirk

GEOFFREY BROOKE

LEO COOPER
LONDON

First published 1989 by Leo Cooper

Leo Cooper is an independent imprint of the
Octopus Publishing Group, Michelin House,
81 Fulham Road, London SW3 6RB

LONDON   MELBOURNE   AUCKLAND

Copyright © Geoffrey Brooke 1989

A CIP catalogue record for this book
is available from the British Library.
ISBN 0-85052-051-7

Typeset by Hewer Text Composition Services, Edinburgh
Printed in Great Britain by
St Edmundsbury Press Ltd, Bury St Edmunds, Suffolk
and bound by Hunter & Foulis Ltd, Edinburgh

To
the late H.S.R. Cunyngham-Brown OBE
and
the late Colonel A.F. Warren CBE, DSC, RM

Contents

Illustrations

Acknowledgements

By the nature of this book I am indebted to many people for giving me permission to quote from their accounts. Sources have tended to fall under three headings: institutions, private contacts and published books.

I am most grateful to the Keeper of the Department of Documents, Imperial War Museum, Mr R.W.A. Suddaby, for effecting the introduction to Mr Leo Cooper in the first instance and for his interest and help, and that of his staff, throughout the research. The following have kindly allowed me to quote from the papers lodged by them or their antecedents at the Museum:
Mr P.G. Cazalet, Mrs M. de Malmanche, Mr R. Dykes, Mr D.P. Eastgate, Mr D. Gavin, Mrs F. Hosking (whose husband, Major F.J. Hosking, recorded a large number of exploits at the time), Mrs E. Innes-Kerr, Mrs S. Lea, Mr J. Lyon, Mr J. Marsh, Mr L. Morris, Mr R.H. Nelson, Mrs R. Ramsay-Rae, Mrs M. Reilly, Mrs X.E. Sharp (whose father, Major W.A. Barnes, also recorded many exploits at the time), Mr R. Trevor, Mrs D.E. Turner, Mrs P. Wallwork.

The Royal Commonwealth Society has kindly permitted quotations from the papers of Lieutenant H.R. Oppenheim and Mr A.P. Ross.

The following provided invaluable information personally, in some cases specially written for this book:
Mr W.B. Bevis, Mr K. Bindoff, Mrs M.R. David, Commander I.D.S. Forbes DSC, Mr R.A. Fryer, the late Mr A.W.F. Grafton, Mr W. Leah, Lieutenant-Commander E. Leather DSM, Mr W.J. Long, Mr D. Macfarlane, Colonel J.L. Nicholson OBE, Mr A.R. North, Major G. Pearse, CPO C.H. Rogers, Mr R. Tall, Mr J. Webb, Mr P. Whitworth.

My thanks are due to the following publishers or copyright holders who have kindly permitted quotations from their books, of more than the statutory number of words verbatim: Angus and Robertson (*White Coolies*), E.J. Burrow (*Singapore to Freedom*), Frances, Lady Smyth (*The Will to Live*), Lennard Publishing (*Quiet Jungle, Angry Sea*) Mr J. Larkins (*A Tribute to Australian Women*), Mrs J. Rivett (*Behind Bamboo*).

I am greatly obliged to the undermentioned for lending or providing the illustrations detailed:

Department of Photography, Imperial War Museum (Sir Shenton Thomas, a Fairmile ML), Mrs M. Allgrove (Australian Nursing Sisters); Commander J.R.H. Bull DSC (*Wu Chang*); Lady Cazalet (HMS *Durban*); the late Mr H.S.R. Cunyngham-Brown (himself); the late Mr A.W.F. Grafton (scenes of Pompong and Indragiri River); Messrs W.H. Allen (SS *Rooseboom* and Doris Lim); Mr B. Howard and the National Library of Australia (Miss V. Bulwinkel's dress); Mr C.V. Holt (HMS *Dragonfly*); Mr M. Passmore (scenes onboard *Sederhana Djohanis*); Mr A. Stewart* (*Kung Wo*); Mr R.D. Penhall (HMS *Li Wo*); Mrs E. Pidsley (Colonel A.F. Warren); Wright and Logan (HMS *Stronghold*).

The late Mr A.W.F. (Bob) Grafton and Mr J.C. Sharp, both of the Far Eastern Prisoners of War Association, were most helpful with contacts and references and lastly, my thanks go to Mrs F. Oddy for her dogged determination in reading my handwriting, to Mrs H. Anstruther for her withering criticism ('Rephrase!'), to Mr John Beatty for his helpful comments and to my wife Molly for her saintly steadiness in the face of dire domestic disruption.

* Prodigious efforts to trace Mr Stewart have not been successful.

Abbreviations

ADC	Aide-de-Camp
AOC	Air Officer Commanding
Bdr	Bombardier
C-in-C	Commander-in-Chief
CPO	Chief Petty Officer
FMSVF	Federated Malay States Volunteer Force
Gnr	Gunner
GOC	General Staff Officer
MRNVR	Malayan Royal Naval Volunteer Reserve
NCO	Non-Commissioned Officer
OR	Other Rank
PO	Petty Officer
RNR	Royal Naval Reserve

Glossary

atap	thatch	prauw	Malay sailing boat
busok	decayed	pulau	island
Emir	chieftain (superior to penghulu)	sampan	small Chinese sailing/rowing boat
juragan	skipper	Selamat jalan	Bon voyage!
keris	dagger	serang	boat owner, boatswain
kampong	village	songkok	Malay velvet hat
kolek	canoe	taikong	skipper (Chinese)
nasi goreng	fried rice with oddments	tongkang	motorised lighter
nonya	Chinese married woman	towkay	headman (Chinese)
pagar	paling (e.g. fishing stakes)	tuan	sir; respectful form of address
parang	chopper	twakow	small junk
penghulu	headman		

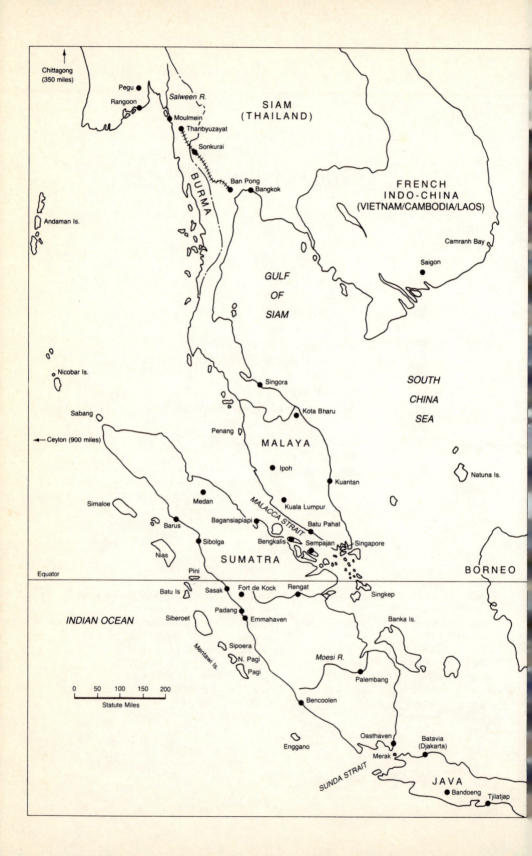

Chittagong
(350 miles)

Pegu ●
Rangoon ●
Salween R.
Moulmein ●
Thanbyuzayat
Sonkurai

SIAM
(THAILAND)

FRENCH
INDO-CHINA
(VIETNAM/CAMBODIA/LAOS)

Ban Pong
Bangkok

Camranh Bay

Saigon ●

Andaman Is.

BURMA

GULF
OF
SIAM

Nicobar Is.

SOUTH

CHINA

SEA

Sabang ●

Singora ●

Kota Bharu ●

◄ Ceylon (900 miles)

Penang

MALAYA

Natuna Is.

Ipoh ●

Simaloe

Medan ●

Kuantan ●

Barus ●

Bagansiapiapi ●

Kuala Lumpur ●

Sibolga ●

MALACCA STRAIT

Batu Pahat ●

Nias

Bengkalis

Sempajan ● Singapore

BORNEO

SUMATRA

Equator

Pini

Batu Is

Sasak ● Fort de Kock ● Rengat ●

Singkep

INDIAN OCEAN

Siberoet

Padang ●
Emmahaven

Banka Is.

Sipoera

Mentawi Is.

N. Pagi

Moesi R.

Pagi

Palembang ●

0   50   100   150   200

Statute Miles

Bencoolen ●

Enggano

Oasthaven ●

Batavia
(Djakarta)

Merak ●

SUNDA STRAIT

JAVA

Bandoeng ●

Tjilatjap

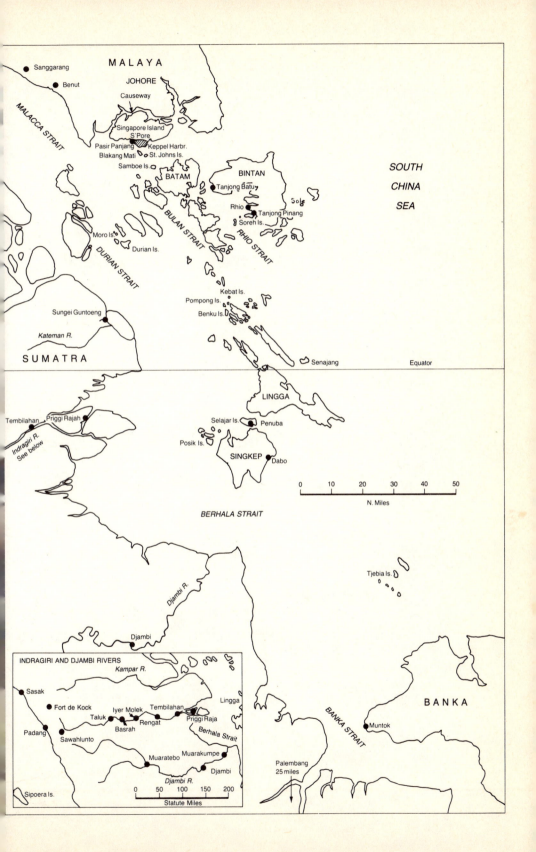

MALAYA

JOHORE

Sanggarang

Benut

Causeway

MALACCA STRAIT

Singapore Island
S'Pore
Pasir Panjang   Keppel Harbr.
Blakang Mati   St. Johns Is.
Samboe Is.

BATAM

BINTAN

Tanjong Batu

Rhio

Tanjong Pinang

Soreh Is.

SOUTH

CHINA

SEA

BULAN STRAIT

RHIO STRAIT

Moro Is.

DURIAN STRAIT

Durian Is.

Kebat Is.

Pompong Is.

Benku Is.

Sungei Guntoeng

Kateman R.

SUMATRA

Senajang

Equator

LINGGA

Tembilahan   Priggi Rajah

Indragiri R.
See below

Selajar Is.

Penuba

Posik Is.

SINGKEP

Dabo

0   10   20   30   40   50

N. Miles

BERHALA STRAIT

Tjebia Is.

Djambi R.

Djambi

BANKA

BANKA STRAIT

Muntok

Palembang
25 miles

INDRAGIRI AND DJAMBI RIVERS

Kampar R.

Sasak

Fort de Kock

Iyer Molek   Tembilahan

Taluk   Lingga

Basrah   Rengat   Priggi Raja

Padang   Berhala Strait

Sawahlunto

Muaratebo   Muarakumpe

Djambi

Djambi R.

Sipoera Is.

0   50   100   150   200

Statute Miles

Introduction

Dunkirk was a picnic compared to the eleventh hour evacuation of Singapore. The numbers were much greater at Dunkirk but there we had command of the sea, sporadic command of the air, the enemy did not press as hard as he might have, the evacuees were all fighting men and the distance to safety only forty miles.

At Singapore the enemy, almost within the gates, had complete command of the air and sea; though for the first few days succour of a sort was the same distance away, proper armed support was more like 500 miles, soon to double; but worst of all, about a third of the evacuees were civilians, including many women and children.

Much is known about Dunkirk, but many details of Singapore are obscure even now. Singapore is, of course, on the other side of the world but an equally cogent reason is the curtain that came down on information from 15 February, 1942, when it fell. Of forty-four unescorted ships of reasonable size that left, mostly on the 13th, only one or two got through. And over the five-day period from the 12th, of about 5000 souls who were evacuated or escaped – the exact number is unknown – not more than one in four made it, the rest being killed or captured. Most of the survivors got to India, those in the services invariably being retained there to renew their argument with the Jap. Though a few escape stories were published during the war, the majority did not get written until the Far East Prisoners of War (FEPOWs) returned in 1945.

There are a good many such accounts, but some of the best are to be found among the private papers given or bequeathed to institutions such as the Imperial War Museum. It is from these, from published sources, and also from the personal experience of the author, that this book has been compiled. It is by no means an exhaustive record, careful selection having been necessary, in a work of this compass, to avoid it lapsing into a list of details. On the other hand, lengthy extracts, warts and all, from original documents have been included without apology, as so often they have more immediacy than could any rewriting.

For ten days, and in some cases more, there was, in a 400 × 50-mile corridor extending south-east from Singapore, a holocaust of individual tragedies that almost beggars description. However, this account is not solely a catalogue of horrors but also of selflessness and heroism, on the part of doctors and nurses as much as anyone else. Several individuals in particular delayed their progress to safety by helping others until too late and this book is specially dedicated to the late H. S. R. (Sjovald) Cunyngham-Brown OBE (then Lieutenant MRNVR) and the late Colonel A. F. Warren CBE, DSC, Royal Marines, without whose successive actions I would probably not be around today. Also to the late Brigadier F. J. Dillon OBE, MC, the late Commander C. C. Alexander RN, and Colonel J. L. Nicholson OBE, all of whom lost vital time shepherding the rest of us across Sumatra. To be remembered for protracted, delaying ferry operations are Lieutenant-Commander A. H. Terry DSC, RN, Surgeon Commander Stevenson DSC, MRNVR, Captain E. Gordon, Lieutenant H. T. Rigden RNVR and Sergeant-Major J. F. I. MacLaren. Every one of the above was taken prisoner to undergo appalling hardships (to be described by Gordon in *Miracle on the River Kwai*) except for Terry and Stevenson who lost their lives. There are others too, like Reynolds of the *Kohfuku Maru* (who got away successfully) and poor Shaw of the *Tanjong Pinang* (who did not). Someone said there are no medals for defeat but none of the above should have gone unrecognized.

Lieutenant-Colonel Dillon, as he then was, wrote (à propos one of his officers getting away to eventual safety in a rowing boat), 'How invisible are the fine threads of fate!' Throughout the research concerned in what follows the truth of these words was continually borne in on me. Time and again pure chance was the sole factor in success or failure (no more so than in Dillon's eventual capture). The last, doomed exodus was on 'Black Friday' the 13th and for me the Bingo cry 'Unlucky for some!' reflects the whole dramatic, fateful business of Singapore's Dunkirk.

G. A. G. Brooke
Beech House
Balcombe
Sussex

Shadows of Coming Events

'I was working at the hospital, on night duty, and when I came home soon after 6 am Eric was up early, making a cup of tea. He said, "If I don't come home after breakfast you'll know I've been sent somewhere else." We didn't meet again for four years.'

*   *   *

'So on the same day that I had promised the NCOs that there would be nothing of the sort, I was detailed to evacuate!'

*   *   *

'. . . told me to pack a suitcase, take a bedding roll and in a quarter of an hour we were on our way like a lot of families were. . . . Being eighteen I couldn't bear to leave some of my things, so I packed my suitcase full of evening dresses.'

In setting the scene for the evacuation of civilians and key service personnel shortly before the fall of Singapore and for the escapees thereafter, it is necessary to stress the breathtaking speed of the Japanese advance down the Malay Peninsula. It was this speed that spread confusion and forced decisions – not least regarding evacuation – that were either mistaken or just not made where perhaps they should have been.

The main enemy landing was at Singora, over the border in Siam (Thailand) on 8 December, 1941; ten days later they had taken Penang, a quarter of the way to Singapore; Kuala Lumpur, the capital of mainland Malaya and well over half-way, was entered on 12 January; and they were at Johore Bahru, facing across the water to Singapore Island by the end of the month. Singapore fell, after bitter fighting, on Sunday, 15 February, a total progress of about nine miles a day.

Had General Yamashita been held up for the 100 days he anticipated instead of only 70, most if not all the harrowing experiences
related in this book would never have occurred. In the first place,
the débâcle of the Naval code books would probably have been
avoided and there would have been time for fuller consultation,
possibly leading to planned evacuation of *bouches inutiles*. As it
was, both GOC and Governor set their faces against this and
in the circumstances of unexpectedly rapid retreat their attitude
was certainly arguable. From the former's point of view at least,
you cannot allow fighting men to look over their shoulders.

At the same time it must be pointed out that, had a pre-planned
and anticipated evacuation been put into force, the resulting
movements by sea would have been before the full power of the
Japanese air force could have been spared from the support of
their army, and the Japanese Navy would not have been astride
the southern escape route, as it was at the fall of Singapore.

The reasons for our poor showing are many, have been debated
ad nauseam, and are only relevant here because of their direct
bearing on the speed of the enemy's advance. Pitiful weakness
in the air, at sea, and our complete lack of tanks – all beyond
the control of the men on the spot – were the main factors, but
there was a military shortcoming which to my mind does not
seem to have received adequate weight in the discussions on
the campaign. This was faulty infantry tactics. Straightforward
European methods based on the maintenance of a 'front' were
no match for the wily, enterprising Jap, who used the jungle
or rubber as often as not for encircling movements. This is not
the place to go into detail, but only three or four units had
the answer, in particular the 2nd Battalion, the Argyll and
Sutherland Highlanders; developed and practised by them, it
turned out to be exactly what the enemy had devised after
much pre-hostilities study, and was subsequently adopted by
our XIVth Army in Burma with success. It should be said at
once that many regiments fought very bravely indeed, but not
with the benefit of the right tactics. Since our original garrison
troops (as opposed to the reinforcements, some but half-trained)
were on the ground long before the Japanese, one feels entitled to

ask why not? General Wavell was to put it like this (perhaps not *quite* fairly): 'If all units in Malaya had been trained and led with the same foresight and imagination as Colonel Stewart showed . . . the story of the campaign could have been very different!' Singapore would still have fallen, as no substantial help was forthcoming, but the end could have been postponed, with all that that would have meant, not least to evacuees.

Though the reasons for the speed of the enemy's advance were almost entirely military, Malaya's civil administration has a lot to answer for. Not only was it little geared for war (with the honourable exception of the volunteer bodies) but the soldiery, who had begun to arrive in large numbers, were even somewhat resented. Of course one must beware of judgement with hindsight. There was no war in the Far East, except the 'China Incident' which had rumbled on for four years (and, incidentally, had not shown up the Japanese in a particularly efficient light) and a peacetime atmosphere reigned serene. Nor were peaceful thoughts the prerogative of civilians. I well remember, as a junior officer in HMS *Prince of Wales*, the battleship en route for Singapore, expecting that at last we were going to get a little relaxation!

General Yamashita's progress was better than anything he had dreamt of and of course worse than anything the British GOC, Lieutenant-General A. E. Percival, and the Governor, Sir Shenton Thomas, had envisaged in their lowest moments. Always bearing on the pressing decisions to be made, often out of date as soon as communicated, was the necessity to demonstrate *sang-froid* to a shocked populace and in particular to Asiatics of whom there were 500,000 in Singapore alone (doubled by the end due to the influx of refugees). For this reason I believe it to have been impracticable to have had a scorched-earth plan prepared in advance of hostilities; such a thing would have been contrary to the spirit of confident optimism exuded by those in authority.*

---

* This originated at the top. Churchill, when asked by the writer – during the trip to meet Roosevelt at Placentia Bay – whether the Japanese would attack Malaya, replied, 'No I don't think so. And if they do they will find they have bitten off more than they can chew.'

From the Governor's point of view, it is not difficult to imagine the appalling dilemma of someone committed to making optimistic announcements about the future, while simultaneously sanctioning demolitions. On the same lines, General Percival set his face against establishing strong defence works in rear of the Army because it would be bad for morale (eventually admitting this to be wrong). Latterly he also had demolition problems. Ordered by the Chiefs of Staff at home to hold Singapore to the last, but at the same time to destroy anything of military use, he pointed out that not only would such destruction have an appalling effect on morale but it would prejudice successful fighting.

Fresh from England only some six months before hostilities began (though with previous experience of Malaya as GSO1), Percival had immediate difficulties with the civil authorities and their business-as-usual attitude. Even late on in the campaign there were some extraordinary incidents like gunners being prevented from cutting down rubber trees to make clear fields of fire and golf course secretaries saying that there would have to be a meeting of the committee to sanction the digging of trenches on the fairway! Astonishing as this sounds today, one has to remember that only a few weeks before, when war broke out, Sir Robert Brooke-Popham (the overall C in C) had announced in essence that there was nothing to fear and the Governor was reiterating the importance to the allied war effort of Malaya's rubber and tin. Perhaps those in high places, whether or not they knew the essential weakness of our position, can hardly be blamed for putting a brave face on it. The sad thing is that this took in our own people, especially regarding evacuation, but not the Japanese, whose intelligence was excellent.

For my own part, following the sinking of my ship (with HMS *Repulse*) two days after the declaration of war, I found myself assisting in the evacuation of Penang by running the ferry *Bagan* to the mainland, her crew having disappeared. Back at the Naval Base on the north shore of Singapore Island, I was given, as a newly promoted two-striper of twenty-one, an independent anti-parachute force of 150 sailors. No parachutists obliged and we were used for a variety of *ad hoc* jobs as the need arose. The Army continued to retreat, but optimistic communiqués made the best of things and surely something would turn up. If pessimistic thoughts did surface one kept one's own counsel. Fortunately there is, in most people, a sort of automatic screen of optimism that prevents one believing the worst. In this connection I had to take a large party to unload crated Hurricane fighters from the MV *Sussex* in Keppel Harbour, the native labour having failed to stand up to the constant bombing. When we had finished, her First Officer said it was obvious Singapore was not going to hold out and would I like him to take home a trunkful of my personal belongings? I was shocked as I had not consciously considered surrender. But he was from the outside world and could view things with a dispassionate eye.

Sir Shenton Thomas, who was a stout-hearted 'good sort', certainly wove an 'everything will be all right in the end' cocoon round his thoughts. Someone in his position could hardly do otherwise, but concerning the evacuation of civilians, especially women and children, it has been argued that he should have faced facts and been more pragmatic. Dead against this was his training as a senior colonial administrator, which crystallized into the paternal belief that he was responsible for all the races in Malaya, not just those with white skins, and that there should be no preference for the latter. In fact, when Penang was evacuated somewhat precipitiously and the garrison commander gave Europeans priority, the Governor was incensed. It was in character, therefore, that he believed Europeans should stay (Lady Thomas broadcast to the effect that the place for women was beside their husbands) and that there should be no official evacuation.

Percival thought the same regarding Service families, but he does not seem to have pronounced on the subject, even when Churchill twice suggested the evacuation of women and children. After the war he wrote: 'It was more than once suggested to me that arrangements should be made for the evacuation in the last resort of important personages and as many others as the available transport could take. This I refused to countenance.

Our job was to hold Singapore for as long as we could and not to evacuate it, and any suggestion that arrangements for evacuation were being made would have had a most disastrous effect!'

Brigadier Simson is on record that one of the first things he did on being appointed Director-General of Civil Defence was to ask the GOC and the Governor and then Mr Duff Cooper (the Cabinet representative) to order all *bouches inutiles* away at once. There was no response from any of them.

There was, however, a considerable exodus of those leaving voluntarily. Shortly after the outbreak of hostilities, instructions had been received from the Colonial Office that evacuation on a limited scale might take place. There was to be no racial discrimination and both civilians and service families were to receive facilities. Destinations were to be the UK, India or Australia. A good number immediately applied, mostly Europeans and military families.

Regarding the latter, though General Percival may not have encouraged them to go, the Army did set up the necessary machinery, as witness the experience of Mrs Frances Hosking (whose husband was to be taken prisoner and to provide many of the accounts in Chapters V and VI).

> Quite some time before the outbreak of hostilities, they sent all wives a form which they had to complete giving details of the family and a first and second choice of where they wanted to be evacuated to, should the need arise. . . . We were never in doubt that contingency plans had been made to evacuate Army families, and I seem to recall it being said that those with the largest number of children would go first, and so on. My husband's role was to visit artillery batteries in the field to carry out adjustments, etc. He was in the Ipoh area, but found it difficult to find the units as they were falling back so rapidly, and when Ipoh fell he reported back to Kuala Lumpur. When K.L. fell, he returned to Singapore. Realising the speed at which the Japanese were advancing, he persuaded me that we should leave as soon as possible, which he arranged, and we left within about a week of his return.

The early ships, limited to families of two or more children, left before the end of December. A good deal of responsibility seems to have rested on the Sea Transport Officer, Commander R. A. Trevor RN (retd) who wrote home on Christmas Day, 'Am in the process of getting some 1500 women and children out of the country . . . have solved the problem of who should have priority. Women with the biggest families regardless of class or service come first. 3 cheers for democracy. Deluges of abuse will no doubt descend on my head.'

Another large contingent of 4000 departed on 30 January in the liners *Duchess of Bedford*, *Empress of Japan*(!), *Wakefield* and *West Point*. As well as these groups of evacuees, there was a steady trickle away – though several ships sailed with plenty of room to spare – until the enemy actually landed on the island. The true state of affairs was then borne in on the most sanguine and there was a rush for anything that happened to be going. But it was still voluntary until three days before the surrender when a few thousand were sent away, first in an organised convoy on the night 11th/12th and then in an armada of separate sailings from the 13th.

On board the patrol vessel *Kedah*, part of the organized convoy, was Mrs Muriel Reilly. The wife of a senior business executive, she was on the Governor's personal staff, and extracts from her highly evocative diary not only provide a vivid description of the last days of the doomed city, but throw interesting light in a number of directions.

I think I can most appropriately start this account by relating a conversation which took place between the Governor of Singapore, Sir Shenton Thomas, and myself on Saturday, 6 December, 1941. I had been Cypher Officer at Government House since March, 1939.

He came into my room and sat down on the edge of my table and very solemnly said, 'Well, Mrs Reilly, I have got bad news for you. We are at war!' I put down my pencil and said, 'Well we've been expecting it for a long time now. Let's be thankful it didn't happen a year ago when we had that scare.' He looked at me over the top of his glasses and replied, 'Oh! but you didn't ask me with whom we were at war.' I answered, 'But of course, you mean Japan.' At which he laughed and said, 'Ha! I thought I would catch you! No, we are at war with Finland.' As he walked away laughing, I called after him, 'Oh! I thought you were going to prepare me to expect a Jap bomb on my head any moment.' At that he returned and said, 'Japanese bombs in Singapore! You can take it from me there will never be a Japanese bomb dropped in Singapore. There will never be a Japanese set foot in Malaya.'

On the Monday morning, about 4 am, 8 December, the Japs bombed Singapore!

We were advised by the Governor in several broadcasts to 'stick to our guns' and set a good example to the natives – and, unfortunately, we did. The result was that hundreds of us lost everything we possessed – and many of my friends, who were not as fortunate as I was, lost their lives, when they tried to get away at the last moment, when the Japs over-ran the Island.

Of course it is obvious now that all women and children should have been evacuated from the Island when the Japs were just having an easy walk through the Malay States – but we believed what the Government told us that 'Singapore would not fall'!!

12 February, 1942. Very disturbed night – listening to troops straggling past the house, obviously retreating before the Japs. Sound of almost continuous machine-gun fire seemed to be hourly getting nearer and appeared to come from beyond the golf course. We had no planes left and no aerodromes, but I did not feel unduly alarmed as I knew reinforcements were being rushed out to our aid and the Governor had repeatedly assured me Singapore would *not* fall and all we had to do was hold on until help came. Front line appeared to be just beyond the golf course – about three miles from our house.

At breakfast, to my surprise, Cookie arrived and said he wanted to leave. When asked why, he replied that his friends had told him the Australian soldiers had run away and that the Japs were through on to the golf course and he wanted to take his wife and child into Singapore, as he had been told we would give in before the Japs got as far as the town itself. My husband and I said, 'Rubbish! Japs are not on the golf course. Take the race glasses and go up on the roof and look for yourself.' However, he took our word for it. My husband pointed out that the servants were much safer with us – open country and a strong, bomb-proof shelter for them in the grounds. Town was being bombed and there was more chance of being killed there. Cookie then turned to me and said, 'Mem, are you staying?' and I replied, 'Of course, Cookie.' He put the same question to my husband and received the same reply, so Cookie then said, 'All right, if the Mem and Tuan are staying, Cookie and the boys will stay too.'

Air raids [were] practically continuous so I phoned Government House to know if they really needed me and was told
several cables were waiting to be decyphered. I waited for a
lull in the bomb-dropping and my husband and I got into the
car and started off. Rather disturbed to see the hundreds and
hundreds of Aussies straggling along the Johore-Singapore main
road – others sitting on the sidewalks – most of them clad only in
shorts – no arms – no equipment. . . .

I found that the cables were in one of the cyphers the books
for which had been destroyed, so I could not decypher them, but
there were a lot of secret papers to be burnt, and I was in the
middle of helping with that job when I was told I was wanted
on the phone. It was Air Commodore Modin who said he had
not forgotten his promise to my husband that he would get me
out of Singapore should conditions become dangerous; that that
moment had now arrived; he had come to my house to get me
and found, to his horror, that I was working. I couldn't believe
that things were so bad and rather demurred at getting out,
whereupon I was told, 'I am speaking from your bedroom and
what I can see coming over the golf course makes it imperative
that you should *not attempt* to return to your house. I cannot
speak more clearly – you are sensible – you must understand
what I am trying to tell you and every moment I stay here the
danger is increasing. I am sending my car now with a bodyguard
to get you from Government House and they will bring you to
where I will be.'

Then I telephoned my husband and when he heard what Modin
had said, his reply was an amazed, 'Christ! I just cannot believe it.'
I said I would still much rather remain with him but he begged
me to go whilst I had the chance and said, 'If things are as bad
as they seem, it means concentration camps and I shan't be with
you. Just imagine my feelings knowing you were in the hands of
the Japs – and I couldn't help you.' I realized I would only add to
his troubles if I stayed and so I said, all right, I would go, but that
I would come down and say goodbye to him – somehow or other.

I then went into the Governor's room and told him of my
conversation with the Air Commodore and that I was getting
away from Singapore. The Governor said he didn't believe there
were any Japs on the golf course or anywhere near the golf course
– that they were miles away (as a matter of fact the Japs were
outside my house that afternoon!) and that, in his opinion, there
was not the slightest necessity for my getting out. He said the
Japs *had* broken through the Australians, but that a small party

of Argyll & Sutherlands had been rushed into the breach and they, together with the Indians on the left and right flanks, had pushed the Japs back two miles. . . . As events turned out, Cookie's information *had* been correct and his trust in us had prevented him from getting his family to safety that morning.

The Air Commodore's car arrived and I went in to say goodbye to the Governor. He shook me very warmly by the hand and said he would never forget and could never thank me sufficiently for all the work I had done for him and expressed the fervent wish that I would get safely home to my Patsy but he again said, 'If you didn't have a child at home I would still ask you to stay on here, but there is always the danger of a bomb getting you – apart from that there is no need for you to leave Singapore – IT WILL NOT FALL!!'

I got into Modin's car and found two of the RAF there, armed with Tommy guns – my 'bodyguard'! We dashed down to Thomson Road and I was informed by one of them that GHQ and RAF Headquarters – both of which were less than 1/4 of a mile from my house – had gone up in flames and that an old Chinese house in Thomson Road was being used as temporary headquarters, but that the RAF hoped to get away to Java that afternoon. We had no planes or aerodromes left and the RAF were going over to Java to continue the war from there. Just as we reached the Chinese house, another raid on and it became obvious that the Japs already knew where the RAF and GHQ temporary Headquarters were, as they dropped bombs all around us – but missed the building completely. I was rushed into Modin's office and he said, 'Thank God you've got here safely, Mrs Reilly. Now you are to stick by my side – I don't want to lose sight of you and I will personally take you on to that boat myself. Meantime I've been trying to persuade your husband to get out with us. We badly want a man of his experience and ability in our Finance Department and I'd get him commissioned right away, but he has scruples. Phone him and see what you can do. I'd like to see him out of here.' I phoned my husband but he said his two partners were staying; he was a member of the Local Defence Corps and had undertaken certain duties, and he felt it would be wrong to run away from them. . . .

Some time later the Air Vice-Marshal came into the room. I was shocked at his appearance. He was obviously in a state of great tension – almost mental it appeared to me – and he kept walking up and down the room, muttering to himself and thumping tables and chairs as he passed, and every now and then stopping in front of me and saying, 'This is a dreadful business – this is a dreadful state of affairs – the whole show is damnable – utterly damnable. An Air Force with no planes and no aerodromes. What the Hell are we to do? What *can* we do?'

The afternoon wore on and then the Air Commodore came back and said he had got all the others safely away. Then Air Vice-Marshal Pulford suddenly wheeled round and said, 'I won't go – I'm staying here.' Then followed a hectic scene with both men losing tempers and shouting at each other. Modin pointed out there wasn't the slightest use the RAF staying in Singapore – we had no planes and no aerodromes left and the reinforcements were being diverted to Java and we could bomb 'Hell out of the Japs' from there. But Pulford kept on saying, 'I won't run away from those yellow B---- B----s', and at the end of a lengthy argument he was still adamant. Modin then turned to me and said, 'That means I must stay too. If the Air Vice-Marshal remains I can't go. I fully intend to personally see you safe, as I promised your husband. Now I can only do my best to see that you get away. I will get you a bodyguard and you will go down in my car – straight to the boat – she is due to arrive any moment now. I will give you a letter to hand to the CO at RAF Headquarters, Batavia and he will look after you.' I asked if I could not stop on the way past my husband's office to say goodbye to him and Modin hesitated for a moment and then said, 'I want you to go straight to the boat. If you stop on the way with these continuous raids on, you will be endangering the lives of the four men I am sending with you and in addition you may lose the boat' – so I knew I would have to leave without seeing my husband. I tried to phone, but the line was dead and so I got into the car and had the heartbreaking experience of passing within a stone's throw of my husband's office. I *nearly* disobeyed orders, and how many times since I have wished that I had!

The town was being bombed as we tore through it and we could see blazing buildings everywhere. However, we reached the wharf safely. I knew we were going to the little *Kedah* – a coastal steamer on which my husband and I had had many happy trips up to Penang for race meetings. We sat on the wharf and waited – and waited – AND WAITED. . . . I thought of my husband anxiously waiting and watching for me to come and say goodbye to him and I got more and more miserable. . . . Then at 3.30 am on Friday the 13th the *Kedah* at last arrived!

Friday the 13th came to be known as Black Friday. Though ships had continued to leave in the last few days, invariably southwards to Java (apart from the shorter distance the many islands en route promised more succour than the Indian Ocean westwards) there was no word of any *evacuation* until this day, when RA Malaya, Rear Admiral E. J. Spooner, took a hand. Having decided that, if any ships now at Singapore were not to fall into the hands of the enemy, they must sail that night, he called a conference. There was accommodation in the vessels available, meaning little more than standing room in some cases, for 3000. He allocated 1800 places to the Army, a few hundred to the Navy and RAF ground staffs and the rest to the Civil Government. Allocations, with passes, were made out by these and communicated to the people concerned, who conformed as best they could, often with no warning at all. The three quotations at the head of this chapter are typical of many.

The first was by Mrs Marjory de Malmanche, an English nurse who returned to her hospital at 2 pm to find the forecourt crowded with baggage, nurses and soldiers, who told her that everyone had to be on board a ship by 3 pm. It was sunk, but she will be heard of later. As many nurses as possible were evacuated on Percival's instructions, a direct result of the Jap atrocities penetrated on nurses at Hong Kong. It would have been better for most of them had they stayed, but no one was to know that.

The second quotation, from the recollections of the then Captain A. R. Stacey, 6th Royal Norfolks, is typical of the Army's experience, as is the following letter from Captain Barham Savory, 5th Royal Norfolks:

> Well we withdrew quite successfully and started to dig and wire ourselves in feverishly on the 'final line'. . . . I was awoken at midnight when the C.O. read me a personal message from the Brigadier telling him to detail three officers and seven other ranks to report to Brigade HQ at 12.30 for special duty. The people selected to have outstanding ability in the field and no consideration to be given to consequent loss of efficiency of the battalion. . . . When the C.O. had finished reading the names he said, 'Well, Barham, are you game?' So all I could say was, 'Yes Sir'. We chose a few good men to come with us and then we all piled into a truck and went off to Brigade HQ where we found

1. Colonel A.F. Warren,
CBE, DSC, Royal Marines

2. H.S.R. Cunyngham-Brown,
OBE, Malayan Civil Service

3. Sir Shenton Thomas, GCMG, OBE, Governor of Singapore.
Behind him is Rear-Admiral Spooner, DSO, RA Malaya

4. Bomb damage to the *Kung Wo* (p.27)

5. Last boat away from the *Kung Wo* (p.28)

similar parties from other battalions. There, everything was very hush-hush. . . . The Brigadier came round to shake hands with us and say goodbye. Then we went off in a truck to the docks . . . it was an attempted evacuation. . . .

After the shelling we collected ourselves and moved off to the docks only to find that the last official boat had gone and taken everyone in authority. We didn't even know where we were supposed to making for.

Great secrecy surrounded these sudden biddings, as of course wide knowledge would have been catastrophic, as Percival indicated, to the morale of the remainder. Yet another account, by Major F. F. Swalwell RA, well describes the confusion surrounding the whole unexpected development:

What specialists were required? Evacuation never occurred to me. Whilst I was stewing over the message things outside had hotted up considerably and there was a lot of mortar fire . . . at that moment a Subaltern from Command arrived. . . . I said, 'But what is it all about?' He seemed surprised at my lack of appreciation. . . . 'You are off, you lucky people.'

Well; lucky for some, I soon realised. Whom to take? If we were to re-form with Javanese troops in Batavia we needed the senior men or those who would be suitable as instructors or who had particular skills. . . . We paraded at the roadside and I told the four Troop Officers . . . to nominate seven from each troop. I vetted the names, but if they had been seven different names I would have accepted them because we had no passengers. I added my own selection of NCOs and BHQ personnel with growing feelings of despair. I don't know why, but I could hear the caller at Housey-Housey ('Bingo' today) saying 'Number 13. One and three. Unlucky for some!' Friday the 13th. By now it was nearly the 14th and all hell seemed to be let loose. The shell and mortar fire had increased. . . .

A Sergeant who was selected soon realized when we reached the dock that we were being evacuated. He came to me and said, 'Sir, I am not going. We can't leave the rest behind.' It had been bad enough for me, this selection business, so I told him, 'Look, *I* am obeying orders and you will damn well obey mine. Get on board.' He was eventually commissioned in India and was, I am sure, a very good infantry officer, for that was where his heart lay, I think, after Singapore.

As was probably to be expected, given the short notice and difficulty in communicating with civilians, action by the Civil Government was even more confused. Added to which it would appear that Sir Shenton Thomas, with his anti-evacuation outlook, did not really want to know. Three months after the fall of Singapore he wrote a statement on the subject, which describes how on 13 February Brigadier Simson told him of the Navy's offer of accommodation 'for a considerable number of civilians on a ship sailing almost at once' and that he agreed to this provided that each civilian was authorized by Simson. Clearly he left it all to the Brigadier (sensible decentralization under the circumstances). Noting 'It was not until we were all interned that I began to learn what had actually happened', he went on to comment on previous instructions to Government servants on sticking to their jobs, the circumstances of a handful of men he had personally allowed to leave and strictures on others who he said had no such permission.

Brigadier Simson came to the Governor a second time on the 13th to say that he had been unable to make sufficient contacts to fill his quota. Sir Shenton says, 'I was not surprised as telephone communication was then bad and many people had changed their addresses. Also experience had shown that most Asiatic women wanted two days rather than two hours in which to make ready.'

Less than one hour was all that Mrs T. Innes-Ker, typical of many civilians, received.

We were still at the breakfast table when the phone rang. It was an MBC girl, 'Will you be at Clifford Pier in an hour with your baggage?' Quite apart from a rushed pack, my first and main thought was that I must speak to Tam. I could not get into direct communication with him on his machine-gun post, but had to ring his beach commander, Philip Holt. I was so choked I could hardly speak, and I can hear now Philip saying calmly, 'Take it easy Enid, take it easy.' I could wait no longer. . . . Maw and Barbara were getting into the car and I was poised on the top step of the bungalow, just leaving, and the phone rang . . . those last few words with each other . . . we were off, leaving a fully furnished home and many prized possessions. Actually there is only one thing that to this very day I regret having left and that is Tam's Rugger Honours cap. It would have meant so much to him if only I had thought to pack it.

If some confusion marked the provision of passes, it soon reigned supreme over the docks as an increasing crowd of recipients clamoured to get past the Military Police at the gates. A passing Naval Officer was beseeched to help the distraught parents of a child who had gone through the gates and boarded a ship about to sail. They could not get through and he could not help them. All the time burning go-downs sent up clouds of smoke round those struggling towards their ships, enemy aircraft droned continuously and shells from both sides whined overhead. The plight of terrified children was heart-breaking. All these presented a tempting target and the inevitable occurred. A string of bombs landed on the edge of the crowd and a good number were killed or wounded; one young man about to embark was seen to take his small child from the arms of his dying wife and go on board in tears, leaving her body on the ground behind him. But the harrowing scene did provide the first of many instances, to be described here, when evacuating nurses behaved superbly; as recalled by another Naval Officer:

> The incident that stands out most in my mind of these last hours was the magnificent bravery and fortitude of a group of Australian nurses who were waiting their turn to be evacuated. The air-raids were following one another in quick succession and causing heavy casualties among the evacuees. To the noise of the guns was added the screams and cries of the dying and wounded. Smouldering and dismembered bodies lay everywhere among the pathetic remains of scattered burst-open suitcases. It was essential to calm and succour the survivors if a complete panic was not to set in. These brave nurses were always the first to answer calls for assistance and by their bearing and spirit were in stark contrast to some of the opposite sex.

Not all the ships got away successfully on the 13th, a few leaving on the 14th. A note on the evacuation is provided by the last issue of Singapore's paper, the *Straits Times*, a copy of which I have. Taken over by the Governor and produced by an Asiatic volunteer staff, it consisted of a single sheet, 14 inches by 9 inches, printed on one side only and distributed free by hand. Dated 14 February, 1942, it has a headline ALL EVACUATION SUSPENDED AS FROM TODAY and then in bold, 'By order of the General Officer Commanding, Malaya, all evacuation from Singapore is entirely suspended. This applies also to women and children.' Presumably this was intended to avoid disappointment; after all, there were no more ships. Along the top of the page is 'Singapore must stand; it SHALL stand. – H.E. The Governor'.'

Up till a few days before, the Japanese air force was heavily engaged bombing and strafing our troops and installations, but their command was well aware of the embarkations (Tokyo radio put out that the British were not going to be allowed another Dunkirk) and as more and more aircraft – now based on Tengah in the north of the Island – became available from the land assault they were switched to attacks on shipping.

Where were their motley and weakly armed targets (except for a few motor launches and gunboats they were all ex-merchant ships) making for? In accordance with their sailing instructions from Admiral Spooner, they were heading for Batavia (now Djakarta), almost the nearest point of Java, about 500 miles from Singapore. A handful of adventurous spirits did subsequently make it through the Straits of Malacca to India, but a glance at the map (page xiv) will show that this was a much more formidable undertaking. It will be seen that the huge – 1000 mile – island of Sumatra runs NW/SE, its top half overlapping and roughly parallel to the Malay Peninsula. Singapore is about opposite its mid-point, a little south of which the Indragiri River runs inland towards Padang, the main port on the west coast. The River Djambi is 40 miles south of the Indragiri, but not so useful for getting to Padang. Further south again is the Banka Strait, between the 150-mile-long island of that name and the Sumatra coast near Palembang. Between Singapaore and Banka are a great many islands, most uninhabited. Generally speaking the west coast of Sumatra was underdeveloped, especially the lower half, with miles of coastline containing little but fishing villages, swamps and mangrove (strong curly-stemmed bushes that grow in the water). Wherever refugees landed in Sumatra it would be necessary to get across to Padang and thence to India, or down to Java and thence to Australia.

The Admiral's decision to direct his exodus fleet to Batavia was therefore straightforward enough. But something – best described as an unlucky accident of timing – had happened which was to have appalling consequences. The officer – normally at Fort Canning – with overall responsibility for the books for decoding secret Naval signals was told on 11 February by Admiral Spooner that he (with several others on the staff and at least one unattached officer) might leave in HMS *Jupiter*, which sailed in the early hours of the 12th (see p. 182). Before embarking it is assumed that he ordered the burning of the code books on his own initiative. From some time on the 11th, therefore, RA Malaya was unable to read coded signals from the outside world.

An early and comparatively innocuous result of this was that on the evening of the 11th the cruiser *Durban*, approaching Singapore, had no acknowledgement of her time of arrival signal, causing the Captain eventually to report: 'It appears, however, that the RA Malaya had already destroyed all I and J tables and my signal was therefore indecypherable.'

A far more serious, in fact catastrophic, outcome relates to the fact that, on the day the code books ceased operation, the Japanese Vice-Admiral Ozawa, with a force of one carrier, three cruisers and several destroyers, was escorting a troop convoy from Camranh Bay in French Indo-China (Vietnam) towards southern Sumatra. Their task was the invasion of Sumatra and Java, beginning with a parachute attack on Palembang and then landings against Batavia. By early on the 13th Ozawa's cruisers and destroyers (the carrier somewhere in the background, her aircraft searching northwards) were positioned in the Banka Strait at its narrowest part, like a gang of thugs across an alleyway.

It is believed that the presence of these enemy ships was reported to Singapore by the Dutch but of course this vital information never reached Admiral Spooner. He himself, until he actually saw them off Banka Island, was quite unaware of Ozawa's presence*. Another twist in this unfortunate chain of events was that the Intelligence Branch of Command HQ was told on 10 February that the Japanese shipping at the Anambas Islands had been ordered to rendezvous in the Banka Strait on the 13th, as a preliminary to the assualt on Palembang. It must be assumed that this was not passed on to Admiral Spooner.

In subsequent conversation with Air Marshal Pulford about the fact that he must have missed an 'enemy report' from the Dutch before he left Singapore, the Admiral said in the hearing of Lieutenant R. A. W. Pool that he had never authorized the destruction of the code books. It must be said that the implied criticism of the officer concerned is hardly fair. The Admiral himself considered on the 10th that Singapore would fall 'today or tomorrow' and when the officers mentioned were sent away on the 11th, all thought the end was near. But Singapore held out till the 15th and no doubt poor Spooner was thinking that if only the code books had been available for another few hours he would not have routed the exodus fleet to Batavia.

---

* Noel Barber in his book *Sinister Twilight* (1968) stated categorically that the Dutch had warned Singapore that Japanese warships were in the Banka Strait, but that Spooner was unable to read the message for the reasons given above. On my enquiring of his source, Noel Barber replied that he could not say after 20 years, but the information was probably in the papers of Brigadier Simson, which he had used extensively. I went through these, but without finding any reference, and had to leave the matter there.

It should be explained that there were also cypher as opposed to code books, the former being of a higher order of security. These were under the Admiral's Secretary at Sime Road. Commander (then Paymaster Lieutenant) J. T. Grist, who was Assistant Secretary, remembers helping to burn the *cypher* books, on the 12th. It is likely that any communication(s) with the Dutch (possibly via the British Commodore Collins at Batavia) would have been in *code*, not cypher. Information on the whole complicated question is far from exact, but the account given here is believed to be broadly correct.

The decision as to when to destroy is of course an appallingly difficult one. Capture of the books could mean the enemy is privy to much that is going on for a considerable time. It will be remembered that at least some of the Governor's cypher books had already been destroyed. I myself was to encounter two premature examples (the Dutch Controleur at Dabo and the British consul at Padang) and the history of the war contains many instances of capture with far-reaching results.

In the event, of the forty-four ships (not including those of harbour craft size) which left Singapore on 13 or 14 February, those that escaped death from the air on the first two days unfortunately ran into Ozawa's murderous arms, only one or two getting through. Thus from Singapore to the Banka Strait there was enacted a maritime scene of almost unparalleled horror; to describe it I cannot improve on the words of Oswald Gilmour in his *Singapore to Freedom*:

> As St Valentine's Day, 1942, was nearing its close, a state of affairs which defies description prevailed in this section of the Malay Archipelago. Perhaps never before in the long period of recorded history was there anything to compare with it. Men, women and children in ones and twos, in dozens, in scores and in hundreds were cast upon these tropical islands within an area of say 400 miles square. Men and women of many races, of all professions, engineers, doctors, lawyers, businessmen, sisters, nurses, housewives, sailors, soldiers and airmen, all shipwrecked. Between the islands on the phosphorescent sea floated boats and rafts laden with people, and here and there, the lone swimmer was striving to make land. All around the rafts and swimmers were dismembered limbs, dead fish and wreckage, drifting with the currents; below, in all probability, were sharks; and above, at intervals, the winged machines of death. . . . It was a ghastly tragedy, a catastrophe beyond measure.

Reading this on the flyleaf of a lurid fictional thriller one would dismiss it as a publisher's exaggeration, but unfortunately it was only too true. The sufferings of some of those who were evacuated from Singapore are described in the following chapters, but terrible as many of them were, for survivors taken prisoner it was only the beginning of worse hardships experienced in captivity.

Remembering that it would have been possible to evacuate all the white non-essential (and a good number of Asiatic) civilians up to about the end of January, was Sir Shenton Thomas right or not? His belief in what would now be called no racial discrimination was based on the sort of ethic on which the British Empire was built; nearer home it was the sort of ethic that sent Admiral Phillips northwards against the Japanese without air support because the Navy could not be seen to be doing nothing; and the sort of ethic that led the young Australian Captain Curlewis, when invited to join General Gordon Bennett's controversial escape party, to refuse on the grounds that he ought to stay with his men. There is the example of the Governor of Hong Kong who sent all European *bouches inutiles* away in good time; a decision that had been taken in July, 1940. 1646 service families and over 1800 wives and children of European civilians were evacuated, so that few were taken prisoner there who need not have been. The Hong Kong situation was more clear-cut in that it was always evident the Colony would stand no chance if attacked, but *bouches inutiles* are useless mouths and better out of the way in any siege.

In the event we lost Malaya and with it enough face among Asiatics to last for ever. So perhaps it would not have mattered much if the Governor had sent his ethics packing. He did not, and some would say more power to his elbow; others that he would have saved the lives of thousands of civilian evacuees; and of those captured, prevented $3^{1}/_{2}$ years of hell. Who is to judge?

The only thing that is certain is that no man, especially an upright, courageous and compassionate, but perhaps not too clever one, like Sir Shenton Thomas – who was to endure captivity with the rest – should be faced with such a decision.

II

Pompong Island

When the Naval Base had to be evacuated at the end of January for a hutted camp at Seletar, what remained of the ship's companies of the *Prince of Wales* and *Repulse*, after successive drafts had been sent to ships and small craft, numbered two officers (Lieutenant-Commander A. H. Terry and myself) and about 200 men. Shelled out of Seletar, we were withdrawn to the evacuated Oranje Hotel in Singapore to continue the sporadic tasks given us by Admiral Spooner. After the enemy had landed on the island and made steady progress, our little band, with nothing really worthwhile to do, can hardly be blamed for waiting eagerly and hourly for the Admiral's word to go. He, however, was in a dilemma. Final evacuation of the last of the regular Navy would be a body blow to general morale and he was hanging on as long as possible.

At last, on the morning of 12 February, we were allocated to, and told to embark in, half-a-dozen ships that evening. As all were sunk, it was a case of consignment to death, captivity or, in a veritable handful of cases, freedom. Terry and I and 100 men were to go in the *Kung Wo*, I to spend the rest of the day with a party among the sampans moored many deep up Singapore's river. Casting them off, we paddled them down to be secured along the adjacent seawall; someone had had the bright idea that they would soon come in useful to enterprising soldiers, as indeed they did.

Probably the first ship to sail on Black Friday, the *Kung Wo*, an old Yangtse river steamer of about 5000 tons, was one of the many small merchant ships 'taken up from trade' by the Navy.

All had Chinese or Malay names – *Kung Wo, Tien Kuang* and *Kuala* becoming a well-known trio in adversity. Our one hope – for some reason unarmed – did not exactly instil confidence. She had been fitted out as a minelayer, though there were no mines on board, and was considerably scarred.

However, I was relieved enough to get on board that evening, after avoiding fires, skirting craters and hiding from bombs on my way from the Oranje Hotel. Those of us who had gone back for a last-minute forage had been chased out of it by a series of explosions – one shattered the big domed skylight in the roof – which must have been artillery fire and it was obvious that there was not much time to lose if we were to get away.

The *Kung Wo* cast off to anchor in the harbour and await the order to sail. Much in evidence was a party of five civilian media people. They were being escorted by the Press Liaison Officer, Captain Henry Steel, a fair-haired, ebullient character whose particular charge appeared to be an attractive Chinese girl in her mid-twenties, who had worked for Metro-Goldwyn-Mayer, called Doris Lim. Neat in blue shirt and trousers, she spoke perfect English and won my immediate approval by treating the whole thing as a bit of a lark. The others were Yates McDaniel, Athole Stewart, a man called Wellby, and Flight Lieutenant Syd Downer. There were also two officers of the Base fire brigade. Darkness descended to accentuate the plight of Singapore. Fires, reflected in the sea, appeared unbroken along the whole waterfront, the flashes of shells winked continuously beyond and every now and again a major flare-up marked some demolition. Accompanying it all was the continual noise of the nearby coastal batteries firing northwards at enemy concentrations.

Two boatloads of women and children hailed the *Kung Wo* but went on to other ships when told that our lifeboats were in poor shape from splinters. The night wore on, with still no order to sail. The Captain reckoned we had been forgotten and just before midnight called up the headquarters ship *Laburnum* by light. For a long time there was no reply and then some answering flashes. It was Lieutenant Pool RN in ML 311, waiting for Admiral Spooner to embark. He passed some information about minefields and recommended that we sail. We were off, in the first few minutes of Friday the 13th. It would normally have been pleasant, a passenger with no ship responsibilities, but as I sat in a deck-chair alongside Surgeon Commander Stevenson of the Naval Office and we discussed possibilities, there was not a lot to be hopeful about. The *Kung Wo*'s destination, Batavia of course, meant 500 miles of probable, if diminishing (so we thought) air attack.

Anyway, in the early hours of the 13th, as we turned in, rubber lifebelts handy, the ship sailed on through a minefield, a fact fortunately lost on most of us. The lifebelts were hastily donned at 7.30 am to the roar of aircraft diving and the shuddering of the ship as the wheel was put hard over and a stick of bombs exploded in her wake. All the passengers lay down among the mine rails as two fighter-bombers turned for another run. This time they hit us squarely, at least one bomb blowing a great hole in the superstructure amidships, but with no casualties. Round they came a third time. The only reply had been two rifle shots from the bridge, which turned out to be an enthusiast with an elephant gun, and this time they came very low and made sure of it. There was a blinding flash, a wave of hot air and the clanging of splinters as a bomb exploded just forward of the mine flat and over the engine room. The shrill hiss of escaping steam followed and clearly the main steam pipe had been severed. Stokers came tumbling up from below and for a time no one could get down to cope. The aircraft were presumably out of bombs as they departed and eventually the 2nd Engineer shut off the steam. The near misses had started her plates, causing leaks and the *Kung Wo* was now taking in water to give her a slight but increasing list. Fortunately there was only one casualty, a Chinese stoker found dead with a sliver of shrapnel in the temple.

The engine damage proved irreparable and the Captain gave the order to abandon ship. Luckily, there was a chain of small, thickly wooded islands only some five miles to the east. There were two boats, which would mean several trips each, if they held. Tinned food and barricoes (casks) of water were collected – supplies of the latter might well dictate our fate – and all preparations made for departure. Anthony Terry took charge and allowed one bundle of belongings per person. I forgot to include a mosquito net, the standard presence of one hitherto tending to make one discount these tormentors. The first boats' crews, heading for the nearest island, were seen to be baling furiously, but they just made it.

During the long and trying wait for their return, a Jap seaplane came and had a good look – one could see the observer examining us through his binoculars – but flew off without doing anything. Of course the ship was superficially, but spectacularly when seen from the air, in a terrible state, with large chunks missing and areas of twisted metal, splintered wood and festoons of rigging. Suddenly a fire started in the bunker, caused by deck planking that had fallen through, but was soon extinguished. The heat was bad enough anyway, but this made it almost unbearable. Eventually there was nothing to do but wait. McDaniel would keep popping up, Leica to eye; this was going to be the biggest scoop of his career. Another correspondent, the girl, the airman and myself drank to the future in a bottle of wine found rolling about, after which we hurled our glasses at the saloon mantel-piece, now at a considerable angle, in the best movie style.

It was getting cooler by the time we were taken off (the First Lieutenant of *Kung Wo*, a fine, close-cropped, Scotch Lieutenant RNR called Jock Monro and a number of volunteer seamen had to stay behind for yet another trip) and the sun was setting as we splashed ashore over sharp coral on to a sandy beach, backed by jungle. There was good news in that a stream had been found and the food brought ashore was estimated to last the 120 of us three to four days. After a meal of bully beef and biscuits we stretched out for the night. All in all, if our ship had to go, it had been a pretty gentlemanly end; one of the first of the 44, she was probably the last of which that could be said.

It was a strange awakening on the beach, with birds twittering and the sea lapping a few yards away, as rows of figures stretched and rubbed their eyes. The *Kung Wo* had drifted a little and had a more pronounced list, but our attention was held by two more grey ships, rather smaller, anchored close in to another

island. As we watched, a launch put out from one of them and
went alongside the *Kung Wo*. This did not look good; presuming it
to be Japanese, some people began the destruction of documents
that might prove embarrassing. The launch left the *Kung Wo* and
headed straight for us. That seemed to clinch matters. It came in
as near as possible and a white-uniformed figure stepped on to the
foredeck and yelled, 'Send a boat out!' Our hearts leapt. It was
Monro. The launch turned out to belong to a Dutch planter who,
while escaping, had seen the three ships and come to investigate.
The other two were the naval auxiliaries *Kuala* and *Tien Kuang* of
about 800 tons.

While a conference on what to do next was being held with
the bearded planter – I never heard his name – a small steam
tongkang (sort of bluff maid-of-all-work) rounded the other point
and came in too. It was decided that as many as possible would
go in this and the launch that night to Sumatra – only some
thirty miles – whence Terry would organize further nocturnal
rescue trips. Sumatra was a vast and friendly country. Onward
transport to its west coast, and British ships to India, were
presumably available and it all seemed too easy. We merely
had to wait for the dark.

I thought it would be sensible to exchange information with
Kuala and *Tien Kuang*, so that, if any of us were not lucky in
getting through, the survivors would be better placed to do
something about it. This agreed, I borrowed the sizeable launch
(it had a Malay crew of four) and set off for what appeared on
the Captain's chart to be called Pompong (ours was Benku),
three or four miles away. The two ships were anchored very
close inshore and to each other, rather too close I thought for
bomb avoidance purposes, in a very small horseshoe bay. I was
met at the gangway of the *Kuala* by Petty Officer Taylor, one of
my anti-parachute force, brandishing a huge spanner which he
said was to keep people off the food stores. The Captain showed
me the course for Batavia, after which I tried to reassure his
navigator, who was very worried about aircraft. The ship was
crammed with people, strewn all over the place, and I thought
how terrible it would be if she was bombed.

About three-quarters of the way back we heard the drone of aircraft and, following the old cox'n's shaking finger, I made out a formation of twenty-seven, shaping for the *Kung Wo*. The deep growl of bombs came over the water and she was covered in a fountain of splashes, only to reappear unscathed. They circled and went in again, hitting her squarely so that she rolled over and sank quickly. I could see, in my mind's eye, the scenes of panic that must be taking place on the unfortunate ships I had just left, and pressed on at full speed to embark the doctor and what other help we could muster.

*   *   *

On board *Kuala* – some seconds before this – Mrs de Malmanche had just finished breakfast:

I took the empty plates to the galley, and as I was coming back some planes flew over. There was nobody on deck except a sailor, who pushed me into a cabin, where I found Captain Hancock, the Governor of Singapore Prison, Mrs Hancock and Mrs Cherry. . . . They were all kneeling on the floor, to minimise danger from blast. Luckily, I didn't stay there. We heard the planes go over again, and then I opened the door . . . as I did so, I saw huge columns of water rising around the wreck out to sea [*Kung Wo*]; and when they cleared, it had disappeared. Hastily closing the door again, I said, 'We're going to be bombed!' and even as I said it, there was an ear-splitting crash and the roof vanished, leaving us in bright sunlight. Nobody said a word, but we all scrambled to our feet, and scattered. The bomb had scored a direct hit on the bridge and saloon, and went straight through into the engine room. The Captain, on the bridge, was flung out to sea, but unhurt; all the people in the first cabin I had been pushed into were killed, and Mrs Curtiss (wife of Brigadier Curtiss) who took refuge in my broom cupboard, had a shrapnel wound behind her ear, in spite of the bucket she had put over her head. Dozens of people were trapped in the wrecked saloon. . . . The casualties in the crowded holds must have been terrible.

Within minutes the ship was on fire, the flames ably assisted by our leafy camouflage. Added to the cries of the wounded was a terrifying shrill scream from the engine room – probably a cracked boiler. . . . We had to abandon ship by either jumping straight into the sea, or sliding down a long rope which the sailors had fastened to the ship's rail. A little boy went down the rope in front of me, so crazy with fear that he wouldn't let go of the rail but had to be forced; he was drowned. I slid down the rope, but seemed to go an awful long way under water; when I surfaced I swam about until I was able to grab a piece of wreckage. Someone had brought a boat out from the shore; it was already full, and many people were clinging to the sides. I made for it and hung on with the others. There was only one oar, which was being used, not very effectively, by an elderly woman. Looking back to the ship, I saw the two doctors sliding down into the sea. The planes were still flying backwards and forwards, dropping bombs on the people swimming around, and on the Air Force ship,* which was now their main target.

There was an unpleasant whistling sound, and, looking up, I saw a bomb falling straight towards us. We all cringed towards the side of the boat, and the next minute we were caught up in a huge wave which flung us on to the rocky beach of the island. Everybody scrambled over the rocks and ran up the steep thickly wooded hillside. Halfway up, the planes came again, and we crouched behind trees for protection. Bombs fell, and our boat and the rocks went up in smoke.

Dr (Mrs) M. J. Lyon and Dr Elsie Crowe were two other passengers. When the bombing started, the former was tending a woman who had been wounded when the ship was bombed the day before.

We hurriedly fixed the patient's splints, and carried her to the gangway with Sears' help, to one of the few boats that was not away getting camouflage. By the time we had her at the boat, the ship was pretty well deserted, and was burning briskly and sinking fast. Sears hurried us off, and we climbed down a rope ladder and jumped in, with not a lifebelt between us. (Us is Elsie and I, Elsie

---

* The *Tien Kuang*, which was evacuating the RAF radar detachment, with their secret equipment.

having turned up after the bombing from the other side.) Elsie was not a strong swimmer, but the island looked to be near, and I assured her I could get her there whatever happened. We set out swimming, with no one near us except the lifeboat which followed us from the ship. While we were still a good way from land the Japanese bombers appeared again and all 27 aimed for our ship and the *Tien Kuang*. Something seemed to strike me on the belly, and I thought I was blown in two, but Elsie disappeared in a sort of whirlpool and I was so busy trying to get her up that I forgot all about it. Her dress tore at the shoulders, and I lost her, but finally got her by the hair. She was unconscious for a few moments and her face was black and blue, with blood and cerebro-spinal fluid pouring from one nostril.

There was no sign of the lifeboat and our ship disappeared too. The waves from the bomb were terrific, and I had much difficulty in keeping our heads above water. Elsie soon recovered consciousness, but was stone deaf for days. However, she very gamely began to swim with her legs, supporting her arms on my shoulders. We managed somehow, and finally grated on the shore, both unable to stand for quite a while. The bombers came over several times and wrought havoc among those who had reached the island earlier. After a while we dragged ourselves out of the water, and my abdomen began to bleed from the blast I had received. I was quite surprised, as I had forgotten all about the blow.

Mr Oswald Gilmour (of the Public Works Dept (PWD)) was one of those who had just got ashore:

A soldier gave me a hand to get up the sharp rocks out of the water, then we both dived for the jungle as the planes were heard again. . . . I made a frantic effort to reach an overhanging piece of rock for cover. I managed this, but just in time. . . . A bomb fell; blast and splinters flew by and parts of the rock I was sheltering under peeled off and fell on my face and eyes. When I got up, the trees around were seared and torn and half a dozen soldiers near me had been killed.

The very strong current swept many people away. Mrs E. Stevenson, another nurse, was one of them:

There were non-swimmers holding on to bits of wreckage, I saw one woman grab a dead body only to let go when the truth dawned. Another lady, a nursing sister, who judging by her uniform was from the Government Hospital, was swimming very well and getting clear of the crowded area when a Japanese plane blew her to pieces. It was unbelievable that men could be so cruel and heartless. Everything seemed so unreal, it was a terrible nightmare, yet in my tired and dazed condition, I realized that if I was to live, I must jump overboard. . . . Top deck seemed a long way from the water. However, there was no alternative, the way to a lower deck was either blocked by dead bodies or frantic survivors. Blood from the casualties made the deck slippery. Without further hesitation, I left my small case of valuables on the deck and slid overboard. It seemed better to die by drowning than be roasted alive. The heat from the fire on board was unbearable. . . .

The sea water was nice and cool, and I was trying to swim away from the sinking ship when a voice called out, 'Help me, I have two children in Australia, I must get to them.' I was a bit hampered with clothing and was tired. I had had very little sleep for days. I knew I could not support a grown woman. She clung to me like a limpet when suddenly a piece of wood floated by: I suggested we each held one end of this piece of wood, this freed me to swim and keep us both afloat.

Mrs Stevenson was helped on to a raft but was then asked to make room for someone else in difficulties:

I jumped into the sea and swam alongside. Two other swimmers and myself tried, in vain, to tow the raft to nearby Pompong Island. What at first seemed very easy proved an impossible task. We had not reckoned for the tidal races which abounded in the area. One minute we could almost touch the undergrowth around the island, the next, as if by magic, we were swept far out to sea. Each attempt became more exhausting. Eventually the gentleman swimmer said to the other nurse and myself, 'Let us three make a dash to Pompong Island, I'm sure we could make it'. Hearing this suggestion, a plea from those on the raft not to desert them, ended in the other two swimming away. I stayed with the raft. I knew I could do very little, apart from keeping up morale. It seemed a terrible thing to desert them. I never met the swimmers again.

There were ten of us left with the raft. Nine on the raft and myself swimming with my uniform belt tied to the end of the raft. I was trying to tow it by swimming on my back. What I would achieve by doing this I do not know, but so long as

we kept moving, there was hope. We were a mixed bag, two
Indian Sepoys or Madrassi soldiers, a Sikh Havildar, two RAF
corporals, an Anglo-Indian lady, the Australian nurse mentioned
earlier, and an old gentleman who had been the chief censor in
Singapore and myself. Cries from survivors in the sea lingered
for a while, but as we got further away, they ended.

We will leave Mrs Stevenson for the time being and turn to Mr
Arthur Ross of the PWD in the afterhold of the *Kuala:*

There seemed to be a general rush for the ladder and a good deal
of scrambling, which I am sorry to say soon developed into panic.
Men rushed to get out first and there was a bit of fighting at the
foot of the steps. The children had a poor chance, and I noticed
a little girl of about ten (about Nita's age) lying in a corner with
her whole leg in plaster, no doubt from a previous bombing. No
one seemed to have remembered her, and I got her up in my arms
and told her we'd get out together. She was in a terrible fright,
poor kid, and screamed once or twice, though I did my best to
tell her everything was OK. We reached the well-deck and turned
towards the starboard side, and then I saw what turned me cold.
Wreckage, bodies and blood lay all around and the deck was on
fire burning strongly. At this time the fire was advancing aft, along
the deck planks. Wounded were being thrown over the rail into the
water below to take their chance of being picked up by the boats.
One woman terribly injured in the hip was thrown over, lashed to
a mattress. We climbed about over debris and bodies to reach the
head of the gangway, which was now a seething mass of people.
    With the child in my arms, I am afraid I walked on the wounded
leg of a girl lying bleeding on the deck; I've never felt such a cad
in my life, but climbing about with the kid in the smoke I really
could not see properly. I saw a Chinaman roughly handled by
four women as he tried to force a passage through the crowd,
and I shouted for someone to take the child from me and pass
her through and into the boats, which by now had come out
from the shore to take people off. No one seemed to take much
notice, so I decided to wait a bit, and soon I was able to get her
over the side and into a boat manned by Mr Husband and Mr
Horsley, PWD, who had come out from the shore. I mention
these names as they were the only two I recognized, both being
PWD. There were others, however, and all doing a very gallant
job. I heard later that this child joined her mother and sisters on
the island, but I cannot say if they eventually escaped.

I then took a header into the water from the rail, complete with tin hat and 45 revolver. The former nearly broke my neck as I hit the water, but luckily broke adrift and floated inside up. On looking round I found myself near a nursing sister, who still wore her headdress. 'Are you OK?' I enquired. 'OK,' she replied, 'what about yourself?' I said I was all right and with that she set off for the shore doing a lovely six-beat crawl. Gee! That girl could swim! Just then the Japs came over again, bombing the water around the ship which was now thick with struggling humanity, mostly women and children. I confess now to feeling a terrible panic coming over me, sheer yellow fright and, taking a deep breath, I went down and down and still down as far as I could get. Every bomb that fell stung my whole body and one very bad shock stung my stomach so badly that I thought I must be hit, and put my hand down to feel for the wound. My head and lungs were now bursting and I shot for the surface, now in a state of blind terror.

My original idea was to make for the sandy cove, but I found now that I was being carried along by the tide rip, and my only hope was to struggle on and make the cliffs which rose in front of me to my right. I was almost there when the Japs made their third attack, this time bombing the cliffs themselves, up which many people were climbing. The bombs seemed to burst just over my head, tearing great gashes out of the vegetation and cliff face, and showering stones and rocks into the water all around me. It seems that I scrambled ashore as this third attack was over. I took cover in a cleft in the rock with a man and a woman (three very frightened people indeed), and was able to collect my wits for a few minutes.

There was an empty lifeboat beating itself against the cliff edge a few yards away and I swam along to her and arrived there simultaneously with an Air Force officer bleeding from the face, and a young aircraftsman with a head wound.

Ray, the aircraftsman, and I then proposed to take the boat out to the stricken ship. I thought we needed more men to pull, so I stood up and called to the shore for volunteers to help. I am sorry to say that no man moved, and I said aloud what I thought of them. Then we turned the boat's head around and moved out. . . . We could not reach the ship owing to the strong current, but soon found ourselves among drowning people who were being swept away to sea. There had been a badly hit airman on board when we took the boat out. He was seriously wounded in the back, and we knew he had not long to live. We did what we could to make him comfortable on the thwarts and told him to hang on. Ray then went over the side to an Army Sister in difficulties about 20 yards away. . . . We got her on board and put her in the stern to recover. Ray went over for several more, each time diving over the side and swimming out to their aid while I manoeuvred the boat – women and children he never passed – Europeans, Chinese, Indians, all these he went for while he still bled from the wound in his head. Most of these people were 'all in' when Ray brought them alongside, and each one I had to curse and swear at to stir them to that final effort to climb on board. This verbal lashing seemed to work; poor souls, we would get thighs or hips over while Ray shoved from below. We saw a woman on a mattress and hailed her; she waved her hand; but we shouted that we would return for her after picking up some children just ahead.

After picking these up, and a few more, we remembered her and our promise. She had drifted a fair distance but we reached her and dragged her in on board. She also came in for her spot of cussing and while getting her in over the side I noticed a wound in her buttock about seven inches long, gaping open and bleeding. It was Dr Thomson who had received her wound during the raid on the Pier the previous evening (13th). Stitches had been put in during the night on *Kuala* but these had now torn apart owing to her exertions while swimming. I wanted to do something for her, but she insisted she was all right and there were far worse cases in the boat that needed attention. 'I'm a doctor,' she said, 'and I know.' That settled the argument. She did what she could for the others, then demanded the end of Ray's oar and pulled with him as he needed help owing to his head.

Next we saw a man floating about some distance away, a Sub-Lieut RNVR – Stuart Sim by name. He was wounded in the leg, a bomb splinter having gone into his ankle and embedded itself. . . . We pulled him on board, and he did magnificent work in helping to manage the boat and rescue others in spite of his wounded foot. We were now drifting with the current on to breakers which marked a reef just awash. The situation was desperate; there were some 39 people on board and we were half full of water. I therefore asked Sim to take command of the boat and be Coxswain, which he did, seating himself in the stern and shipping the rudder. What magnificent work he accomplished too, giving commands from the end of that crowded boat. I was pulling starboard oar, and Ray and Dr Thomson pulling front oar, while he swore at and praised us each in turn, but always encouraging

us to our damnedest efforts to clear those rocks. But for Stuart's
seamanship I am prepared to say we would never have got clear
of that reef, but been upset and all drowned. We did at last clear
them, however; but we then found that we could not get back to
either the ship or the island, though we had already been pulling
for two hours.

Everywhere the sea was dotted with swimmers, each engaged in a
personal battle, making their way as best they could to the far
from hospitable shore. Among them was a 'QA' (British Army
Sister) destined to become famous, in a way she would not have
chosen herself – Miss Margot Turner. She had jumped into the sea
from *Kuala* with her matron, Miss Russell, who, though thought
to be a strong swimmer, was not seen again. An Australian Sister,
Gwen Dowling, also jumped, to find her hand caught in the hair
of a dead Chinese girl who had lost one of her legs. Another sister,
Brenda Wells, who was with her, swam strongly to begin with but
suddenly disappeared, probably hit by machine-gun fire. Joining
a Canadian sister, Gwen Dowling climbed into a lifeboat full of
women, the two nurses taking over from the two male rowers who
were exhausted. They got the boat round to one of the island's
beaches, where they were joined by Margot Turner, who had
been tending a badly wounded British soldier until he died.

As soon as they could, those who got ashore climbed up into
the jungle to hide from the bombing, and on to the top of the hill,
which to the best of my recollection was about 200 feet high. As
described by Mrs de Malmanche:

> When we got to the top of the hill we found a very pretty little
> grassy plateau; the sun was shining through the trees, and in
> normal times it would have been an ideal picnic site; now it
> resembled a small battlefield, with wounded lying about all over
> the place. All the able-bodied women were dressed only in pants
> and brassières, as they had torn up all their outer clothing to
> staunch wounds and make bandages. Several nursing Sisters
> were there, but there was really little that could be done.
>
> After a little rest, I carried on over the top of the island and down
> the other side where I came to a nice little sandy beach. Here I was
> delighted to find the two doctors, but they were both wounded.
> . . . There were several other badly wounded people lying on the

sand. Just then I saw Miss Brebner, Matron, Singapore, dressed
in pants and bra, with her handbag under her arm, struggling
down the hillside. She said how happy she was to see us alive;
she was heartbroken about all her nurses and Sisters killed and
injured. She herself was killed two days later. . . . Before leaving the
ship, Dr Lyon had taken all the morphia and hypodermic syringes
and tied them round her neck. She now got up, although feeling
ill and in pain, and did a round of all the wounded, giving pain
relief where necessary. On our side of the island we got all the
wounded into little groups; some of them were very bad cases,
and at this stage we didn't even have drinking water. The only
uninjured doctor was dealing with casualties on the other side
of the island. Miss Jones, an Australian nursing Sister, swam
back into the sea eighteen times to rescue people who were
either wounded or in difficulties; when she was too exhausted
to swim any more, she went out in the boat to help. She was
extremely brave, as bombs were dropping all the time, and the
under-water blast was terrifying. . . .

Some time later we heard the sound of an engine, and word
passed that the Dutch Controleur from one of the bigger islands
had come, bringing a few blankets. . . . The Controleur went away,
taking with him some of the worst cases, who had a chance of
living. There was a Miss Doughty, a young schoolmistress from
Malacca, with both legs smashed and one of them amputated on
the beach with a pair of scissors; and a young airman named Hogg
who had tried to launch a boat to help some people and had got
his arm blown off at the shoulder.

The Controleur must have come to one side of the island at the
same time as Lieutenant-Commander Terry from our party was
on the other. Anyhow we will now return to Benku for a while.

When I got back with the launch – just after the attacks on
Kuala and *Tien Kuang* – Terry, Surgeon-Commander Stevenson
and a Sick Berth Attendant with a first aid box boarded it and set
out for Pompong Island, telling me to get everyone ready ashore.
They were gone a long time and the light was beginning to fade
as we saw them returning. Terry shouted for us to come out;
we were to embark as arranged. The launch had many badly
wounded women on board and some who had died on the way
over. The tongkang was slow and it would not be feasible to load it
up at Pompong after dark. Help from Sumatra was the important

thing and it was decided that the launch and tongkang would set out, each towing one boat.

Everyone was mustered at the water's edge and a long crocodile began to wade out, slipping and blaspheming at the sharp coral. The two boats ferried to the larger craft, which was very slow work. Doris Lim, still taking everything in her stride, went on board one of them with her press entourage and it soon became apparent that there was not going to be anything like enough room for all of us. Jock Monro and I then said we would stay behind with a rearguard and I called for volunteers. Eventually about thirty men were taken into the tongkang and the same number in the boats. The rest of us, wet and silent now, stumbled back to the beach.

The unfortunates on Pompong would of course have to be taken off before us and the future looked bleak; though to the good could be counted fewer mouths to feed, which increased our ration to eight days, and the call for volunteers had had the effect of providing a hard core of reliable men. Except for Monro, one of the ship's engineers ('Tommo' Thompson, a rifle shooting enthusiast; it had been his elephant gun that had greeted the aircraft) and the two British officers of the Naval Base fire brigade, the sixty remaining were almost all ex-*Prince of Wales* and *Repulse* ratings. The senior fireman, Macintosh, was fluent in Chinese and Malay, so we were unlikely to have language problems. After the senior rating had organized the men for various duties we turned in.

Daylight revealed that *Tien Kuang* was no longer there, we hoped having got away with all the survivors to leave us top of the list for nightly rescue. Also that one of the lifeboats was high and dry. It proved to be holed and battered and shortly the other boat was found in similar state some distance away. Our hearts sank. It looked at first as though they had foundered but close inspection indicated evacuation in an orderly manner, with such details as a pair of gym shoes, dry, in the stern sheets. So it was possible they had just proved too unseaworthy and their occupants somehow taken on board the towing craft. Later the sound of an aero engine sent us diving into the undergrowth; a reconnaissance plane circled low over Pompong and then our island, but seemed satisfied that we could be left to whatever devices we might have. He paid us a visit daily thereafter, a confounded nuisance. I took three others on a jungle exploration to try and discover anything edible, but without success; about the only plus was that the stream had been found to have a pool inland which was excellent for washing.

These conditions were paradise compared with those on Pompong. No one was able to wash there because the sea all round was covered in oil fuel from the ships. Only one small fresh water spring had been found. Pompong turned out to be a 'most unfriendly island' in Gilmour's words, 'nearly all hill', in curious contrast to ours, which was not so. Both were covered with inedible jungle, but Pompong's shoreline, except for the one strand, was all jagged rocks and boulders, made dangerously slippery by the oil.

The *Tien Kuang*, surprisingly, had not been hit, though holed by near-misses and taking in water. Nor, unfortunately, had she 'got away with all the survivors' as Mrs de Malmanche explains:

> Some of the men decided to go to the Air Force ship, to see if it could be got under way. It was too badly damaged, so they brought back everything they could; this included drinking water, tins of fruit juice, corned beef and ship's biscuits, clothing and of course all the medicines and dressings they could find. There wasn't much variety; rolls of cotton wool, aspirin, morphia and some tins of M & B tablets. Just before daylight they opened the seacocks and scuttled the ship. If it had been left afloat, the Japs would certainly have started bombing again; as it was, they left us in peace.
>
> As soon as it was daylight we were able to start work. The steward from Government House was elected Commandant of the island; he was a very competent man, and had an honorary wartime Air Force commission. He soon had jobs allotted to various people, and a food and water rationing system under way. The badly wounded were given the fruit juice and allowed as much water as they wished; the rest of us were given half a cup of water and one small biscuit smeared with corned beef, morning and evening. Several people had died during the night.

Their graves were dug, and the latrines made, by men from the PWD, who also constructed beds for the more seriously wounded from branches. Somebody gave me a saucepan from the ship; this I used as a washing bowl cum bedpan for my patients, scrubbing it with sand between functions. The wounded were mostly messed up with blood and faeces, and were thankful to be cleaned; an RAMC orderly saw to the mens' toilet arrangements, using half a large coconut as a urinal. When I had finished my jobs, I went for a walk along the beach. It was a perfect day, and the sea and islands looked absolutely beautiful. In the distance I saw a ship moving, and hugging the shelter of the land; a few minutes later there were jets of water, and a roar, and the ship disappeared. Continuing my walk, I came upon a soldier kneeling on the sand; he was fully dressed, quite young, and dead. There wasn't a mark on him – he had been killed by the blast. When I got back to camp I reported it, and a squad buried him. . . . In the afternoon I saw to several patients, among them a nice newly-married young woman, Mrs Hawes, who had a hip wound and a severed sciatic nerve, which meant that she would be permanently crippled.

That night I had to look after a woman who was delirious with malaria; it was all very difficult in the dark, and during the night somebody crept up and stole most of the aspirins from the medicine chest. After that, we Sisters took it in hourly watches to hold on to it. In our little camp there was a beautiful Eurasian girl, about sixteen years old. In the ship I had noticed her, brimming with life and vitality, and very excited at the idea of being aboard. Now she was dying of peritonitis caused by belly blast. Miss Spedding, an Army Matron, sat with her and did all she could to help her, but she died during the night.*

As well as 'Sandy Beach' there was, on another part of the island, an unpleasant bumpy site among mangrove roots, but with the inestimable advantage of the spring mentioned. Pompong's new inhabitants gravitated towards these two

---

* I read this with special sadness because a few days before the surrender I was taken pity on by a young RAF flight-sergeant and invited home for a good meal. He was married to a truly breathtaking Eurasian girl who looked about eighteen and I couldn't help wondering what would happen to her when the Japs arrived. The *Tien Kuang* was full of RAF personnel, she could hardly have got a pass to leave without strong reason, and I fear it was her.

areas. Initially, those on Sandy Beach had water from the lifeboat barricoes, but when this gave out they moved to 'Well Site'. The former was under Squadron-Leader Farwell, a firm but approachable officer much approved of by Gilmour. The senior PWD officer, an honorary Group Captain Nunn, was at Well Site in general charge. (It is thought that he was Mrs de Malmanche's 'steward from Government House'). An attempt was being made to record passengers' particulars when the bombing began but this was lost; Group Captain Nunn started another ashore but this has not survived, so there are no records and years later relatives were still trying to piece bits of information together. Oswald Gilmour states from memory that Nunn's list contained 200 women and children, 30 or 40 civilian men and some 400 of all three services.

The story of Pompong, to last nearly a week for some, is one ranging from gross discomfort to death. Most of the women had torn up their outer garments for bandages and nearly everyone seems to have lost their shoes while swimming (though a farsighted individual had brought a bolt of canvas ashore and this provided footwear of a sort). The nights were bitterly cold, aggravated by the inability to light fires or dry clothes in the open for fear of attracting attention, forcing people to sleep clasping each other for warmth. The wounded, though tended with the greatest devotion by doctors and nurses, lacked suitable medical supplies and several died every night. They lay unburied because the ground was too rocky for digging at the hilltop 'hospital' and the effort, on starvation rations, of carrying bodies down to the shoreline too great, though graves in the sand were scooped out for those who had died nearby and for bodies and limbs washed up. Perhaps this is partly explained by the fact that the men were apathetic and, apart from a willing few, not prone to volunteer. The women had a blind faith that they would be rescued, not shared by Gilmour's friend Sid, who after a while asked him, 'How long do you think we should give it before throwing ourselves into the sea?' One should remember that the morale of these unfortunate people was probably poor, after all they had been through, before they even embarked, and near-starvation is a well known reducer of the spirit.

However, all was not lost. Though there had been no w/t communication (the *Kuala*'s radio was defective and the *Tien Kuang* does not seem to have got any message off) Terry, who had promised to be back, would have spread the word, providing he had got through. One happening on the debit side, and naturally to cause much pessimism, was the appearance of a junk which came in quite close and then sailed straight on. It looked at the time as though the local Chinese were unhelpful, or too frightened to get involved. Eventually Anthony Terry appeared in his launch after dark (almost certainly with Surgeon-Commander Stevenson, as there are several references to 'two naval officers'), took on board a number of wounded and then came over to us on Benku.

We had heard or seen nothing for the two days, when a little after midnight there was a shout 'Boat ahoy!' and, wonderful to hear, Terry's roared reply. He could take about twenty and I sent these out – to their deaths as it happened (it is thought they left Padang in a ship that was sunk). We had a few shouted words – he said that Singapore had fallen the day before, 15 February – the enemy had landed in Sumatra and Java, the *Tien Kuang* had been scuttled at Pompong and there were still survivors there. The launch turned, accelerated into the darkness, and he was gone.

There was no sign of Terry the following night, nor the one after that and it looked as if he had been captured. There was now only three days' supply of food left and the ugly prospect of starvation loomed closer. Anxiety gnawed at us and the ration was cut. It was a strange sensation and one being mirrored on a dozen islands in the vicinity, as a very unpleasant death approached inexorably, but in the most idyllic surroundings – the warm turquoise sea and beautiful near-white sand, backed by a myriad different greens; above, a hot sun beating down out of a cloudless sky. The weather, fortunately, was good for most of this traumatic month. Though the very heat of the sun was to be a scourge indeed to some people, the unsettled conditions that accompany the change of monsoon

had hardly begun to appear (though some accounts talk of brief
bouts of bad weather) and we on Benku had that at least to be
thankful for. The mosquitoes did not come into this category, nor
the hermit crabs that trooped out of the sea in nightly droves to
eat in the vegetation, and back again at sunrise. I constructed a
stockade of twigs stuck in the sand and lay down inside it, but
the larger ones got through and were even more trouble, prowling
round and round.

That night we were sure we heard noises at Pompong but when
the sixth day on the island dawned the prospects looked grim.
We were down to a biscuit or two for breakfast and supper and a
little of the Army's 'meat and veg' in the middle of the day. The
noises must have been the major embarkation in HMS *Tanjong
Pinang*, a small naval patrol vessel that had suddenly turned
up. Gilmour, ever active, went out to assist – 'From all parts
of the dark jungle they came in high spirits. This was rescue
from appalling conditions. This was the route to freedom. The
embarkation of about 170 women, some children and a few badly
wounded men proved extremely difficult. The only suitable route
. . . to the little row-boat was half covered with slippery boulders
and the other half with jagged rocks. . . . The men formed a chain
and passed the women and wounded along . . . torches could only
be used sparingly so for the most part embarkation was by sound
and feel. I well remember the hopefulness of those women. One
said, "You men are so wonderful the way you help us . . ." and
I thought, well, if there is anybody to be praised for their work
on this island it is the women doctors, sisters and nurses.'

For the background to the tragic episode of the *Tanjong Pinang*
we must go back to Singapore on Black Friday evening where
she was taking on board Army contingents. One was under
Major Swalwell, last heard of receiving the unexpected order
to evacuate:

The docks were a shambles. Fires everywhere and under constant
shell fire. We came to the 'little' ships, but ours seemed to be the
'littlest' of them all. I cast envious eyes at a couple of gunboats
which seemed so superior, humming away at the quayside. Our
HMS *Tanjong Pinang* was some 133 tons, a nondescript diesel-

engined job. She mounted a tiny 3-inch gun forrard. Aft there was a 40mm Bofors. The skipper was a young New Zealand RNVR Lt-Commander, his name was Shaw. He already had an RAOC Major and party of, I think, 50 RAOC ORs aboard. Shaw said to me, 'You are OC Troops; my idea is to travel by night and shelter in some island creek by day. We have some camouflage nets'. I asked, 'Where are we going anyway?' His orders were to make for Java and if necessary he said he would go to Australia! He had enough diesel fuel and canned food aboard to go anywhere! I was content to leave it at that.

The shelling became worse, with several landing very close, so Shaw set sail, heading into the smoke that was drifting over the water. He was unsure where the minefields were but with a shallow draught thought 'it should be all right'. Two miles off they ran aground, not surprising with visibility nearly nil and there was little to do but wait for the tide to rise. Dawn saw the *Tanjong Pinang* making good progress among the islands of the Durian Straits, Shaw having decided to press on rather than hide by day.

Several of the usual twenty-seven bomber formations passed high overhead, seemingly for Sumatra and then single planes appeared flying very low. Except for a Bofors crew everyone had been sent below, a fortunate move as two aircraft that buzzed them did nothing more. Lack of size was certainly an advantage on such occasions.

Meantime I had noticed bomb bursts on the far side of an island we were passing. Shaw couldn't guess what they could be, nor could I. He said the island was called Pompong and uninhabited. . . .

On we sailed and saw ahead more small boats and one or two bigger ships of 750 tons and upwards. Soon we saw planes diving at them and bombs bursting around. One of the bigger ships was hit and then another. Soon we were fast catching up on the bombed ship which turned out to be *Shu Kwang*, 788 tons. She was stopped and had a list. Shaw hailed the skipper who indicated that his ship was helpless, as a bomb had gone right into the engine room. Wounded and others were drifting away on mattresses etc. (I remember thinking how odd that mattress just floated!). We skulled around, picked up the wounded and then returned to the ship for the others. Shaw said we would proceed to Sumatra, 'dump this lot, and get on to Batavia'.

We made for Sumatra and continued, well into the night . . . there was not an inch of space on deck to lie down. At midday a

smart R N launch appeared and Shaw was told that the Indragiri
River was ahead and he should go up it to Tembilahan. When they
arrived our *Shu Kwang* folk were disembarked and I remember the
cries and moans of a woman who had lost a leg. I had not realised
there was a woman in the wounded. Shaw went ashore and told
me to wait his return. We would soon be on our way again. Later
he came back looking rather crestfallen and serious. I looked at
him questioningly; he said, 'You will have to disembark, I have to
go back.' I was incredulous and said, 'What! back to Singapore?'
He replied, 'No, but to some island (actually it was Pompong)
where hundreds, including women and children, are stranded. I
am afraid we may break down; will you let me have your 'mechs'?'
Taken aback I stammered a little and said I was afraid I must keep
my party intact, I had my orders too. I felt rather badly about it
as he had so little support on his little ship. We parted company.

When the *Tanjong Pinang* arrived at Pompong, Sid, who had
been rowing the dinghy, was told by Lieutenant-Commander
Shaw that he was going to make for Batavia. Presumably he did
not know that Palembang, this side of Batavia, had fallen, thus
barring the way. All were on board by 3 am when the *Tanjong
Pinang* disappeared in the darkness. The off-duty nurses had
gone with her to look after the wounded and among them was
Margot Turner. The next day passed uneventfully except that
the nurses bathed under a hose, their first wash for five days.

They had settled down to sleep on deck after dark when,
without warning, the *Tanjong Pinang* was lit up by a searchlight
and there were violent explosions as two shells hit the ship. Miss
Turner found there were dead and dying all round. Sister Beatrice
Le Blanc, beside her, had a nasty wound in the buttock, but she
said nothing about it at the time. In Miss Turner's words:

The ship was a ghastly shambles of mutilated bodies. My first
thought was for the women and children in the hold; but a
V A D, struggling up from there to the deck, her dress covered
with blood, said that the hold had had the full force of one of
the shells and was absolutely smashed. In any case I realised
that there was nothing I could do as the ship was already at a
steep angle and obviously just about to turn over. Beatrice and
I just stepped into the sea and were very lucky not to be sucked
down when the ship suddenly turned over and sank. This time,

however, I had been taking no chances and had gone to bed in my lifejacket.

Just before the ship went down the ship's officers had managed to throw a few small rafts overboard and Beatrice and I got hold of two of these and tied them together. This sinking was much worse than the *Kuala*; the cries and screams of the wounded, the helpless and the dying, were quite terrible; and the fact that it was in the middle of the night made it all so much worse. Dead bodies and debris from the ship were floating everywhere. During the night we two Sisters swam around and managed to pick up fourteen people, including six children, two of whom were under one year old. There was room for two people to sit back to back on each raft, each one of them holding a child in their lap. The rest of them were in the water hanging on to the lifelines. I instilled into all of them the importance of never letting go; but when dawn broke I found that two of them had gone.

The captain of the *Tanjong Pinang* hailed us from one of the ship's lifeboats but he said it was stove in and already leaking badly. He said that if he didn't sink he would try to get help. He told me to cling on and not give up hope – perhaps a Dutch plane would fly over. We never saw him again.

Beatrice, who had insisted on being one of those in the water, looked so ghastly that I hauled her on to the raft and found she had a desperate wound. She died that afternoon – as bravely as she had lived.

The tropical sun was beating down on us and, despite my efforts to hold them, two more of the women let go and were carried away. There was only one other person on the raft whom I had ever met before, when she was in Alexandra Hospital in Singapore. She died at the end of the first day; and on the second day the children went mad. We had a terrible time with them – and lost them all. I examined each of them with great care before committing their small bodies to the sea. The last one was a very small baby and it was difficult to know when it was dead. I thought, 'This is some woman's precious child; I must not let it go until I know it's dead.' But in the end there was no doubt and it had to go with the others. One by one the other women had gone and on the second night, 19 February, I was left alone with a Mrs Barnett, whom I had never seen before, but felt that at least I should know her name.

As we could now see no single soul on the face of the ocean we decided to let one raft go and both sit back to back on the other one with our feet in the water. Our lifejackets had made our chins absolutely raw so we took them off and tied them at the side of the raft so they trailed in the water. It was our third afternoon on the raft and we could now see a number of little islands round about; but the currents were terrible and we didn't know how we could possibly reach any of them. We managed to catch two pieces of driftwood and with these we began to paddle feebly towards one of the islands. Mrs Barnett let her paddle slip from her grasp and, before I could stop her, she had plunged into the sea after it, clutching the two lifejackets with her as she went. I was much too weak to swim after her. I called and strained my eyes to catch sight of her – but there was just nothing. I was now all alone. . . .

I prayed that help would come and felt very definitely that some unseen power was watching over me. Why me, and not those others who had drifted away? I managed to collect a few drops of rain-water in the lid of my powder compact and also ate some seaweed which floated near the raft. Night came and I watched the stars and soaked up the rain that beat down on me. I thought of home and my family and the happy things in my life.

On the afternoon of the fourth day Margot Turner was more dead than alive but could make out a ship approaching. Too weak to wave she managed to sit up, realizing that she was burnt black by the sun and must look like a Malay. As the vessel drew near she saw it was a warship and hoped it was British, but when it slowed and came right up to her, all the faces peering over the side were yellow. A rope was thrown but she was unable to do anything and a Japanese sailor came down, tied it round her waist, and she was hauled up like a sack of coal.

Fortunately there was an English-speaking doctor on board who looked after her very well. Though raving with thirst she was not allowed to drink too much too soon. What was left of her dress disappeared but she was given a shirt and trousers. When the ship came to anchor she was told to get up, but could not walk and the doctor carried her down the gangway and on to the long pier at Muntok, Banka Island. To her astonishment she heard English voices calling. They were British prisoners of war. She was then put on a stretcher and taken off to the civilian prisoners' camp where some nurses took over. One of them, Miss

6. The *Kuala*, sunk off Pompong Island (pp.30–37)

7. Tembilahan, collecting point
on the Indragiri River in Sumatra

8. Refugees boarding boats
at Rengat on the Indragiri River

9. The railway line
between Sawahlunto and Padang (p.74)

P. M. Briggs, recorded: 'We were called up to attend to another group of people . . . one girl was . . . the only survivor from a raft . . . her eyes were sunk into the back of her head and it was sometime before we realized she was English. This was Margot Turner, a QA.' The Japanese doctor visited her every day and was most kind; one day he arrived with her dress 'cleaned, pressed and on a hanger'. Miss Turner recovered from this grim experience, only to suffer the hardships of three and a half years' captivity under very different characters to the doctor. (Years later she was to become a Dame, RRC and Matron-in-Chief, QAIMNS.)

For the three days, or rather nights, after the ill-fated *Tanjong Pinang* had left Pompong, the steady trickle of rescue visits continued, though each was too small to make a real impression on the 400 or so still there. It looks as if Anthony Terry made at least four trips in all. He was seen by Petty Officer Leather (who had been in the *Prince of Wales* with us) on arrival at the Indragiri River on 15 February in the yacht *Tenggaroh*: 'A low boat came alongside and in it was Lieutenant Commander Terry and PO Daley from my mess . . . they had quite a few nurses and other women on the boat – some of them were dead – which they unloaded on this small jetty. I do remember Lieutenant-Commander Terry saying he was going back to continue the rescue as there were many people still in the water. I gave him a box of chocolate, and some other foods, and after a whole they turned the boat and the last I saw of them was going back down the river.'

Virtually doing a shuttle service with Terry was a great Australian character, William Reynolds, in his own ex-Japanese fishing vessel *Kohfuku Maru*, the doings of which are more fully described in Chapter VIII. On his first trip on the 17th he took off seventy-six and subsequently lifted all the remainding wounded and nurses. One of the earlier lifeboat trips had contacted a Malay Tungku (Prince) who sent a small prauw over with a little rice and fruit. Half a dozen civilians decided to leave in this, including Oswald Gilmour and his friend Sid. They were landed at Senajang, an island in the Lingga group with a large kampong, whence they got eventually to the Indragiri.

It will be remembered that many unfortunate swimmers were

swept away from Pompong by the powerful current. For those who were not drowned almost at once, the hardships were if possible worse than for those who made the shore. One raft had twenty-six people on and around it. All died, one by one, until there was but one survivor. He eventually swam ashore and lived on coconuts until rescued. Mr Cairns of Penang (the man whose wife had been killed on the dockside at Singapore) kept himself and his two-year-old son afloat for seven hours before being picked up. One hopes and imagines they reached eventual safety, because he was to tell Gilmour that the little boy went to sleep lying on a lifebelt in the water! Of course it was very warm.

Mr J. B. Ross, a Singapore bank manager, was the same sort of time in the sea. Though some swimmers were picked up, a considerable though unknown number were not and for those in boats or on rafts it was heartrending to see others being swept away, for whom they could do nothing. Though the sea was infested with sharks, there are, curiously, very few incidents of people being taken by them. Sharks are frightened by explosions and probably dislike oil fuel, of which there was a lot about.

We left Mrs Stevenson swimming beside a raft with ten people on it, being fast carried away from Pompong:

> Cries from survivors in the sea lingered for a while, but as we got further away, they ended. During the afternoon, a Japanese plane flew overhead. We thought our time had come. Silently I prayed to God that after the ordeal we had come through, he would spare us further trouble. My prayers were answered. We saw the plane disappear and could scarcely believe it, perhaps we were not seen, or maybe not worth a bomb. This gave us renewed strength of will to survive. Various distractions occupied our minds as we floated along. A strange fish jumped on to the raft, it was wedge-shaped and pale pink in colour. We kept it, possibly we would be hungry later on. On two occasions, the old gentleman at the rear of the raft decided that he was a nuisance and dropped into the sea. 'He's in the water, miss,' was the cry. I untied my belt, swam round and rescued him. In spite of his remonstrations that he was a hindrance and had 'lived his life' I knew that if one person left, others would follow in despair. We got very thirsty as the sun beat down. The raft was just a few strips of wood nailed together, it had no provisions or water supply. With the sea all round us, there was

temptation to drink, but we knew the consequences of this. For some hours our spirits flagged. Suddenly there was a refreshing breeze. One of the RAF men took off his shirt, threaded it over a piece of wood and propped it up for a small sail. It proved quite useless and was soon carried away. When it was beyond reach, the owner said there had been two hundred dollars in one of the pockets. When the reality of our position became apparent, each of us got frustrated and cross. The Punjabis and Madrassi did not speak English and communications were difficult. They tried to help by paddling with their hands in the sea. I prayed throughout the day, vowing that if my life was spared, I would try and be a better person, never to let opportunities to help others pass me by.

It was getting dark and must have been nearly 6 pm. No one had a watch that was working, but in those tropical regions there is usually twelve hours' day, followed by twelve hours' night. I felt very heavy and tired. My tissues must have been getting waterlogged. What could I do? – to sleep in the water was out of the question, there was no space on the raft, had I tried to get on it those already there would prevent this. However useless this proved, it was taken for granted that I would stay where I was, towing the raft.

Suddenly a tiny 'speck' showed on the horizon. What could this be? My first thought was Japanese looking for survivors. We all yelled with what force our dry throats would permit. It was really too dark to see clearly. At first we thought the boat was going away from us, but in a short time, it was alongside our raft. It was impossible to see what nationality these men were, and when they produced a knife I wondered were they going to kill me. In our nervous state we expected the worst. Soon they cut my twisted belt and pulled me into the boat. The others called, 'Leave her – she can swim'. How they thought I could last any longer was beyond belief. At such times people are irrational and think only of themselves and their own survival.

Another woman was also helped into the tiny boat. It was then full and the fishermen rowed away. They were Malays and hearing our cries for help had left their work to come to our aid. They rowed to a sandbank and returned to collect the others from the raft in relays. From the sandbank we were taken to a small island a short distance away. On our way they passed their hats round for any jewellery, or money we had. . . . I was, however, only too pleased to have something with which to show my gratitude. Especially when the Malays had been so insistent that I should be rescued first.

Mrs Stevenson and her party were eventually deposited at the mouth of the Indragiri River to join an escape route to Padang. Her feat, saving those people by sheer force of personality and physical strength, was surely worthy of substantial recognition. The same can be said for Arthur Ross, who we left handling a boat with an RAF officer and an aircraftman. The boat was full when he discovered he could not make the beach against the current:

We decided to conserve our strength and turn about, running with the current towards another island we could see on the horizon. Ray had all along addressed me as 'Sir', probably because I was in uniform. He was very exhausted with the pulling, loss of blood, and continually going over the side, so I definitely forbade him going over again. However, he disobeyed my orders soon after and in so doing perhaps *again* saved the lives of most of the people in the boat. He spotted a water-cask some distance from the boat and without losing an instant dived over and swam for it. We soon had it aboard and found it to be half-full of fresh water. This was probably belonging to a boat I had seen receive a very near miss from a bomb. It was full of children when it capsized. I saw it in the distance bottom up and on fire. I sincerely hope that most of those little ones were killed outright. I sent up a silent 'Thanks' to the Almighty for this cask. There were wounded children and women among us, and God knows what suffering lay ahead of them without water. It was truly an astonishing Act of Providence.

Our little company was now suffering much. The sun was very hot, and there was little room in the boat to move, and the bilge was full of a mixture of blood and salt water which the women were trying to bale out with their shoes. I erected an improvised sail made from two shirts lashed to a boat hook, which I think eased the efforts of rowing a little. Three of our people had died. The aircraftsman with the wounded back went very quietly. Sim had rolled his shirt as a pillow for him. A sister felt his pulse and put her ear to his chest. She pronounced him dead, and we put him gently over the side. The Army Sister whom Ray had just rescued, was dead; she never recovered and probably died from drowning. Two sisters rolled her into the water. Another wounded airman died in the bottom of the boat, died while lying in blood and salt water nearly 12 inches deep that lapped round our legs. A Sister lay down beside him, taking his head on her arm and clear of the foul water that threatened to drown him as he lay. Just another heroine among many that day.

It was getting on to dusk, and we were nearing an island (Kebat, as I discovered later). We were steering for a little sandy beach and the water was getting shallow, when four enemy fighters came into view; we all knew what that meant. Would they slaughter us with machine guns now, after all our pain and suffering? I don't think anyone cared. I certainly did not. On they came, diving on us as they approached. Thank God I had an oar to pull and something to keep my mind from the terrible suspense of waiting on certain death. No one spoke and I believe even the kiddies knew. They came from the bow and the drone increased to a great roar, and I waited for the bullets to crash into my back. They held their fire.

The strain seemed to have affected me as the next thing I knew I was being soused with water over my head by a Chinese woman. It tasted of blood, having come from the bottom of the boat, but it brought me round and I felt better. In about ten minutes we ran into the shoal water and I went over the side for sheer joy, and shoved the boat aground. It did not take us long to unload and take stock of our surroundings. First, there were the wounded and another magnificent job of work by Dr Margaret Thomson. We had no dressings of any kind and the only lotion was salt water. Splints were cut from driftwood with my sheath knife under her directions, and all wounds bathed and cleaned in the sea. Our great problem was dressings and bandages, and here again the women came to the fore. There were no shirts among the men and the women had cast off most of their dresses while swimming in the water and many stood bravely in only brassières and pants.

Of the thirty-six people, there were only nine men, and of these three were wounded and one just out of hospital. Two were soldiers, and I am sorry to say not inclined to be very useful. Of the women and children the oldest was close on eighty and blind, and the youngest only one month old. We had no matches for a fire, and night was coming on. I tried the friction stunt with dried sticks with no result. (I had been voted Commander of the party soon after landing.) The wounded were very unhappy. The girls were all suffering from severe sunburn all over their bodies. Ray Frazer's head was hurting badly and Sim's ankle had become stiff and cold. One poor lady with a shattered forearm must have suffered the agonies of hell, but silently.

During the night a woman came over and whispered to me that she had seen Japs looking at her from the bushes; I told her to go back to her place and go to sleep, as she was simply overwrought and seeing things. In about an hour she came again. This time she informed me that the girls at the end of the line were being raped by Japs. I rather went off the deep end, told her not to make a blasted fool of herself and took her by the arm and led her back to her place. Next morning I told Dr Thompson who said she would keep an eye on her. Later she started raising a scare among the women of 'headhunters' and Chinese pirates etc. Dr Thompson slapped her face with a left and right. Two great wallops. After that we had no more trouble.

As soon as it was light enough to see I set off to explore the island, and find water, as our precious cask would not last very long among so many. . . . I judged it to be near noon, and I was contemplating on the prospect of making our presence known to the Jap Aircraft, and making distress signals. It didn't seem fair to the children to carry on when all seemed so hopeless and the water finished. I went up to take a look when I caught sight of the upper part of a brown sail coming around the island into view. I let out a yell that roused everybody. Then a great Chinese junk had come into view bearing past our camp about half a mile from the shore.

One sister was wearing an old theatre overall which was once white. This I called for, and she pulled it off in a jiffy, and we hoisted it aloft at the end of a long pole and kept it waving from side to side, at the same time counting one, two, three, and all yelling together, which made a great volume of sound. Still the junk bore on, though I was certain we had been seen and heard. Suddenly she went about, and returned on the opposite tack, as if she wanted another look at us, for I could guess they were suspicious and taking us for Japs. It was neck or nothing now to make them understand, so I decided to swim out. . . . The water was calm and it was easier going than I expected. Had I thought of possible sharks I should have funked it completely.

After a time I got across to the reef as the junk came by – then I heard a strange sound coming from the shore. The Chinese were singing. The junk seemed to hear it too, for the sail came down and two men got a little sampan over the side. We were saved, and then I sat down and cried like a child. (The junk captain said he would have continued on his course had he not heard the Chinese song. It seemed to be a particular distress call of their own, only used in dire necessity. Our little Chinese nurses did their stuff too). The swim back was easy; in that joyful state of mind I could have swum anywhere. Dr Thompson pulled me out of the water and put the cigarette tin to my head. It was the last tin full of water she had drained from the cask.

Mr Ross (and one presumes the others) got to Padang and safely away, after as stout an effort as any among the tragic islands. He must have arrived at the Indragiri about the same time as Gilmour and Sid, who found they were behind those they had left on Pompong, because in the meantime there had been exciting developments. These started with us on Benku. It was now 19 February. Nothing had happened since Anthony Terry had taken a few off three nights before.

I was sitting on a dead tree-trunk, thinking of nothing in particular, except how hungry I was, when the lookout shouted; he was pointing at a speck which materialized into a man in a kolek, heading our way. We crowded round as he landed, a youngish Malay in horn-rimmed spectacles, with no shirt but smart khaki shorts and sandals. I understood him to say he was a local government Minister (eventually discovered to be, almost certainly, Tunku (Prince) Mohideen of Kalantan) and was making for somewhere further south. He thought he could send junks. We had a whip-round for him to pay for them and he was on his way, paddling strongly.

This was a tremendous fillip but crowned next morning by a repeat performance. Another shout heralded a largish sailing kolek with three naval khaki-uniformed Europeans, one of whom, with a cap at a rakish angle, was standing in the bows directing the cox'n along the pale channels of sand that wound among coral. Willing hands ran the boat up the beach and out stepped a fair-haired young man with an engaging smile and confident air that gave the impression that he looked on it all as a seaside jaunt. He was Lieutenant Sjovald Cunyngham-Brown MRNVR, First Lieutenant of HMS *Hung Jao* (a small ex-customs vessel) which had left Singapore on Black Friday and, after picking up survivors from several ships, had landed them up the Indragiri River. There, they had heard of the horrors of Pompong and decided on a rescue operation. Shaw of the *Tanjong Pinang* had been there too. Cunyngham-Brown, an experienced Malaya hand, said they should go to Singkep Island and arrange junks to Pompong from there, moving as much as possible by night. Shaw would have none of this and said he was going to go straight to Pompong; which he gallantly but unfortunately did.

Cunyngham-Brown's best bit of news was that his four junks were now on their way, in fact at this moment they were anchored on the other side of the island. He had found a motor boat, the engine of which needed expert attention and, on hearing that Thompson was an engineer, asked him to come with them – the other two were naval ratings – to try and put it right. 'Tommo' agreed and in a moment of generosity gave me a .22 rifle he had with him. Singkep, we learnt, was the biggest island of the area, the Lingga Archipelago, with a town – Dabo – a w/t station in contact with Batavia, tin mines, a hospital and other amenities. Its Dutch Controleur was being most helpful, a vital advantage to the many shipwrecked refugees from Singapore who had congregated there. Commander Charles Alexander RN (whom I had been under at the evacuation of Penang) had taken charge at Dabo and Cunyngham-Brown strongly recommended that we make contact with him rather than plough a completely lone furrow to Sumatra. He himself was going to Pompong via the junks, so I decided to go with him and bring one of them back.

We were shoved off by a happy crowd and it was not long before the junks came in sight, clustered in a little bay. I boarded one, Cunyngham-Brown spoke to the skipper, a wizened old Chinese, we wished each other luck and he was away. I admired him enormously. It seemed nothing was going to hold the rampaging Japanese down to Java or even Australia and that every day would see them further. While we were thinking, pardonably, of nothing but getting to safety, here he was doing a Scarlet Pimpernel act among the islands. Used to this part of the world, he did not, presumably, feel lost as we did, but it was nevertheless a fine performance. We did not meet again for 45 years.*

The junk was about forty feet long with a big open hold and two masts with brown lateen sails, which were soon being hoisted.

---

* Though we have corresponded. Minor differences between this account and that in *Alarm Starboard!* are thanks to his information.

Alone with the crew of three I began to wish I had brought someone with me and sat down in the stern, ostentatiously opening the flap of my holster. When we arrived, the first boat load came out baling furiously and when Monro climbed on board from the last, and the anchor was coming up to the tok-tok of wooden palls, we looked back at the friendly island with mixed feelings. It was exactly a week since we had first set foot ashore but seemed like a lifetime.

No sardines were packed tighter in the smelly hold, under a tarpaulin until dark, but later we slept well to the steady slap of water against the bluff bow. Islands, mostly uninhabited, were passed all the following morning and what looked like one of the other junks was in sight far astern, when in the afternoon the old skipper pointed to a long green streak and said 'Singkep'. The anchor splashed down half a mile off a waterside kampong, at which two native policemen in green uniforms with straw hats and cutlasses came out in a boat and took Monro and me back with them. They spoke a dialect he did not understand too well, but it appeared that several boatloads of white tuans had arrived recently and gone on to Dabo by road. More boats could be sent out and motor transport arranged. We came alongside a bamboo landing stage, scattering some very English-looking ducks which Monro and I eyed greedily. Among a few battered boats was one with *St. Breock* on it, the name of a tug last seen alongside the *Laburnum*. Two white men were working on another and we went over eagerly for news. It was not reassuring. There were at least 150 shipwrecked servicemen and some fifty civilians still at Dabo. They did not know of any ships coming to our rescue, in fact Jap aircraft were over every day and they did not see how any ships could make it. They were getting out as soon as possible.

Deposited opposite a stone building at Dabo, I went to look for whoever was in charge, with a sinking feeling that if Commander Alexander had moved on it might be me. However, he was there, exuding his usual *sang-froid*. I learnt that we were completely isolated; there was no longer communication with anywhere else as the Dutch had prematurely destroyed the w/t station. The Controleur, though first class, was a very worried man.

Food supplies were inadequate for his Malays, to say nothing of the sudden influx of Europeans. He was concerned that the troops behaved well; we were the last Europeans likely to be seen by the Asiatics, perhaps for many a long year.

The other junks must have arrived, with spare capacity, not long afterwards because Alexander called a conference. Present were a dozen officers from as many sunken ships. The goal was to be the Indragiri River, about fifty miles due west and we all pored over the one chart, of which I made a copy as best I could on the traditional back of an envelope. The Japs had set up a seaplane base at an island on the route; the only other difficulty – the passage should be possible in one night – was actually hitting off the river mouth, a featureless gap among miles of mangrove.

In the course of this, one of my Chinese crew presented himself and announced that they did not want to go any further. Bearing in mind the Controleur's warning against violence, things looked awkward for a moment. However, he had provided Alexander with a trump card, which was now played with fine theatrical effect – opium. The production of a black box, full of little tubes like water-colour paints, changed the Chinese's attitude markedly. Future procurement was apparently in jeopardy and so a good supply invaluable to these people, to whom it was next to life. He acquiesced and we were soon back on board, covetous eyes following the magic box that Alexander had given me, together with a pass from the Controleur, addressed to all local headmen, and 50 guilders.

I did not see Commander Alexander again. He elected to stay at Dabo, organizing the onward passage of the likes of me, and then bringing up the rear to Padang, where he was taken prisoner. We also said goodbye to Jock Monro who had agreed to go in one of the other junks and bring it back if numbers made this necessary. Having volunteered first to stay on the *Kung Wo*, then on the island and now to return, he too was taken prisoner. The behaviour of these fine officers was typical of a dedicated few whose doings illuminate the otherwise rather sombre story of *sauve qui peut*.

III

The Indragiri River

Our Chinese had never been to the Indragiri and it looked as if the last part of the trip was going to be somewhat hit or miss. Moreover, if we pressed on, the dreaded seaplane base would be passed in broad daylight; accordingly, I decided to lay up for a day so as to time our passage right, anchoring up a little channel between two islands. There was a charcoal burner's family there, in a little house built on stilts over the sea. Macintosh the fireman was soon chatting to them and we went ashore to be fed on rice, sweet potatoes and cane sugar. Several times it was necessary to hide under the house as enemy planes came over.

At sea again just before darkness fell there was a bad moment when a large ship was thought to be bearing down on us, but on approach she was found to be hard aground, another victim of the Jap 'air'. As instructed, I handed out opium every few hours. One smoker offered me his long pipe, the bowl of which he kept over a little fire. I tried a few sucks to show willing and was nearly sick; my only venture into drug-taking! Minutes later, just before dark, the shout 'Jap destroyer!' sent a shiver down one, but it was one of the gunboats from Singapore, beached and with wreckage and black stains where a bomb had burst forward.

Though my opium-smoking friend had considerable trouble holding the course and my envelope chart seemed woefully inadequate, dawn found us opposite the mouth of the Indragiri. Mudflats and mangrove bushes stretched away into the haze each side and to have missed the mouth by as much as a mile would have been no joke.

As we proceeded, a lone native came out in a kolek to meet

us. Wearing only a loincloth, he rasped alongside, chest heaving, and passed himself down the junk's side, jabbering hard between gasps. Macintosh looked interested. 'He says he'll pilot us in. Lots of tuans have passed this way in the last few days.' We hauled the Malay on board complete with kolek and he sat down to chatter away with hardly a pause. The sun glistened on his brown body and caught the water drops which flew as he gesticulated. His large black eyes took in every detail of us and his good humour (had not the last tuans paid well?) seemed to be a good sign. Hundreds had indeed come through Priggi Raja, which was the waterside kampong we could now see, in all sorts of craft. He would take us to the village headman who would be able to provide food; also he would show us a message from one of our predecessors.

The tide turned against the junk and progress was very slow. I decided to go ahead with the native to pave the way for the 'ship's company', so we launched the kolek. He steered right over to the north bank where the current was negligible, to glide along under overhanging boughs and surprise all manner of birds with our sudden approach. The muscles played powerfully under the oily skin in front as my guide drove his paddle and I blinked continually as the chequered shadows of the branches ran flickering down the canoe. Our going created a refreshing breeze and with it came contentment; life had certainly taken a turn for the better.

This was confirmed after we had landed at a rickety pier under a battery of curious stares. A little Eurasian in white ducks and topee introduced himself as the headman, saying that some food could be provided, but that two or three thousand people from Singapore, mostly soldiers, had almost cleaned out the shops. He then showed me a sheet of written orders tacked to the wall of a hut. Signed by a Major Campbell they were to the effect that one should keep going up river; there were officers at different stages who would give further instructions; the first was Tembilahan. This was terrific, an organization to help us! I had heard that Sumatra was a pretty wild place once one got inland and the idea of getting sixty sailors, not good footsloggers anyway, from one coast to the other, was one that had appalled. Nor was this all. The headman said he could provide a small steamboat to tow the junk to the next stop. Expecting to be behind them – on account of our delay – I was surprised to hear that the other junks had not arrived. Ours anchored off and the men were soon being ferried ashore to large helpings of curry. After a bit we re-embarked, distributed a little of Alexander's money and said a grateful goodbye to the friendly kampong. The steamboat puffed manfully up river, its passage marked by the ponderous ascent of large birds of the crane variety, and groups of wild pig beating hasty retreat from stretches of mud into the thick jungle which crowded each side. Peculiar fish with fins that looked like rabbit's ears scurried about in the slime and once we saw a crocodile. Eventually the sun was extinguished by a black fretwork of trees and so was our interest in Sumatran fauna, or anything else.

Sometime before midnight harsh Chinese voices and a slight bump ensured the unwelcome return of consciousness. Bright moonlight showed us to be alongside a landing stage among other craft, and a cluster of huts ashore. A large figure materialized, approaching gingerly over slippery planks. 'Hullo! I'm Ernest Gordon. What do you consist of?' He was surprised when I said we were sixty with two or three more junk-loads to come. 'That's awkward; we thought we were about at the end. Anyway, the situation is . . .' and he explained that there were 200 soldiers here and more at the next stop, Rengat; others were at various places up river, all moving on by slow stages. The Dutch were being splendid, arranging somewhere to sleep, scratch meals, and most important of all a couple of motorboats; we had a landing craft and all three were engaged towing motorless craft full of men. When those at this place, Tembilahan, were cleared, the organization was moving on up river. We had really just arrived in time. 'What about money?' I asked. 'Oh that's more or less looked after; you'll meet Major Campbell at Rengat; he's under Colonel Warren who is in charge at Padang, our goal on the West coast.' 'Have you seen Lieutenant-Commander Terry, a big broad man with a yellow beard?' 'Yes, he's been doing great work collecting people from the islands and towing backwards and forwards, but he's gone on now.' It was good to get news of Terry and I felt sure we'd meet up soon.

Next morning a food queue was formed in a nearby square; it led to a large barrow from which a Sergeant was giving out an egg and some rice apiece. Soldiers and sailors took their rations to a corner and eagerly finished them off. Malays stood on the outskirts in interested groups and I felt the first pang of shame. What could they be thinking of this mass influx of khaki tuans, shabby and haggard, queuing for food, when hitherto their impressions of Europeans had been formed from respectful contact with Dutch planters? We were to learn that, staunchly as they rose to the occasion, the Dutch authorities were naturally ill pleased to have us as guests, this lowering of the European standard, and worse, being one of the reasons.

I jumped as a hand landed on my shoulder and turned to the smiling face of Norman Crawley, a Gunner Captain. We had both been concerned in a projected raid on the Japanese positions across the Johore Straits (forestalled by the enemy's attacking first). The story of his (and Captain Dudley Apthorp's) escape was one of the best and is described in Chapter V. Dwarfing the others, Crawley's 135-ton junk *Hiap Hin* lay at the head of the line of miscellaneous craft. One of the other junks from Singkep arrived at mid-day and it was learned that another had made the river mouth. I paid off ours, to which we owed so much, the old man stowing the magic box lovingly away.

In the evening everyone was told to board the *Hiap Hin* and another boat, and when the thick rattan cable tautened there were over 250 in the clumsy but well-found craft, packed in the hold, on deck and under a big canopy aft. Though hardly eventful, the trip was not without its moments. She was steered by a huge tiller which came chest high and was operated by two men walking back and forth. They could not see the towing boat under the junk's high prow, so one of us stood on the canopy roof to which a twig was nailed so that it projected over the edge. This was kicked to port or starboard and followed by the helmsman below. Rounding a very sharp bend the junk swung right out, the tow parted with a bang and we drifted onto the mud. The original soldier crew were anxious to show their mettle and Crawley, who they called Skipper, asked me, as I started up with some hands to recover the end, to let the soldiers do it. They eventually secured the awkward, stiff rattan cable to bitts in the bows and after much straining the towing boat got us off. Rounding another bend the cable began to render and then slipped off the bitts. We ran aground again. 'Aw, for heaven's sake let the Nighvy do it,' said an Australian subaltern and we went forward to help amidst much good natured banter. Eventually the 'Bosun', a very large, congenial Bombardier who appeared to be Crawley's right-hand-man (his name was Rawson) wiped the sweat out of his eyes with 'Blimey, I might o' thought o' that' and on we went again.

Some time during the early morning the anchor splashed into the yellow and now narrowing stream at Rengat – quite a large place – and a voice hailed us: 'Who's that?' – I happened to be on watch – 'Lieutenant Brooke, a big junk-full'. 'This is Campbell; you can come ashore or stay where you are. Probably going on in barges tomorrow; we can't get that thing up any further.' A bustling and efficient King's Own Scottish Borderer, who I was to get to know very well, Major 'Jock' Campbell was at the door of a warehouse taking down details of the various parties and allotting numbers, which would be our sequence of movement across country. 'The next step up river will be in those' – he indicated some flat wooden barges moored astern of two steamboats. 'I hope you'll get on this evening but it all depends on the Dutch. They are doing wonders but we are a damn nuisance at a tricky time. They only have to forget us for a few days and that's it.' He said the next step was Iyer Molek. 'There's a lot of us there, under Colonel Dillon. The Dutch have something on and the transport question is getting difficult, but I hope it'll be all right.' Someone asked if the Japs were near. 'They're not far,' he said. Palembang, to the South, had in fact just fallen to an attack by parachutists, but we did not know this.

It was a tight fit, though fortunately not a long journey to

Iyer Molek. A very oppressive atmosphere had built up and soon the rain began to descend as it only can in the tropics. It was still raining when at about 10 pm we squelched ashore on to a muddy verge. A man with a torch led the way to some large buildings which he explained was an evacuated rubber factory, and there we were dished out with some excellent soup. He then took us to the rubber storage barn, where we wrapped ourselves in latex sheets and slept like hibernating caterpillars.

The self-appointed CO of this makeshift camp was Lieutenant-Colonel F. J. Dillon, RIASC. Always calm and tactful, but firm, he sat at a table facing the entrance and wrestled with all manner of problems, assisted by a Sapper Major, J. L. Nicholson. It had been he with the torch the night before, a very youthful, fair-haired little man in dark green riding breeches, presumably procured from the Dutch. They explained to each party on arrival the necessity for good behaviour and insisted on a 6 pm curfew for Other Ranks.

Dillon was a very remarkable officer; though he eventually became a Brigadier I would venture the opinion that his impending incarceration was a loss to the Army on a par with that of his General, Beckwith-Smith, Brigadier Paris and certain others. Nowadays almost anyone is called a veteran, but 'Andy' (also 'Dillo') Dillon really filled the bill. Of course I did not learn this until much later, but after being a Battery Commander on the Western Front at 19, he was continually in action on the NW Frontier of India until 1935, being awarded the MC and Mentioned in Despatches seven times. Having transferred to the Indian Army, he was AA and QMG 18 Division, destined for the desert but redirected at sea to Malaya, where they arrived two weeks before the capitulation. One of those chosen to carry on the war in Java, it fell to him to organise, as far as possible, the embarkation of the last few hundred in whatever could be found at the docks.

From then till I met him at Iyer Molek, Colonel Dillon was continually arriving to find a dangerous situation and staying to sort it out, first on his arrival at Batoe – a focus point off Sumatra

for boats heading South, then at Rengat and then at Iyer Molek.
At Batoe, in his own words:

> The trouble had started when some without money, being refused
> food, took it by force, only to be copied by others who had money
> but were prepared to loot rather than to buy. The shopkeepers
> themselves had not been blameless because they had seized the
> opportunity to demand fancy prices. . . . I soon found that the
> worst-behaved were not necessarily the deserters or Other Ranks
> and one had to be pretty tough with individuals. . . . There was
> a distinct air of *sauve qui peut* abroad among some civilians, some
> men and some officers and it was obviously only a short step to the
> armed man with no money saying to himself 'My gun is as good as
> anybody else's cash when it comes to getting necessities'. Rengat
> was worse. The Dutch Controleur was polite, but emphatic, 'You
> cannot land here.' The white concrete river-side quay was hot
> under the Sumatran sun. Shops a few yards away were all barred
> and shuttered, and groups of tough-looking Indonesian troops
> were posted at every vantage point. I could see a few refugees
> and troops lolling aimlessly about the Customs House straight
> across the road from the quay. On the ship behind me, I had a
> couple of hundred armed men quite desperate enough to force
> the issue for the moment, but the Dutch were our allies and
> were engaged in fighting the same enemy as we were. Moreover,
> any precipitate action would have made it quite impossible for
> anybody else to come up the river later. Negotiation was the only
> possible course.

It was the same old trouble – a party of refugees, many of them
destitute but armed, had taken what they wanted forcibly from
the shops and had commandeered transport by force. The local
inhabitants were terror-stricken, had closed their shops, hidden
their lorries and called for protection. There was no possible
going back and no other course open except to land at Rengat,
and cross Sumatra by road for 300 miles to the coast if the men
with me were to be got away from the western ports to fight
again.

For me it was a thoroughly bad moment. Unless someone took
charge, it was clear that few, if any, would get across Sumatra,
and as odd men of my division were involved, although the
party for which I had any direct responsibility were already
many days ahead, there seemed to be only one possible decision. I stood cursing inwardly, for it was obvious that getting
involved in the clearance of this mixed bag of refugees and

military parties would entail waiting until the job was done, and that would only happen when the process was stopped by the Japanese.

What had to be done was quite clear – someone had to stay in Rengat and someone had to go to extemporize administrative arrangements for those that came afterwards. I undertook to be responsible for their good behaviour and that we would see that there was no more looting. The Controleur was finally persuaded to let our shipload land on these conditions and he in turn promised to arrange transport to take all our parties from Rengat to Iyer Molek, a rubber station and factory some 30 miles away, where a transit camp might be set up. I landed first of all a small party of mixed Australians and British selected by eye on the spot, and had these stand by on the quayside while I went out to talk to the troops in the Customs House.

These were some of the worst troops I had met up to date. They were mixed Australians and British, were very truculent and had obviously been in the course of screwing up their courage to take on the local garrison; some of the civilians were as bad as the troops. I had a very unpleasant half hour including the nasty experience of hearing the bolt of a rifle push the cartridge into the chamber with the muzzle pointing at my stomach from about two feet away. I hope I did not show what I felt! However, in the end they came round, but I could see that trouble was to be expected from some.

True to his word, the Controleur produced some lorries, and I got away all those who had been there before we arrived with Philip in charge and then landed our own shipload after explaining very carefully to them the rules of the game. The Assistant Controleur gave me enough money on my personal signature to make a small issue to each individual who had none and we had enough food from Lyon's organization which, with the cash issue, sufficed to ensure that every one would be fed and could keep himself clean. The Indonesian troops were withdrawn, the shops re-opened and things were a bit easier. I had a notice drawn up and hung outside the Customs House stating that the penalty for looting was death, and would be enforced. I am glad to say that we only had to apply this order once.

Up river at Iyer Molek, a Colonel Palmer had been in self-appointed charge when Dillon arrived. During discussion as to who should remain, it came out that the former had several children, while Dillon had none; so he decided to take over. (Palmer was to have his jaw broken at Padang while trying to separate British and Dutch soldiers fighting, and subsequently died when his rescue ship was sunk.)

One was to discover later that the two original organizers of the escape route belonged to the (Singapore) Special Operations (SOE) under a Colonel Warren, who had sent them over some days before the surrender to 'set up shop'. Apart from those – Major H. A. Campbell whom I had met, and Captain I. Lyon – the continued operation of the scheme relied entirely on volunteers such as the two colonels mentioned above, Nicholson, Terry, Reynolds, Ernest ('Tiny') Gordon – who was a captain in the Argylls – and others I did not run into. These included another Gordon (Captain J. – known as Gunner), Lieutenant H. T. Rigden RNVR, MSM J. F. T. MacLaren RASC, and Sergeant H. Pearce. 'Tiny' Gordon had co-opted Rigden and MacLaren, the three forming a highly efficient team collecting parties arriving at Tembilahan from the islands, ferrying up the Indragiri and generally providing support. They did not escape, though Gordon nearly made it, as we shall see. All three were recommended for recognition after the war, but nothing came of it. As well as Sergeant Pearce, mention should be made of two young unknown planters who ran a rescue launch among the islands; also a similar launch's crew of gunners from Changi, Singapore, under a Corporal Clarkson; both must have saved many lives and can hardly have escaped.

The story of the doctors and nurses who made Singkep Island and the Indragiri after their ships had been sunk is the same one of selflessness. A Dr Kirkwood with nurses from the gunboat *Grasshopper* more or less took over the native hospital at Dabo and some of them spent many days in the various rough and ready hospitals encountered in Sumatra. Colonel (eventually Sir Albert) Coates RAAMC, who was to become a legend, not only in the FEPOW world but internationally, began his herculean labour in a small dispensary in Tembilahan. One of those ordered to evacuate on 13 February, he had left in the *Shu Kuang* with ten other medical officers, British and Australian.

Attacked twice, the ship was hit by three bombs which caused dreadful casualties on the crowded decks, the second attack leaving her sinking and Coates in charge of a lifeboat full of wounded. Sjovald Cunyngham-Brown in the rescuing *Hung Jao*, which was full up, shouted to him to keep rowing and soon they were picked up by the yacht *Tenggaroh*. On being landed, Coates immediately took over a small Indonesian dispensary and, having called for help, started operating with four other doctors, one of whom, Major Kilgour, was proficient with chloroform. By dusk he had performed fifteen operations: '. . . had to have his right hand amputated. I may say there was no saw in the place. For that and for two thigh amputations on British boys, I had to rely on a chopper for bones.' Thus began the Albert Coates saga of similar, brilliant, surgical improvisations in Sumatra, Burma and Thailand that ended only in 1945. After thirty-six hours without food or sleep, he was ordered by his superior to leave and escape; but he refused, and as most of the others passed through, made his way across Sumatra, continuing to operate in appalling conditions.

The indefatigable Dr Lyon and Mrs de Malmanche, having been taken off Pompong by Reynolds, did likewise, moving so slowly with the wounded and other nurses, in conditions of supreme privation, that they also forfeited their freedom.

The two women and their charges had transferred to a small river steamer, as described by Mrs de Malmanche:

Dr Lyon and I arranged to be in the cabin in shifts. . . . I had only been there about fifteen minutes when Mrs Warre woke up and went completely mad and violent. In the dark I struggled with her, restraining her with one hand and preventing her removing her bandages with the other. This went on for the rest of the night. . . . About noon we came to a little town, where there was an ambulance at the wharf; in it we put Mrs Warre, but while we were going back for Dr Crowe, the Greek family rushed into the ambulance, which then drove away. However, there was a stretcher on wheels, so on that we pushed Dr Crowe to the hospital. There were no doctors or nurses around, but we met an elderly American woman who took us under her wing. . . . I was put on night duty. . . . Like all the other village hospitals we saw, this one seemed to be in a state of complete disorganization;

defective plumbing, no noticeable administration, and I never saw a nurse. About 10 pm a Dr Bruna, a German, came round with a bottle of morphia in one hand and a syringe in the other; he scarcely spoke to us as we accompanied him on his rounds, but he gave each patient – in whatever condition – a generous shot of morphia, before going back to his house. . . . We were not once given any food at the hospital; I was all right, staying with Mrs Hawthorne, the American, but I only found out much later that Brenda was living by herself in an empty house, with a large bunch of bananas (given to her by a British sailor) as her sole food supply. Each day looters came and removed more of the furniture, until only the bed – with Brenda in it – remained. . . . During our entire stay we had been completely ignored by the Dutch population.

One afternoon some sisters arrived with the patients; one of them, Paddy Clarke, we knew. She eventually reached India, where the first person she met was Eric; she told him I was somewhere in Sumatra; and that was the only news he had of me during the whole war. [Eric will be remembered as having said at the very beginning of this book: 'If I don't come home to breakfast you'll know I've been sent somewhere else'].

At the next stop we were met by Major Davies, RAMC, a very nice man. He apologized for the ward we were all put in, which was not at all clean and infested with bedbugs, but he had no authority there. We were, however, given a plate of soup, the first time we had been offered food of any kind at these wayside hospitals.

Back at Iyer Molek the river had started to flood and navigation further up was considered impracticable. Road transport had been found for our predecessors, who were taken to the railhead at Sawahlunto and thence to Padang. There had been no difficulty about this, some dozen lorries being at British disposal until the day before we arrived, when Colonel Dillon had been politely informed that they were required elsewhere. A vague promise of some in the future had been made, and the matter left at that. He looked worried. Rumour of the state of affairs was already round the camp and faces were long. Though there was a large kampong nearby, prices were going up – native boys wanted five guilders (about 20p) for a duck's egg – and there was little to occupy the men.

I amused myself watching some giant toads in a ditch. Also a strange little band of swarthy, bandy-legged Japanese prisoners. In the charge of an intelligence officer called Clarke, they had been sunk in one of the gunboats and he was hoping to get them to India. At least one was a fighter pilot. All behaved very well; in fact, another brought a loaded rifle to Dillon, saying he did not think it should be left lying about within reach of Japanese prisoners! As the Japs were not allowed to surrender, perhaps they were not looking forward to being reunited with their kind.

On the second day a Dutch captain arrived, looking for the Colonel. He was enormous, blond and bronzed; a bandaged foot showed through the cut-off toe of his left boot, and his tidings were in keeping. The Dutch had decided to withdraw into Fort de Kock, about 200 miles NW and every available vehicle was wanted for the transport of troops and ammunition. All local lorries had been commandeered. He did not expect to get us away in the next few days, but he would try. The worst news was that the Japs were pushing on to cut the mountain road at a place between us and Padang. He limped disconsolately away.

Colonel Dillon's load was now heavier than ever; there was food for a week, dumped earlier by Captain Lyon; after that it would be a case of further begging off the Dutch. He put me in charge of the cookhouse in succession to an officer who had just left. Camp life centred round the cookhouse and it took some handling. We had a tight drill, unbeloved by those who would rather have scrummed and I had a row with one officer which ended in his going before the Colonel. The third day some lorries arrived and took off the fortunate few at the top of the roster. There was nothing for the rest to do but stroll round the kampong, and life was very irksome. The younger men grumbled at the camp restrictions and some were openly doubtful of the whole system. By the fourth day there was considerable talk among the soldiers that we were wasting vital time and would do better pushing on individually or in very small parties.

In the afternoon Petty Officer Pickard came to me and reported that about 50% of the camp had decided to depart that night. I immediately told Colonel Dillon who ordered a parade and gave a convincing speech on the situation and why it was suicidal to attempt any individual action. He said that we were still hundreds of miles from the coast and that the intervening terrain consisted of mountains, dense jungle, rivers and at the best bad roads. Our one hope was the Dutch, who could be relied upon to do their utmost, who were annoyed at the independent and bad behaviour of previous groups and who had specially insisted on our being formed into a collective body. His words went down very well and all except a handful resigned themselves to waiting. I did lose one Able Seaman who decamped that night. We never heard of him again.

The following day was a tough one. Some lorries turned up and, being now at the top of the list, we were preparing to leave when Colonel Dillon said my party could not be spared. Another left in our stead and the men got into an ugly mood, not without reason. They were unimpressed when told it was an honour and I was more than relieved when, mainly under the senior ratings' influence, the situation was grudgingly accepted. There were no lorries the next day and a hundred more men came into the camp; some had made their way along jungle paths from a point on the coast a long way north, which was a stout effort. One such group of nine airmen were thought to be the sole survivors of the *Chang Tei* (except for one civilian picked up by Cunyngham-Brown's *Hung Jao*). They had reached the coast in a grossly overcrowded boat; taking it in turns to be towed behind it, some had been 25 hours in the water and were suffering from exposure.

By noon on the fifth day the Colonel decided that something had to be done, if only for purposes of morale. The river was in flood at about 5 knots and it was arranged for an old steamboat and the landing craft to tow the two barges. Accordingly half the camp, which included my party, set off, making good about one knot. The bank could just be seen to be going past! Conditions were even worse than before, there being more bodies to fit in. The river wound and twisted and by nightfall we had probably come five miles in a straight line; but the following afternoon, on rounding a bend that disclosed a large kampong, we could hardly believe our eyes; recognized khaki figures were wandering about at the water's edge. The news was unbelievably good. Several buses had turned up soon after our departure and brought all the rest of the camp up here to Basrah; some had been taken on already to the next place, Taluk. Iyer Molek camp had been closed.*

My party of fifty-nine was then allocated two small lorries and climbed aboard for a twenty-hour drive of nightmarish discomfort. Our driver, a very young Malay, went as fast as the old Ford's engine allowed, with a permanently open, laughing mouth, almost devoid of teeth. The springs were non-existent, every board and plate rattled and our jolting passage over roads that were little but mud and stones was murder.

At midday, when we had all ceased to take much interest in life, one became aware that we were entering the outskirts of a small town and then climbed painfully down when the lorry stopped in the main square. This must have been Taluk. Through the open verandah of a substantial building, I could see Major Nicholson sitting at a table, and went up to him. He smiled, 'Not so good Brooke, I'm afraid,' he said, pointing to a big lorry ahead of mine which was being loaded with green wooden boxes. 'That's ammunition going up to Fort de Kock; they've got to get it all there tonight, and want our transport. There is just a chance of course that it will all go into their own, but not much.' We waited, watching the ammunition coming out. To lose our transport now might mean never to regain it, especially since the Japanese must be close. An hour later there were a few boxes left when Nicholson said something to the officer in charge, who nodded. Nicholson nodded to me and we were off.

---

* No account of the place would be complete without a tribute to the manager of the rubber factory, a Swiss by the name of Von Aesch. Nothing was too much trouble for him and his family; he had in fact produced the steamboat.

That was the last I saw of him. I heard nothing of Colonel Dillon either until after the war. Both stayed behind (though they come into the story later) and were the victims of the cruellest bad luck.

Just before nightfall the lorry rattled down for the tedious crossing of a broad river where we boarded a raft to be winched across by means of a wire and handwheel (see page . . .). Thereafter the road began to rise, up and up, as the last light faded. On went a pair of yellow lamps. Speed was not slackened. We had had nothing to eat since the morning but I began to feel sick. An occasional glance at the dusty features beside me, whenever they showed in reflected light, revealed the same gleam in the eyes; only the mouth was closed now with a purposeful grin in place of the laugh. And then we saw the most beautiful sight of my eastern experience. After grinding uphill in bottom gear the lorry burst forth into bright moonlight. For miles below us there was jungle and mountain and more jungle. It looked soft and feathery in undulating rolls, losing detail until coming up against a mountain chain; here and there a jagged hilltop thrust its head up to send black shadows over the tree-trops behind and to the right was a streak of silver that looked like a lake.

Then we were back in shadow and sleep must have overcome me, because I woke to realize we had stopped and it was terribly cold. My left arm and hand, still clutching the little rifle given to me by Thompson, were quite numb. The driver was gesticulating to a hut off the road, the lights of which picked out his central tooth like a milestone. We stumbled inside to find it a small tea house full of British soldiers drinking coffee. There was also fish to eat. The coffee was bitter and the fish dried kipperlike miserables that stared forlornly in the candle-light, but both tasted like the Berkeley's best. Then on again. The surrounding country became flatter and occasionally cultivated; then there were bungalows with gardens, and just before 4 am we could see the lights of a small town immediately below. It was reached by a corkscrew route and in a few minutes the lorry had stopped beside Sawahlunto station. Climbing slowly down, we thanked our Jehu suitably, at which he refuelled the old bus, turned her round and, with a cheery wave, drove straight back to Basrah!

Hard-boiled eggs and soup were doled out, followed by a welcome few feet of floor space in a large warehouse already loud with snores. A few hours later there was general commotion; a train for Padang was just coming in; it would take all of us. Padang, our goal! It was almost too good to be true. For the hundredth time Chief Engine Room Artificer Roper mustered the party, who were in high spirits. There had never been any question of difficulty after Padang. The train came in, a tall ancient thing, and we climbed up to the carriages via several steps; there was a puff and a jerk and I settled back with a Squadron-Leader Farquharson onto the comfortable cushions. The journey took about four hours and was very pleasant. After twisting round mountains and lakes the line led across terraces of straight-furrowed *padi* fields that descended the lower slopes in long steps, with workers in large straw hats straightening up to stare as we passed.

About midday the train drew into Padang – by far the biggest place encountered in Sumatra, about 60,000 inhabitants – and was met by two British army officers. They explained that all 'refugees' were billeted in two evacuated schools, the Malay School and the Chinese School, both virtually empty as our predecessors had been taken off by ships. Being somewhat junior, I was surprised to be informed that I was in charge of the Malay School. A Major Rowley-Conwy commanded the other. I was to have about 100 sailors and 300 soldiers, mostly Australian. After all other ranks had been made to hand in their arms – a most unwelcome procedure – we marched there and settled in. I was then taken, with a light heart, to the British Officer in Charge, Padang, Lieutenant-Colonel A. F. Warren, RM. All the officers of the new 'draft' were gathered there and we went into his room. He was a fine figure of a man, very dark and sunburnt with a black moustache, and great force of personality. Our hearts sank at his words:

> The situation at the moment is not good. We have about a fifty-fifty chance. I have wireless communication to Colombo, but cannot get anything through *from* them as the consul burnt his cypher books prematurely. Ships have been in fairly regularly, taking off refugees as they arrived, but nothing has been here for five days now. We do know that one was sent from Colombo, but she is two days overdue, and I have just had a report from further down the coast that the last one to leave, which was for Java, has been torpedoed. There is daily Japanese air reconnaissance here and it looks as if they have pretty well sealed off this port either from the air or by submarines or both. The enemy are about 60 miles away by road, though not yet in strength, and the length of time we are left unmolested depends entirely on whether the early reduction of Padang is included in their strategy. So you see we are in rather a poor way.

He smiled at our rueful faces and I could not help feeling that here was a man equal to anything. Then he got down to administrative details. Rowley-Conwy and I received our orders (only half the men to be absent at a time; always at five minutes notice to go) plus a few guilders for expenses; after which, somewhat pensively, we went our different ways. It was hard. The whole thing had been a race against time, and presumably we had lost.

The Malay School was a white stone building built round a grass courtyard with a big tree in the middle, under which a couple of native barbers were constantly at work. The large rooms lent themselves readily to allocation to the various parties, each under an officer or two. These were soon organized and set to cleaning up. Good food, brought in a Dutch military van, the opportunity to wash myself and my clothes properly and the feeling that the future was somewhat out of my hands, went some way to counteracting the nasty taste produced by our prospects. A night on hard boards was no hardship now and the next morning Warren produced enough money for officers to have eight and men five guilders to refit their uniform, or what was left of it. I went shopping for domestic requirements of the school with PO Hobbs. There was a Dutch barracks on the way, at which I had arranged to call in and listen to the radio with the Orderly Officer, who translated with anxious features. The news got worse and worse. The fighting in Java was clearly going badly. Nearer home the enemy, somewhere in the hills we had crossed, was taking this and that place. One seemed to have heard it all before, but it was an antidote to have lunch at the Oranje Hotel, stood by Alex Lind, a Lieutenant MRNVR on Warren's staff who told me something of his boss.

The Colonel was the head of a War Office secret unit, actually separate from the Special Operations Executive (SOE) in Malaya, but working closely with it. The SOE's Freddie (*The Jungle is Neutral*) Chapman was training Chinese communists (some released from gaol!) as 'stay-behind' parties to harass the Japanese from the jungle and two other SOE officers, Richard Broome and John Davis, had been secreting arms drops for these when the speed of the enemy's advance cut the ground from under their feet. Meanwhile Warren, seeing that Singapore was not going to last long, decided to set up an escape route through Sumatra, dispatching Captain Lyon (with Sergeant Morris RAMC, who did sterling work on survivor casualties) to establish the food dumps on Moro and the Durian Islands and elsewhere, and Major Campbell to liaise with the Dutch, as I well knew.

Warren had obtained a small coaster, the *Hin Lee*, officered by Alex Lind and Brian Passmore – another of his lieutenants – and on 6 February she sailed for Sumatra with Broome and Davis, who wished to contact their stay-behind parties, and two other SOE colleagues, Ronald Graham and Frank Vanrennan, whose ends were sabotage. The *Hin Lee* put back for more charts at which Colonel Warren embarked as he wanted to liaise with the Dutch Colonel Overaakers on clandestine matters. On arrival two junks were hired and the two pairs returned to Malaya. Tragically, Graham and Vanrennan were betrayed and executed, but Broome and Davis were successful, bringing some Chinese back with them. (After escape to India both were landed by submarine to carry on their work; living in the Malayan jungle, latterly with Chapman, for two and two and a half years respectively, they ended up as colonels with well deserved DSOs).

When the advance guard of the unruly element among the refugees, of whom we have heard in connection with Colonel Dillon, arrived at Padang, the authorities were naturally alarmed. On top of disgraceful behaviour, some were suspected of selling arms to the natives; there had been an uprising fifteen years before and the Dutch were very sensitive on this issue. They had asked their Java command to send a senior British officer to come and take charge of all the British and Australian servicemen now pouring into Padang, and Colonel Warren, already there and now without a clearcut role, was the obvious choice. He had arrived, with Lind and Passmore, on 24 February, to be joined by Davis and Broome and then as the stream of refugees began to dry up, by Lyon and Campbell.

Warren had made his headquarters in the Eendracht Club; most officers were accommodated at the Oranje Hotel, with Other Ranks in the two schools. Order was very soon restored; certainly by the time I arrived on 7 March, everything (except the school heads, which were quite unable to cope with the influx – or should one say exflux) was very shipshape.

As darkness fell on the 8th, I went to a hotel for a drink with three subalterns, taking with me my knapsack containing my pistol and a few other things. Java had just fallen, it was pouring with rain and we were a pretty gloomy quartet. Conversation had dried up when a hotel boy asked if I was Lieutenant Brooke; someone wanted me on the telephone. Major Waller, a 'refugee' officer who was on Warren's staff told me to report to the Colonel at once. Others were arriving, having had the same summons, as I got to the club: Rowley-Conwy, Clarke (the Intelligence Officer from Iyer Molek) and two new to me, in addition to Waller and Davis. When there were eight of us 'refugees', Major Campbell came in and said we were to make our way unobtrusively to Warren's room.

He stood there looking at each of us in turn as we made a semi-circle round him. I could feel my heart thumping. 'I have decided,' he said, 'with the help of information received, that if any of you are to escape, it is useless to leave it until after tonight. The Japs can be expected at any time, and there is no hope that a ship will get through at this eleventh hour; still less that she would get away. It is likely that all personnel here will be made prisoners of war. There is just a chance for some of you. Some days ago I authorized the purchase of a prauw* which is provisioned and has been lying up the coast so as not to attract attention. I had intended to sail for Ceylon in her, with my officers, having turned over the responsibility here to Colonel Dillon. The latter has not arrived; I fear he may have been captured, and I am staying.

'I have got you eight here because there is room for you in this boat. You have been selected as the most useful to the war effort in other theatres, and I am ordering you to go.

'You will sail tonight. It is a very long way and there is considerable risk. This is just the end of the suitable monsoon weather. You may make it before the S W monsoon breaks or you may not. Personally I think you have a sporting chance. Has anyone got anything to say?'

You could have heard a pin drop for some seconds. My mind was in a turmoil. Then the silence was broken by Clarke saying he had promised Singapore Intelligence not to let the Japanese prisoners out of his sight. Colonel Warren said, 'I over-rule that. You are to go.' I said I did not see how I could possibly leave my men at this juncture. He said, 'I'll deal with you in a minute,' or something like that. I went out on to the verandah to think, followed by one of his officers, muttering about not being rash; but I did not take it in. I knew I had only seconds in which to make an appalling decision. Warren came out. 'I'm ordering you to go!' he said. Then, 'Anyhow they'll segregate the officers from the men, so you wouldn't be any use to them.' I had been steeling myself to disobey him but his last remark – almost an aside – suddenly decided me. It would be pointless to go into captivity to no avail and rightly or wrongly I said I would go.

* Pronounced 'prow'.

'Good,' he said. 'Campbell,' turning to the latter, 'everything in order? Right, get going. Absolute secrecy; we don't know what orders the Dutch authorities may have had from Java which has just fallen, and it is quite possible that surrender terms, if there are any, include the handing over of all allied nationals, so keep away from everybody. Goodbye; good luck to you all!' And that was the last we saw of Colonel Alan Fergusson Warren, Royal Marines.

Outside it was still raining, dim reflected lights lending the scene a Wagnerian quality as we climbed into a number of gharries (small traps) already hired. Campbell indicated the last one and settling beside him I suddenly remembered the two subalterns. 'No, we can't stop for anything,' was his reply. 'Anyway a slip at this juncture might wreck the whole show.' After a while the ponies' hooves ceased to ring on the back-street *pavé* and we appeared to be heading into the country.

Though anything was on the cards, we had some chance; the men left behind had none. The feeling that I was a deserter was to be somewhat alleviated $3\frac{1}{2}$ years later, when I received letters from many of them saying they were glad I had got away; but I anticipate a low mark on the slate when these things are the subject of final judgement.

IV

Prauws from Padang

Two hours later we were climbing, with great difficulty, out of a dancing kolek onto the deck of the prauw. The moonlight showed a substantial attap (bark) roof amidships and, ducking through a small opening into the lantern-lit interior, I found a dozen forms asleep on the bottom or on half-decks at each end, was given something to lie on and 'knew no more'.

Waking to the strange creaking of the gear and jumble of voices, I wondered where the hell I was and then the immediate past rushed back. In overall charge was R. N. Broome, ex-Malay Civil Service. The starboard watch was to be under himself and the port watch under Ivan Lyon, a sandy-haired Gordon Highlander captain (who was to receive the MBE for setting up the Indragiri escape route). Jock Campbell was in charge of the victuals, such as they were. John Davis (ex-Straits Settlement Police) and A. V. Lind I had met before. Together with Brian Passmore, a tall dark Lieutenant RNVR, all these were SOE. We new arrivals were: Geoffrey Rowley-Conwy, the Gunner Major (who had done good work among the islands); his side-kick, Lieutenant D. C. A. Fraser; Major W. R. Waller, who had been on General Percival's staff; Captain G. J. C. Spanton of 1st Manchesters: H. M. 'Tojo' Clarke, the Intelligence Officer; Major L. E. C. Davis RAMC, last heard of with Mrs de Malmanche; A. J. Gorham, a swarthy Lieutenant RNR whom I did not recognize with his new black beard but turned out to be the *Kung Wo*'s second officer – he had saved his sextant and acted as navigator*; H. E. Holwell and R.

---

* Accounts describing Ivan Lyon as the navigator are incorrect.

10. "Arrived at a suitable island,
we said goodbye to the crew and paid them off" (p.83)

10–17. The Sederhana Djohanis (pp.82–89)

11. In the sternsheets: Waller, Broome, Gorham, Davis and Lind

12. From the bowsprit: *left* – Major Geoffrey Rowley-Conwy
(now Lord Langford): *right* – the author

13. Looking forward; note the state of the rigging

Cox, both MRNVR Lieutenants from the minesweeper *Trang*. The only RN officer on board, I was also the youngest by several years. The crew was completed by Jamal bin Daim, Davis's Malay orderly and Lo Gnap Soon, a Chinese protégé of Broome's. At the outset there was also the Malayan crew of three, an old jurangan (skipper) and two boys, to give us a crash course – exactly what it was! – on the gear.

If little Doris Lim, who had so captivated us in the *Kung Wo*, had been present she would have given the good looks palm to either John Davis or Richard Cox, but more important – both had considerable sailing experience. So had several of us, but none more than Ivan Lyon. A very keen long-distance solo yachtsman in these waters, he was in his element. After many hours together in the long night watches I was able to get to know him well and develop not only professional respect but considerable affection. Undoubtedly a Wingate in the making, he was already planning a guerrilla-style return to Singapore; Colonel Dillon, who was most impressed, records a long conversation at Iyer Molek with him on the subject.*

Gorham, who had a chart of the coast of Sumatra, not of use for long, and a wind map of the Indian Ocean torn from a pocket dictionary, had copied out the relevant pages of navigational tables on board the Dutch S.S. *Rooseboom* that had put in. He told me that Anthony Terry had been back to our island again, probably on the very night after we got away. This seemed unfortunate, but in the event the loss of time, plus the ensuing delay at Iyer Molek, saved us from leaving Padang in the ship he did. Its identity is unknown, Warren's lists giving no indication.

---

* Taking a glimpse into the future, Ivan did raise, train and command a special operations force in Australia that in 1943 used old Reynolds' boat to carry canoes to Singapore. They stuck limpet mines on to the bottoms of ships, sinking a total of 37,000 tons before getting clean away. The following year a repetition, using a submarine, was foiled and they all lost their lives. Some, including Ivan were killed in action (see page 129) the remainder being caught and beheaded. Ivan's wife and little son, Clive, had unfortunately sailed from Australia to join him in India even as he was going the opposite way. They were captured at sea and imprisoned in Tokyo. By then in a Pacific carrier, I met them in Sydney on their release in 1945. Part of this book was written in Clive's Norfolk garden.

In fact, both Terry's end and that of 'Doctor' Stevenson have remained one of the tragic mysteries of those black days. Both were awarded the DSC for their self-sacrificing labours among the islands and up and down the Indragiri.

The plan was to work up the coast some 200 miles to a latitude about that of Ceylon and then sail due west, using the NE monsoon, a steady favourable wind which did not, however, extend far enough down to allow us to start west straight away. If all went well the voyage might take three weeks, but two factors were likely to extend this. First, the notorious character of the west coast of Sumatra with calms, squalls, currents, reefs and every other horror (after detailing them, the area Pilot Book recommended sailing craft not to venture thereabouts, and if they must, to anchor at night) and second, the change of monsoon from north-east to south-west in April. As will be seen, south-west was no use to us and the date being 9 March there was a real danger that if precious days were spent off Sumatra early on, we might find ourselves halfway across the Indian Ocean being blown towards Rangoon, now in Japanese hands. In fact, as Colonel Warren had intimated, the whole thing was a gamble.*

The boat herself looked all right at first glance. *Sederhana Djohanis* (roughly translated as Lucky John), whose function had been general trading, was a sailing ketch with masts of about thirty feet and twenty feet and carried a very large head of sail with main, mizzen, fore and jib. She was roughly forty-five feet at the waterline, with a beam of sixteen feet and draught of four; with no keel the result was very saucer-shaped. There was a tremendous bowsprit. The central roof sloped down at a steep angle, so that the only flat exterior route from one end of the boat to the other was along the six-inch top of the gunwale.

We soon discovered that her sailing qualities were strictly limited. She would not sail nearer than some eighty degrees to the wind and made the most devastating leeway closehauled. But

---

* Rubbed in when Alex Lind, who had just bought and prepared the prauw, confided in a Dutch Merchant Navy officer, to be told, '*U bent idioot, mijnheer; Ik ben zeevarenlui; Ik kenn het zee!*' ('You are mad, mister; I am a real seafarer and I know the sea!').

running free, which seemed to be the only method really favoured by Malays, she went well and to make six knots goose-winged (sails set on both sides) was not unusual. *Djohanis* was not intended to go out of sight of land, however, being designed for shore breezes; in fact she had seldom been under way at night – there were no lights – and our initial insistence on continuing after dark kept the old skipper, *Bapa* (Father) in a state of continual jitters.

Provisions consisted of a supply of bully beef and tinned salmon (I cannot now touch either!), biscuits and a limited amount of extras such as tea, coffee, sugar and rice. The problem would be drinking water. There were two large drums and some petrol tins which worked out at a pint a head for 42 days, with a little left over for cooking the rare hot meal. Brian Passmore produced a Leica, though surprisingly he was not very interested and I borrowed it to take most of the pictures that now exist of our ship.

The boat's second great weakness very soon became apparent, the shocking state of her canvas and rigging. To begin with the sails were made of cheap, thin canvas, now rotting, that tore if poked hard with the finger! And all the cordage was on its last legs. It was obvious that what sufficed for pottering around the coast was quite different to that required for an ocean passage at the change of monsoon. This meant that our existence would be one of the finest judgement on the question of reducing sail; and eternally refitting. When carried out on the Equator on two biscuits for breakfast, a diminutive portion of meat for lunch and supper and a pint of water a day, this turned out to be tough.

Arrived at a suitable island we said goodbye to the crew and paid them off. *Bapa* shook hands all round, made a speech of benediction and obviously thought us all quite mad. The rest of that twenty-four hours is taken from Broome's log. It represents the daily fare until we struck westwards and frequently thereafter.

The night was bloody. We were beating up N, about 2100 when a squall came down and we had to lower mainsail. Wind went all round the compass and by am fell to a flat calm, and we had to lower all sail to prevent chafe. Rolled like hell. Nearly lost all our water. . . . Wind still non-existent at dawn. All

sails required work on them. Finally hoisted jib and got away
for a short time to S wind. Then hoisted mizzen and found
mizzen halyard one strand gone. Hoisted nevertheless. Hoisted
main starboard side and immediately had to lower to change
of wind. Tore a large hole while lowering, through catching in
wire strand on starboard runner. Mended this. Hoisted again.
Tore a large hole through catching boom. Repaired this. Finally
1030 hoisted by which time no wind. On shore breeze began
1130. A bloody night and a bloody morning. Seriously worried
re sails and gear. May make for Nias and see what we can
do.

However by 12 March we had come 180 miles from the starting
point, felt moderately safe from that direction and struck west
for Ceylon (about 1000 miles as the seagull flies). There were
still some islands to be cleared, and one dawn found *Djohanis*
in a light breeze off Pulau Bansalan, an unusual plateau-like
coral formation about a mile square. Approaching this we could
see the emerald-green streaks of a reef but decided, with our
shallow draught, to try a passage rather than the alternative
wide detour. A sudden shout from myself at the end of the
bowsprit proved discretion the better part of valour and we
returned as we had come. It was none too soon for one could
see great coral shelves and clusters a few feet under the boat.
Even as we watched, multi-coloured fish scattered in a flash and
a long grey shape glided into view. It came up under the hull as
if in silent warning to the potential survivors of a holed boat, kept
company for a while, and then disappeared with two lashes of an
ugly sickle tail.

Not long after this a fresh south-westerly breeze came off the
land and showed signs of blowing up strong. The jib downhaul
jammed when the storm arrived with a rush to tear the sail right
down one cloth. The foresail was soon lowered too, the wind
reaching about force seven. In two and a half hours we covered
twenty-six miles under bare poles; no mean performance and a
very thrilling, though uncomfortably runaway sensation. After a
few days near-calm the setting sun saw the prauw racing under
bare poles again for a group of islands and those who could
conjure up enough fatalism went to sleep with their fortunes

in the lap of the gods. Navigation was impossible; we just sped along hoping for the best while the land loomed up all round. This blind rush went on until daylight when we found ourselves clear of the islands and out at sea, having passed clean through the lot!

So far we had done 300 miles in the first week. This was up to schedule, but on the debit side with the continuous sail-reducing and hoisting, mostly unmentioned here, the one pint of water per twenty-four hours was certainly proving a minimum. For a few days the results of currents and unfavourable northerly or southerly beating took us back to the north-west of the last island and it began to look as if we might be chained to the land after all. This was fortunately not to be as 18 March found us bowling along again in the right direction. The Navigator announced that we had done ninety-six miles in the last twenty-four hours. The words were hardly out of his mouth when the drone of aircraft engines sent us all below except Jamal the Malay orderly, who took the tiller, an invidious but logical procedure as our one hope of immunity was to be taken for a trading prauw about her lawful occasions. This seemed to work as the big Japanese 'Army 87' reconnaissance bomber flew steadily past and did nothing.

A period of several days sweltering flat calm now set in. All were suffering acutely from the shortage of water and the feeling of helplessness was depressing to a degree. The sails hung motionless and the masts creaked to a minute swell with a regularity that made one want to scream. All the while precious time was slipping away. There was still some 900 miles – in a straight line – to do. With 1 April only nine days off we would have to do ninety miles a day, when the average to date was not forty-five. Eventually the horizon sprouted isolated black clouds and it looked as if we would be involved in a storm coming down from the north. It turned out to be a small cyclone which approached at high speed. The mizzen and jib had just been lowered in record time when someone shouted 'Waterspout!' and there, sure enough, was our first sight of one, a few miles away. The sea at its base was whipped into a whirling cone that dwindled to a stalk about thirty yards in diameter. This rose drunkenly to the angry clouds above which stretched down to meet it. The apparition, new to most of us, made good progress in our direction and all eyes watched with some interest. A discussion ensued as to whether the water went up or down but fortunately we did not have the chance to prove either as the spout sidled off, bending and swaying like a sleepy reptile, before dwindling to an hour glass and disintegrating in the middle.

When the storm hit us the boat heeled and moved forward as if a clutch had been engaged. She flew in its grip for a short time and then was relinquished as abruptly. An exasperating twenty-four hours was then spent sailing nor'-nor'-east with our destination on the port beam. The navigator's announcement that we had done two miles in the opposite direction to Ceylon brought morale down to rock bottom. It was 24 March and the first pang of real apprehension made itself felt. A new trouble arose when everyone began to go '*busok*', as Jamal called it, coming out in sores. I caught my wrist on a rusty nail and immediately went septic, saved by the MO's production of 'M and B', then brand new. Two enthusiasts jumped into the water as an advance on the dipper bucket, but that was the last time anyone did; a twelve-foot shark was on the scene in seconds though he may have been there unobserved all the time. Two immense blue-nosed whales then provided another scare, rolling and spouting in concert; they came straight at us and rifle bolts had begun to chatter nervously before they passed close astern.

By now we had got the measure of the prauw's and our own capabilities. Nevertheless it took several minutes, when available, to get off all sail, with spare hands stationed at the notorious tearing points. As probably the nimblest, I made the bowsprit my job. Gathering in the jib from the end of it in a hailstorm, usually with nothing on so as to lose no opportunity of a fresh-water shower, was quite an experience.

All at once, on 28 March, a steady breeze arrived. The northeast monsoon at last? And then from the heights of hope we were shot to the depths of gloom. 'Aircraft!' We dived below and Jamal took the tiller as usual. The bomber approached slowly from astern but with any luck. . . . ratatat . . . . . . ratatatatat!

Bullets crackled on the water, on the hull and a few smacked round inside. He circled the prauw three times, giving us in all five long bursts. When it ended we could hardly believe that no one had been hurt. The sails suffered most, their expanse probably drawing the gunner's aim high. For a period, as a precaution, only one man was allowed in the open, the congestion below adding to our discomforts.

'Easter Day' I heard with surprise; only three days short of a month out of Padang. The watch on deck were entertained by a big swordfish jumping, its great silver body flashing like a torpedo and tapering to a gnarled spike with which they fervently hoped to have no closer acquaintance. Jotted notes about this time read 'Night, squall to squall. 1200 calm after big squalls. Rolling. Exhausted and seasick. G's wireless check on the time put us back 110 miles. Bad!' That was worse than being shot at, wrecking the gear, or suffocating in calms. As with all sights, the navigator had to know the time exactly and as long as a car radio, stolen out of a taxi, gave the time signal this was all right. When the battery began to fail so that the radio only worked for a few seconds we set up a wrist-watch pool to help him switch on as near as possible at the right moment. He had had no luck for days until hearing on this occasion 'Colombo had its first air raid yesterday'. This was bad enough but anxious calculations, based on the fact that the announcer was well on with the news, revealed that the watch time was minutes out, putting us back 110 miles. However, we were spared the shock of arriving at the estimated position of land with none in sight.

The breeze then varied for a few days, though coming mostly from the right direction. It was exciting when frigate birds wheeled overhead, their split tails forming encouraging 'Vs' but as usual the fates did not permit anything on the credit side for long. The shout of 'Aircraft!' produced, for the first time, a thrill of delight. We were 250 miles from Ceylon (based on a snatch of 'Roll out the barrel' which always preceded the time signal; when carefully resung it indicated a minute before and proved a good guess). There was a scramble for something to wave at this single-engined and obviously friendly aircraft, but as it banked to come at us, the sun caught the ugly red 'poached egg' on its side. Down again, cursing, among the ballast. He roared down in a shallow dive, pulled out, flew round a few times and then disappeared westwards. The solution to the air raid announcement, he was clearly from a Jap carrier. Unless Ceylon had fallen to the enemy!

A group of tankers hove in sight some distance off. A distress signal was constructed and frantically waved from the penthouse roof, but they either could not or would not take any notice and steamed majestically on. Gorham effected a dislike of the Royal Navy and I did not miss the opportunity of pulling his leg about the merchant service keeping a poor lookout. We cursed the tankers but at least felt reassured by their presence.

Later the distant rumble of bombs and guns came to us, which turned out to be the sinking of the luckless carrier *Hermes* and her escort, by the Japanese fleet then in control of the area. The north-east wind then alternately died and came fitfully back again, bringing all the 'opposite monsoon' calculations to the fore, but it served to push *Djohanis* slowly westwards until there was but some eighty miles to go.

And then it happened. The helmsman, who had been scanning the horizon through glasses for some time, said quietly, 'I don't think you'll all be disappointed if you come up here and see what I see'. But there was a tremor in his voice that had the penthouse cleared in seconds, those with sores and bandages scrambling in the wake of those more agile. Land! That cynical horizon was broken at last. A faint but definite mauve triangle (it proved to be the mountain 'Friars Hood') was just discernible. In confirmation, the air at sunset was heavy with a most intoxicating scent. Ceylon. We turned in very happy. Even so, our evil genie could not resist a last fling. That night Fraser, trying to free the foresheets, slipped on a rope's end and fell overboard, splitting his chin open on a fluke of the anchor in passing. The doctor had to put in many stitches – sailmakers' twine and heavy needle! – by lantern light.

The only serious disagreement of the whole trip occurred as we were closing land. Basically Lyon and the sailors wanted to go on and sail triumphantly into Colombo harbour; most of the pongoes were for terra firma and the 'touter the sweeter'. The latter were in the majority and won, but approach revealed impossible breakers and on putting about the mainsail caught – no doubt we were over-confident – and split for fourteen feet. This was the last straw but at the same moment a merchant ship was seen coming straight for us and to cut a long story short we went alongside and clambered aboard to 'Where are you from?' 'Sumatra' 'When did you leave?' '8 March' 'Crikey, they've been over five bloody weeks!'

The skipper of the *Anglo-Canadian* was in a hurry for fear of submarines, but stood off and shelled *Sederhana Djohanis*, now a danger to shipping. Though hard hit, she did not actually sink before we left the scene. There were lumps in our throats as the remains dwindled. We had hated and cursed her, her bugs, her smells and her unfathomable ways, but she had come to the aid of eighteen desperate men and brought them 1,659 miles to safety. Who were we to be pleased with the achievement?

*   *   *

The Japanese did not in fact turn up at Padang for several days after our party had left, days of intense frustration for the 900 or so men accumulated there. The Dutch appear to have thought that by declaring Padang an open town and offering no resistance they might obtain better surrender terms. To this end (though Warren offered a fighting force more than once) all our men were disarmed and prevented from taking any ships or even small craft. There were ships idle locally, much British naval talent available and there is little doubt that with Dutch connivance all at Padang could have been got away. Petty Officer Hobbs wrote to me after the war: 'Lieutenant Monro reached Padang on 11 or 12 March – that same evening he came to ERA Roper and myself and told us of his ideas. He wanted a crew of 30 and you can say for sure we were all for it. We had to muster at midnight. Lieutenant Monro then got the boat stored and watered. Just after midnight Monro reached us and was he mad. The Dutch had foiled us. We

returned to the school, knowing full well that we should be
made POW.'

The same happened to AB 'Taff' Long of the gunboat *Dragonfly* who told me: 'Lieutenant-Commander Eustace said, 'There
are some small docks at Emmahaven – let's go down there and
see if we can commandeer a junk and make a go of it for Ceylon.'
He pointed out that everything was against us, the monsoon was
blowing across the ocean from Colombo and we had no provisions
of any kind; but everyone agreed there was no alternative. On
our way down the coastal road we were halted by a road-block
manned by native Javanese troops under Dutch officers. They
told us to return to Padang and if we made any attempt to reach
the docks we would be fired upon. Commonsense prevailed and
we made our way back.'

However, it would be quite wrong to criticize the Dutch too
much. Far weaker than the British anyway, they had been caught
completely off balance by the sudden collapse of Singapore. As
Colonel Warren was to put it:

> They deserved a tribute for their co-operation and forbearance.
> They had up to then seen nothing of the war or demoralization
> that follows defeat and disaster. There was a lot they couldn't
> understand and much we could not explain. Certainly there
> was little in the situation for *us* to be proud of. But they did
> everything they could and, in the main, refrained from insults
> and recrimination.

The last straw for the anxiously waiting hundreds was the news
that the S.S. *Chilka*, sent from Ceylon to rescue them all, had
been sunk.

When Colonel Dillon duly arrived at Padang, he did not feel
inclined to accept Colonel Warren's initial invitation to take
over; he had, after all, his own direct orders about escaping
and it was only his unselfish behaviour that had prevented him
accompanying his unit to safety. However, he offered to toss for
it! By then the question of escape was becoming academic and
Warren decided that, with all his experience of affairs at Padang,
he would remain. He provided Dillon with money with which

to buy a prauw at Sasak, 150 miles up the coast, and wished him God Speed. The Dutch then helped with two cars and various smoothings of the way; presumably Sasak was beyond the Padang pale.

Colonel Dillon picked a crew of nine in addition to himself. 'I put it to each one that, given a sound boat, good tackle, charts, instruments, food, water, an auxiliary engine and luck, the chance of success was about ten per cent. The lack of any one of these aids I reckoned would cut chances by half and so on progressively. I had a few refusals and I do not blame them; it was not up everybody's street. Some others refused because they would not leave the men for whom they were responsible. More power to them.' The nine were (with the Colonel's little comments): Hooper – to be skipper, MRNVR Captain of the *Jarak*, sunk. 'He thought for some minutes and then, half to himself, "I think she would prefer me to try". A first class officer'; Nicholson – Sapper Major. 'True metal through and through. If I had a son I would hope that he would grow up like Nich'; 'Tiny' Gordon – 'Never flinched, ex-theological student, he lived on extraordinarily matey terms with his maker'*; Thompson – Rubber planter and Air Force. 'He also had stayed with me to help. A good companion and handy man "I'd rather be dead than a prisoner." He died as a prisoner on the Siam railway'; Sheepshanks – Regular Signals officer. 'He refused to leave his men . . . but I ordered him to come . . . a tower of strength'; Crawley – Gunner subaltern. 'He had stayed with Warren and we agreed he should be one of those asked'; 'Uncle' – Merchant Navy officer. 'Chosen for his knowledge of navigation' (Not a success); Salmond – Businessman. 'Had done wonders organizing the survivors. Spoke Dutch and Malay. Never wavered'; Shellard – First Lieutenant of *Dragonfly* he had been in hospital at Djambi. 'Hooper and Warren both asked that he be included. Earned his place.'

The party left in the middle of the night of 15 March, giving a lift to Sjovald Cunyngham-Brown and his CO, Robin Henman,

* Gordon took holy orders after the war.

whose intention was to bring back another prauw to collect the rest of their ship's company.*

Arriving in Fort de Kock at eight am, Dillon's party were told that the Dutch had suffered an overwhelming defeat; all organized resistance along the road to the north-east had ceased and the Japs were expected by nine o'clock; they were also advancing down the north-west road from Sibolga, off which ran the route to Sasak. The race for this crucial junction was only just won. Having turned down the side road they stopped and, peering round some rocks, saw the leading element of the Japanese column tearing down the road they had just come up.

At Sasak, where the Controleur provided valuable assistance, two prauws were bought. Dillon and his men spent the day feverishly provisioning theirs, which was called *Setia Berganti*† and sailed at dusk. Cunyngham-Brown and Henman started back for Padang at full speed to collect their crew, but, approaching Taluk at midnight, they were stopped by a light in the middle of the road. It was the local Controleur who had waited for hours to let them know that the Japanese were encamped at the other side of the kampong. They were cut off. However, they were able to telephone Warren who said, 'You are on your own now,' and then, not for the first time, 'Goodbye and good luck to you'.

Back on board their new acquisition, Henman and Cunyngham-Brown were woken in the early hours by the sound of engines, shouts and the general hubbub of Japanese soldiery. Lying on deck they were suddenly aware of another prauw gliding alongside with whispered intimations that it would take them to the

---

* After organizing the rescue of such as myself throughout the Rhio Archipelago, Cunyngham-Brown's *Hung Jao* had arrived at Rengat to find the Jap net closing from both north and south. Having unshipped her three-pounder gun and mounted it on a lorry, they sank their ship across the Indragiri and set off for Padang. Near Fort de Kock they got word of approaching Japanese and waited with the gun trained on a bend in the road, overlooking a precipice. An armoured car appeared and they hit it first shot to send it over the cliff. The gun fell on its back but they roared off to Padang, just in time to contact Dillon before he started for Sasak.

† Thought by Dillon to mean 'All the Zephyrs' but more like 'Faithful Successor'.

other side of the estuary. They were in the middle of disembarking there when suddenly attacked with staves by their supposed benefactors. But they struggled free and outdistanced them over padi fields to another part of the coast. The treacherous Malays had obviously had an eye on ransom money. Befriended by the headman of a small kampong who was at loggerheads with the Sasak people, they had to do another midnight flit when a Japanese appeared. But they had been given a good sailing kolek with provisions and in six days, still aiming to collect their crew, the staunch pair were off Emmahaven, the port for Padang. Only to find it in enemy hands.

Heading back north for the Nicobars, they met bad weather, needing constant baling. The boat suffered and they had to land for repairs, were betrayed again but just got away. For weeks running into months they made painful progress, becoming weaker and unhealthy on a diet mainly of seaslugs. Their sores would not heal, their gums became soft and they had perpetual diarrhoea. Forced to land again for repairs somewhere north of Barus, they saw in the dark a large new sail and were in the act of stealing it when both were felled from behind, to wake up trussed in the native gaol. Taken to Sibolga, Cunyngham-Brown and Henman were handed over to the Japanese. So ended the exploits, at least those in the realms of freedom, of two resourceful and gallant officers to whom hundreds of men, women and children – though none more than me – owed their safety and often their lives.*

Dillon's *Setia Berganti* was a few feet smaller than *Sederhana Djohanis* (which also hailed from Sasak) but, except for the presence of a wheelhouse aft, was similar in all respects – especially the shocking state of the canvas and rigging and, of course, the devastating leeway made when the wind was not aft. Starting from further north, they had the advantage of being able to strike westwards almost at once, but, before clearing the coastal

---

* Resourceful as ever, Sjovald Cunyngham-Brown survived captivity to go from strength to strength in Malaya after the war. Henman died soon after release, but Cunyngham-Brown lived until April, 1989, when this book was in its final stages.

islands, had the same traumatic introduction to 'sumatras', the sudden inshore squalls. As described by Dillon:

We were on the port tack and it was very dark. Suddenly there was a screech like a train going through a tunnel and the wind hit us on the starboard side. The mainsail boom came up against the main mast and under the huge press of canvas she went right over on her beam ends. Everyone had an exciting time . . . mine was this. I was in the after well deck when it happened and as the sea came over I jumped for the roof of the deckhouse and grabbed the axe which we kept handy at the mainmast and stood by for the word to cut. The spare end of the spar carrying the mizzen sail cut into the mainsail and it split from top to bottom and I think that relief saved the ship. She came up a little and the helmsman started to try to work her round away from the wind, but the big mainsail was too much for the rudder, so he tried the other way with the same result. Then came about five seconds silence and WHAM the wind hit us from the opposite side. At that moment I was spreadeagled on the mainsail, trying to stop worse damage to the sail and in the next split second I was outboard hanging on to the boom for dear life with my legs in the sea. However, I managed to get along the boom and back to the ship hand over hand along the sheet, mostly through the water. As I landed on deck the skipper arrived aft and said, 'Where the hell have you been?'

Now we saw how she really could move. In spite of the torn mainsail she was fairly hurtling along in the gale and, though I suppose it could not have been more than ten knots, the impression of speed was tremendous. Half an hour later there was just a light breeze. We got in the mainsail and rigged a trysail and went on westward. In the incessant lightning (it is continuous in Sumatra) we could see we were gradually closing in to a lee shore and it was a bit doubtful whether we could make a headland that we could see on the starboard bow. As yet we knew nothing about our leeway. We held to the course and it looked all right . . . but just as we got to within about half a mile of the headland, dawn came . . . and then close on the starboard side there was suddenly a great WHOOSH and an enormous rock appeared out of the water, to be covered again with the return of the wave.

Hooper was at the tiller and he acted very quickly. He turned her head up into the wind, shouted to me to drop anchor, which I did in a split second and then we downed sails. Even in these few seconds we saw a lot more rocks all round and as the tide ebbed we discovered that we were lying in a patch of water in a small dent in a coral reef that stretched for miles in every direction. The patch of clear water . . . was not much bigger than a tennis court and had we been to the right or left of it we would have finished then and there on the coral.

The prauw was not more than 200 yards from the shore, soon discovered to be Pulau (Island) Pini, and as there was no hope of getting away until the wind changed, most of them went ashore in the kolek they carried, spread out the sail among some coconut trees and started the 'very dull job of stitching it up', just what was happening in *Djohanis* a couple of hundred miles away. Gordon and Salmond walked to a small kampong; it had not much to offer but a one-eyed fisherman they immediately dubbed Nelson paddled them over to a bigger kampong, whose headman undertook to pilot them out of their predicament to Telok Island, the gateway to the open sea. The sail-mending party did a good job, aided by Malays ('who, judging from the state of their own sails,' wrote Nicholson, 'had very considerable practice').

On going ashore at Telok the Colonel was met by a missionary, who explained that the Controleur was on a visit to Nias with survivors from a torpedoed British merchant ship. (They were from SS *Chilka* – actually sunk by gunfire – a boatload that ended up in the same gaol as Sjovald Cunyngham-Brown. Another of her boats, under the Master, reached India, as described in Chapter VI.)

An unexpected and unwanted interlude materialized when, just as they were leaving, the headman of Telok, who had been most helpful, came out to ask Dillon's assistance in quelling a riot. Two villages were taking advantage of the Controleur's absence to carry on a blood feud, and he, the headman, would get the blame. So the Colonel landed with his five soldiers, armed, and Salmon as interpreter and duly stopped the fighting, threatening to fire on anyone who started again. The prauw left next day, Nicholson noting 'We last saw land on the evening of 28 March. The visit to Pulau Telok had proved most satisfactory except for the waste of time.'

As things were to turn out the last few words were prophetic, but for the present things did not look too bad. Thanks largely to having only ten mouths instead of *Djohanis*'s eighteen, there was no food or water problem. Dillon was to write:

> Most of our breeze at this time was coming at night and it was very pleasant when the ship got up to about four knots, which is enough to get a breeze through the cabin. It was so pleasant in fact that it gave me very strongly the feeling, which I have not lost yet, that I would love to do the trip over again in a properly equipped boat. There obviously is a great satisfaction in just having yourself and your tiny boat against a wide ocean. Sometimes at night porpoise would come along the side of the ship rubbing themselves against it. . . . If you were quick you could lean over the side and pat one on the back and he would dart away for a short time, but soon come back. They were really quite unafraid and I imagine could soon be tamed.*

Two things in particular did get them down. Dillon:

> Our dud was at work again and this time he was trying to convince some of the others one by one that it was madness to go on and to work up a majority to decide to turn back. As he was the most experienced sailor onboard, his word naturally carried considerable weight, and to give him his due, he was suffering badly from an abscess . . . was running a temperature and was delirious at times. Personally I wished he would go off his head and jump overboard. I told him what a chicken-hearted, lily-livered scoundrel I thought he was and what I would do to him if I had any more of it. Nick was all for bumping him off there and then, and when I demurred, went off disgruntled muttering something about being 'Too bloody British!' Very, very unpleasant days!

Though the idea of bumping a man off may sound extreme, it was not so at all: there were several instances. The Argylls shot a Chinese found giving their position away; we did the same at the Naval Base to a spy; an Irish nationalist in the

---

* I was intrigued to read this because, when originally writing up the story of our prauw, I remembered the same thing, but could not be sure I had not dreamt it and so left it out.

RAF was shot for treachery at a northern airfield; and it seems that Colonel Dillon had previously had to have a man shot for looting. Unpleasant days need unpleasant deeds. However, 'Uncle' appears to have done his stuff otherwise, with only an atlas, a compass and his tables, as will be seen.

The second minus was that nearly all of them fell sick. 'At first,' says Nicholson, 'we thought it was sunstroke but finally when all except the Colonel, "Uncle" and myself were affected, it was obviously more serious and it turned out to be malaria. . . . Unfortunately we had no quinine. Gordon was worst, being continually sick. . . . "Uncle" developed a poisoned hand. Altogether we were a pretty sorry ship's company but normally five or six were available for watches.' This was awkward when the weather turned nasty, with the change of monsoon making itself felt. Fortunately they did not have our experience of hostile aircraft, though according to Dillon:

> A daily horror was the air reconnaissance. Suddenly one night as the sun went down we at last got the breeze we were waiting for and we were now at a comfortable bat on the course we wanted. It was a tremendous boost to morale and even the sick perked up. Dawn broke and the breeze still held. The sky was overcast and cloudy. There was a thin drizzle of rain and the visibility was scarcely half a mile. Salmond was at the helm and I was boiling water for a morning cup of tea, when I looked up and there, out of the mist and haze half a mile away came a ship, another and yet another. . . . They were naval tankers – either British or Japanese. Unfortunately the way they were heading, a course a little north and east, they could be only Japanese. Our only chance was that they either would not see us in the murk, or if they saw us, pay no attention. They passed us a mere half a mile away, their big figures dim in the rain. They held their course and disappeared to the east, and we started to breathe again. Geoffrey waved them a sarcastic farewell and everybody relaxed after the strain of these few minutes.
>
> Then all of a sudden I looked round, and out of the mist behind us came first one and then another, then another. They put a shot over us and we hove to.

'Tiny' Gordon's account does not put it quite so laconically:

'Sapper! . . . You're the shorty of the outfit. Get into that coolie coat and that big straw hat and take the tiller. The rest of you get below.' With beating hearts and constricted stomachs we waited. All we could see through the hatchway was the sapper's coolie hat. . . . 'Where are they now?' the skipper asked. 'They're still coming in our direction.' We held our breath. Then, 'Still coming . . . still coming . . . still coming . . . they're about a mile off . . . they're abeam . . . they're enemy all right, blast it! . . . They're drawing away from us . . . still drawing away . . . still drawing away . . . they're well past us.'

'With a bit of luck we may make it yet,' said Crawley. 'We just might,' we all murmured. 'Oh my God,' the Sapper groaned, 'one of them is turning'. I peered over the coming and saw a tanker steaming towards us, her prow throwing up a wave of snarling white water. I could tell from the slack position of my comrades that their hopes, like my own, had reached their nadir. My stomach felt full of ice – cold, hard, raw. We had failed.

Colonel Dillon again:

It was bad luck finishing that particular way. If they had been half an hour earlier, it would have been dark and they would not have seen us at all. If they had been half a mile further away they would not have seen us through the mist and rain, and in any case, the odds against their crossing the one course within a mile or so of us must have been thousands if not millions to one. However, we had 'had it', although we did not learn that expression until three and a half years of horror later, in August, 1945, when we were released.

Their bad luck hardly bears thinking about. Considering that we in *Sederhana Djohanis* had actually tried to attract the attention of these same tankers, the threads of fate are indeed fine.

Taken on board a tanker they were shortly transferred to one of the others. Crawley, being too ill to climb the ladder, was hoisted in with the boat. After being carefully questioned, they were quite well treated, one incident in particular reflecting credit on their captors. As described by Dillon:

We had declared that we had no arms and they did not search our kit. Crawley was flat out with fever and when looking for something else in his kit we suddenly shook a service pistol out of his kit bag right under the nose of the Japanese sentry. He immediately grabbed it and went off to the captain. I immediately asked to see the captain and said that I was exceedingly sorry that it had happened, that the officer himself was far too ill to be held responsible, and that if it left any doubt in the captain's mind that others of us had not told the truth, we would be quite amenable to have our kits searched. He, however, sprang to his feet and with a bow and the inward hiss, said 'No' and that he was quite prepared to take our word. He finished with 'I know English gentleman'. I met no other Jap like that in the next three and a half years.

The captain scrutinized Uncle's dead reckoning track since leaving the Sumatran coast and pronounced the position when captured as only 15 miles out. Pretty good after several hundred miles! Landed at Singapore, they all had a very rough time subsequently, three of them dying. Colonel Dillon in particular made an honoured name for himself in charge of camps in Burma, Siam and Singapore as witness various reports by officers, now at the Imperial War Museum; but I think he would have chosen as his epitaph (he lived until 1975) an unpretentious letter that is among his papers, from a corporal on release. It goes:

> I hope you will excuse the liberty I am taking in writing to you. I got your address from Colonel Hutchinson who sent me some photos.
>
> I feel I couldn't but write, as I didn't get the chance to see you before you left us so sudden. In my humble way I would like to thank you from the bottom of my heart for the wonderful work you did for myself and many others in those grim days. Your gentlemanly and always soldierly bearing, your kindness and good example was of the finest order. And has left imprinted on thousands of minds both British and AIF the memory of a man they shall never forget.
>
> May God bless you. And may you have many years of Health and Happiness with your family whom I am sure are as proud of you as myself and so many others.

*   *   *

Captain Dudley Apthorp, who at Singapore had swum out with Crawley to commandeer the junk *Hiap Hin*, did much the same at Padang on 17 March – the day the Japs arrived – except that this time it was a case of scouring the docks for a boat. With

Captains Purvis, Dicker and Tranter and sixteen assorted men they were investigating a prauw in the early hours when a Dutch police officer, Van Dyl, and two or three others appeared on the same quest. 'Hurry!' was Van Dyl's message and they soon saw why. A line of lights against the black mountain, moving steadily out from Padang, denoted a Jap convoy coming to take over. Their small store of provisions was rushed on board, the rudder shipped, the rattan mooring ropes cut and they were away.

They were hardly under precise control as no one had a real knowledge of sailing or navigation, but the tide swept the prauw out to sea, parallel and close to the road down which the Jap convoy was now only too plain. Apthorp's account,* quoted hereafter, describes the moment vividly: 'We held our breath. Those on deck lay flat. The few minutes we took to pass seemed as many hours, but at last the final tail light dwindled in the distance and we were alone.' The sail was hoisted as the first streaks of dawn revealed the prauw as the *Bintang Dua* (Two Stars), very similar to the two already described. It had been decided to aim for Colombo, in spite of Apthorp's 'In my estimation she was totally unsuitable for a long sea voyage'. Purvis, who had 'some knowledge of small boats', was elected skipper, Tranter was in charge of stores, with Dicker, Apthorp and two NCOs heading the four watches.

That night a sudden squall heeled the prauw right over, throwing most of the men into the watery bilges and splitting the mainsail. By good fortune the anchor fell overboard and brought her up short of some rocks, allowing makeshift repairs to be made on the sail. When they started off again, course was set for an island which their one chart indicated was Siberoet, the idea being to fill up with water before attempting the 1000-mile voyage westward. On the way a kolek with eight soldiers in it was nearly run down in a rainstorm. These were taken on board, the leader, Sergeant Strachino, proving to be the man the *Bintang Dua* needed – engineer, soldier and seaman, he had at one time served on a coaster and now took over as skipper. Thirty-six hours later

* See *The British Sumatra Battalion History* by Mrs D. Apthorp.

they made fast alongside the primitive wharf of a kampong on Siberoet Island where the display of a bundle of guilders secured a shipwright and large bamboo water containers. A central rail was constructed across the hold, to which these were lashed.

Time was pressing; it was presumed that the owner of the prauw had reported the loss and that either the Dutch or the Japanese would be looking for them. In spite of this, a significant proportion of the crew had discarded any pretence at discipline and 'every order resulted in discussion, argument and interminable delay'. Progress, not surprisingly, was slow and it was 21 March when they regained the open sea. Three days later it was cloudless and very hot; it appears that the lookout was taking a nap when the helmsman indicated a patch of troubled water on the port bow. 'Only a patch of brown water,' said the former but it was rocks and too late. A grinding and shuddering wracked the hull, the mainsail came down with a crash and the *Bintang Dua*, drifting sideways, continued to bump and grind against a reef. 'Over the side!' roared Strachino, meaning to lighten and push her off, but only the officers and a few others responded. In the midst of this, half-a-dozen men took Strachino's original kolek – towed astern – and rowed away. The tide ebbed, the prauw settled firmly on the reef and they were stuck. However, there was another, smaller kolek and this was launched to take most of them ashore, where somewhat unwisely they lit a fire. In the early hours of the next day the prauw refloated, little damaged, drifted shoreward and was anchored for the men to rejoin.

Sergeant Strachino distinguished himself again by diving repeatedly to ship the rudder on its submerged pintles and they were just about to weigh anchor when the party who had done a bunk reappeared and climbed on board – to a frosty reception. They were 'court-martialled', there was a show of hands and Purvis pronounced that they should have a quarter of the provisions and arms and then go to the devil. With Strachino fingering his revolver, the miscreants declined to argue, tumbled back into the boat and were gone for good.

Progress was very slow against the northerly wind. For two days the prauw was becalmed. Then they realised that, though

the flotsam around was hardly going past, the low lying coast
was indeed moving considerably. The only explanation was that
they had reached the southern entrance to the Strait of Siberoet
and a current was taking them through. Strachino altered course
and 'our spirits rose mercurially, and for a short time – such a
very short time – it seemed that we might indeed escape'. Then
– it was 30 March – the lookout reported a patch of haze on the
horizon. This turned into smoke from a small vessel, wearing
no ensign, which closed inexorably to circle the prauw and
let go a burst of machine-gun fire. They hove to. A launch
manned by small, dark-skinned men was lowered and came
alongside. The silent watchers could now see that these had
'Koeniglyke Marine' on their hat ribbons – it was an offshoot
of the Royal Netherlands Navy. Nothing was said, but a piece of
paper passed up with 'Please send your commander unarmed'.
Captains Apthorp and Purvis climbed down into the launch and
were taken back. The ship proved to be the SS *Banggai*, 662 tons,
whose peacetime occupation was servicing lighthouses. The crew
were mainly Indonesian and there were seven armed police, but
what astonished Dudley Apthorp was that the officer in charge
was Van Dyl!

Politely formal, he told them that the owners of the *Bintang
Dua* had complained to the Japanese and that the *Banggai* had
been sent to recapture her. Purvis was to return to the prauw
and arrange for the men to come over unarmed. The Malay
sent back with him suggested that the British take the *Banggai*
by force but he was told that Purvis had given his word. The
British officers tried to persuade Van Dyl to say he had failed
to find the prauw but the latter was afraid that Indonesians in
the crew might tell the Japanese and his wife and children were
hostages in Padang. The captain of the ship said he was happy
to go anywhere ordered, even Colombo, at which the captives
seriously considered taking the *Banggai* by force. Apthorp was
keen, but outvoted: it might have worked with complete unity
among them, but unfortunately this was not the case.

So they were taken back to Padang to join the others as prisoners, a process leading to Dudley Apthorp's inspired leadership

of the 'British Sumatra POW Battalion'. This provided slave labour in Sumatra, Malaya, Burma, Thailand and Indo-China, remaining for three and a half years, a 'disciplined, organized and when necessary, well-turned out unit'.

*   *   *

A fourth prauw from Padang – there may well have been others – was encountered off Siberoet by the kolek party whose story starts on page 221. This prauw, with a Lieutenant Dainty, Indian Army and twenty-seven soldiers on board, was passed by the kolek some days later – it was 28 April – heading straight inland. Before anything could be done to stop her, she crashed onto a reef before their eyes. The kolek crew could do nothing to help and it is not known what happened to those on the prauw.

*   *   *

We left Colonel Warren at Padang, having dispatched Colonel Dillon to Sasak, and then telling Cunyngham-Brown on the telephone that the Japs were all round and expected hourly. They arrived on 17 March. Warren, with a Dutch army Captain and the Governor and his staff were waiting tensely in the latter's office, when:

> 'They're here Sir!' from my interpreter (the Colonel's vivid account goes). They entered noisily and we stood up as the sentry banged his butt. . . . The Jap commander entered followed by about twenty others. They strode purposefully in with the air of conquerors, kicking their legs in front of them, their muddy boots striking heavily on the floor, their curved swords jangling as they walked. . . . Treating us all as if we did not exist the general sat . . . to the accompaniment of noisy throat clearing and hissing intake of breath. . . . I glanced about me. . . . These were good fighting men, crude, fierce, proud and confident. There was little about the undersized myopic Jap in this bunch with the broad, flat, yellow faces with cruel eyes and long whispy moustaches.

Mrs de Malmanche, who, with Dr Lyon and the nurses had arrived at Padang a few days before the enemy, tells of her last day of freedom as follows:

The Japs took over the town quietly. . . . That night, however, we were all rudely awakened, at about 1 am, by a tremendous crash, and found the whole place swarming with Japanese soldiers, who had crept up silently and broken down all the doors simultaneously. We all had to assemble in the hall. Dr Lyon was slapped for daring to fold her arms over her flimsy nightgown. . . . The next day we were told that we were internees but were to remain and run the hospital until further notice. [Her story goes on to cover the coming years of devoted nursing.]

A B Taff Long of the *Dragonfly*, it will be remembered, had been turned back from an escape bid to Emmahaven:

Some Dutch officers, accompanied by a couple of dozen Jap soldiers, called upon us to fall in outside the school. We marched through the town past jeering, gesticulating natives to a gaol where they used to incarcerate native criminals. There were already several hundred Dutch colonial troops inside. In this gaol started three and a half years of despair, degradation and malnutrition; of working on a railway; but that is another story. Of the fourteen Naval men of our party from Rengat five eventually survived.

Commander Alexander, having brought up the rear of the refugees all the way from Dabo, declined any chance of escape at Padang, a supreme example of devotion to duty that went completely unrecognized. He commanded a camp on the Railway, being with Colonel Warren most of the time. The latter, writing to me after the war, remarked 'Bad in parts, but we had some fun sometimes'.

Warren's assumption of command at Padang – at the request of a Colonel Field at GHQ, Java – had been in no sense an appointment; several more senior officers had passed through with no inclination to take over, and he was well known to the enemy in Singapore (Malaya being full of sabotage orders and cheques signed by him) who had put a big price on his head. I myself heard him say, 'They know how to make people talk,' and it is not surprising that he was looking forward to moving on. In the event he was questioned closely but pretended to be another officer of the same name, shaved his head and moustache and somehow got away with it. He was sent to the Burma/Siam (Thailand) Railway early on, where he commanded a camp (one of his officers being the irrepressible Jock Monro).

The end of a promising career was as nothing compared to the very grisly death in prospect if found out, as it seemed he must be. In short, Colonel Warren's staying to face the Japanese music was an act of sacrificial, cold-blooded bravery that must rank in its way with any VC of the war.

V

Do It Yourself

In my opinion the palm for enterprise at Singapore's Dunkirk goes to the small parties and even individuals who set out at short notice, with no preparation, in anything they could lay their hands on. The pity is that, with so many small boat stories, there is only room for a few.

As already intimated, some 1800 Army officers and men, preferably of special merit or qualification, were detailed for evacuation to Java on 12 and 13 February. Insufficient time for organization, allied to accurate enemy shelling of the harbour area, disrupted their embarkation, some ships leaving early when full up, so that a number of units were left stranded. Typical was the situation of a party from the 9th Battalion, Royal Northumberland Fusiliers:

> At about 1900 hours (it was the 14th by this time) it was officially made known that no craft were available . . . all ranks were given the chance of returning to their units or making an individual effort to leave the island. All risks and hardships that might be involved . . . were explained . . . by Major Leech. All men elected to got through with the venture.

As it happens, Wavell's last message to Percival, agreeing surrender, on 15 February, ended, 'Just before final cessation of fighting, opportunity should be given to any determined bodies of men or individuals to try and effect escape by any means possible. They should be armed.' The unfortunate Percival cannot have had time to do much about this, but there were many who needed no official spur. So the exodus which had begun on Black Friday, the

13th and continued on the 14th, became a veritable do-it-yourself flood on the 15th, when the eight-thirty pm surrender dropped the flag for some 3000 and changed deserters (who had for the most part been turned back by 'red caps' at the docks) into bona fide escapees whose soldierly duty it was to get away. Though the general military situation had deteriorated fast since the enemy had secured a foothold across the Johore Strait, most had contrived a sort of mental block against thoughts of disaster and the news of the surrender came as a great shock to many, e.g. 'We were horrified when ordered to cease fire at about 5 pm. I do not think any of us had visualised a surrender. We were previously ordered to fight to a finish – so thoughts of escape were in their infancy,' and again, 'Mr Cook came into the shelter . . . and said "In a quarter of an hour the war's over, we surrender." At first I didn't quite catch what he said and thought it was the enemy who had surrendered.' Thus virtually no escape plans had been made.

The getaways were surprisingly successful because General Yamashita undertook, at a dramatic parley at the Ford Motor Works, not to enter the city until the morning of the 16th and, in fact, the bulk of his Army never did. It appears that only small parties penetrated to the waterfronts in the first crucial days and in any case the Japanese were themselves exhausted, short of ammunition and no doubt only too glad of a respite. They were not, therefore, very energetic at rounding up prisoners or preventing escapes at the outset; nor, of course, could they be everywhere at once, seeing that they were outnumbered by nearly three to one.

The map on page xv shows that there is a mass of islands and islets (many unnamed) stretching for about 40 miles over a broad front south of Singapore, then a thinning – it can hardly be called a strait – followed by another large group of islands extending roughly south-east for about eighty miles. The big island at the southern end of this is Singkep, the town on which, Dabo, became an unplanned collecting point for shipwrecked mariners. In peacetime yachting enthusiasts, both officers on the station and civilians, had been used to sail out to these islands – some of them very beautiful – for picnics in idyllic privacy. Some boasted Malay fishing kampongs or Chinese villages, and fishing stakes and *pagars* (bamboo platforms) were not uncommon. Ivan Lyon, with his passion for sailing, must have known many of them and so was well placed to choose Moro for a food dump. Of course, few escapees knew of it before setting out.

As well as high-flying bombers with other targets in mind, Japanese fighter-bombers and reconnaissance seaplanes were over the exodus fleet most of the time. They did not often attack the junks, sampans, launches, yachts and dinghies spread out beneath them; but one never knew, and many of these emulated the big ships in taking the 'seamanlike precaution' of laying up by day, camouflaged with branches.

The commonest vehicle of the exodus was the sampan, simply because so many were available. To a Westerner it is not the handiest craft. One anonymous soldier recorded: 'We went in all directions; the sampan is a cross between a canoe and a rowing boat, has no seats and no rudder, and you cannot tell bow from stern.' And another: 'It is designed to be rowed from a standing position facing forwards, but from the stern end. Rowing like that is an art that takes some time to master but we got over the difficulty by . . . sitting side by side and shoving brutally.'

Sergeant Denis Gavin of the East Surreys, with three others, took a sampan of only nine feet, 'We didn't know anything about sails or sailing but we began to learn the hard way of course.' Fortunately for everybody the wind was blowing from Singapore to Sumatra (a nice example of the Naval expression 'a soldier's wind').

Two others

noticed about 50 little rowing sampans moored together about 100 feet off the quay. Quite half of them were burning but lots looked whole. Jarrett-Kerr and I immediately scrounged a lift . . . found an apparently sound one with oars. We collected some spare oars, a pole for a mast, and several rush mats which are used as sails . . . we soon loaded our meagre belongings onto the tiny craft. With the three of us and our haversacks and water bottles

it was below any plimsoll line it might have had! Getting out of
the inner harbour was easy because it was almost as bright as
day. There was no current. . . . We had set sail at 3.30 in the
morning and by 4.30 a decent breeze sprang up. In the darkness
Jake managed to rig some sort of sail. I never saw it in daylight but
presume it was something like that. Anyway, it was a stout effort
on his part. We had no map but each of us possessed a compass.
We knew that Sumatra, or the nearest point of its coastline, lay
about 45 miles to the SW.

A little vignette of two more military mariners makes pleasant
reading. They landed, from a small rowing boat, on an island
to rest.

The sun was overhead when I awoke with a terrible thirst and I
was just going to search for water when I heard voices just below
me. I woke Charles Bailey and decided to remain under cover as
they might still be Japs. After ten minutes the undergrowth parted
and much to our relief some Chinese approached with a large mug
of cool water and plenty of biscuits. By God, was I thankful to see
that water! We ate like pigs and the Chinese told us to come down
to their small huts. They were absolutely grand. When we landed
they had seen us and after we were asleep they had rescued our
boat which had drifted out to sea, mended a small hole, built
a sail and replaced the three oars we had lost. They made us
coffee and gave us tinned sardines, and when we were leaving
told us which island to make for. I offered them money for all
their kindness but they would not accept anything.

Sergeant A. R. North, originally of the East Surreys, was yet
another who left at no notice and with no preconceived plan.
He kept a diary from which the following is extracted:

By ten pm on 15th, most of the men in this area had been disarmed.
An hour later Sergeant Healy, an operations clerk, asked me if I
would like to make an attempt to escape with two FSO Officers
who had had permission to go; the answer was obvious. We left
Fort Canning at about 23.30 hours and proceeded to Raffles Hotel
in Singapore, where we made plans. We decided to go through
the Japanese lines to Changi Yachting Club, but later gave up
the scheme as it was too risky. A Chinese waiter in the hotel said
that he had a small flat-bottomed boat – enough to carry three

people – and said we could have it. We went to inspect the boat and decided to take a chance with it.*

We left the hotel and carried the boat along the beach road to the sea. It had to be lifted over the barbed wire, some five yards wide, which we did with the aid of a bullock cart. . . . We headed due south the first night, each taking a turn in rowing. There were floating mines which didn't help. . . . We made for the Kalapa Islands and hooked up in a mangrove swamp at about midday, very tired and hungry.

The two officers went inland exploring next day and found a kampong where they were given food. After the four had spent an uncomfortable night in a swamp, badly bitten by mosquitoes, they finished the last of their bully beef and procured footwear that North badly needed and Chinese clothes and hats. They kept on with blistered hands and fitful stops for snacks from friendly Chinese fishermen, while Japanese bombers continually droned overhead, until, one evening, they were approached by Europeans in a small sailing kolek.

They said that they had a large Chinese junk called *Hiap Hin* which was anchored off one of the islands in the distance, and if we could make the junk before darkness they would take us with them. We could hardly believe our luck. We eventually reached it by 7 pm. [This was the junk of the seemingly ubiquitous and undoubtedly enterprising Captain Norman Crawley who] then proceeded to give us the rules and regulations of the boat. . . . Everybody had to pool cigarettes, food and money so that they could be shared equally. If anyone was caught hoarding these articles they would be put ashore at the nearest island with a little food and left there. Everybody had to work and were not allowed to carry revolvers. These had to be handed in. There were 72 men on the junk, British, Australian and Indians and about five wounded men. The skipper told us his plan. He said that he intended to make for Australia. The ship had a good supply of water and rice. We were to set sail in the morning. Each of us was allotted his job.

* The two officers were Major Waller (a Gunner on Percival's staff who had just signed the surrender order, it having been passed down by reluctant seniors), and Captain Spanton; both were to escape from Padang with me in *Sederhana Djohanis*.

Everybody was up at dawn and we had breakfast of some watery rice, bully beef and some very weak tea which we drank out of a coconut shell. A Malay fisherman came aboard stating that for $100 he would take us to an island where there was plenty of English food. This island, named Moro, was some 25 miles away. The skipper decided to take a chance on it. . . . We hoisted the mainsail, the two anchors were pulled up and we set sail. There was a lovely breeze and we were making a few knots. This was really marvellous, something I had wanted to do all my life. The islands we passed were very pretty and colourful, typical of the Indies. At 5 pm we anchored off Moro and sent a party of men, armed, to have a look. They came back with the good news that the food was plentiful and there were cigarettes and medical supplies. All this had been put there about eight days before the fall of Singapore for men attempting to escape after the capitulation. There was also a map showing us an organized route to Sumatra, where arrangements would be made to take us to Padang on the west coast; there the British Navy would pick us up. This sounded too good to be true. The skipper called us all on deck and asked us what we wanted to do, Australia or the organised escape route. It was decided to go to Sumatra.

This they did (my naval party joining them at Tembilahan for the trip to Rengat, where the junk had to be left). Poor North was taken prisoner at Padang, becoming a member of Captain Dudley Apthorp's Sumatra battalion. To return for a moment to the boarding of the junk at Singapore – Apthorp himself was an 'original member' of the *Hiap Hin*, having swum out to a mole near the anchored junk. Crawley, who could not swim, followed behind, clutching a baulk of timber. They found a boat but also that the current was too strong for them. Some thirty soldiers had gathered on the mole by this time and eventually a boat's crew made the junk. A rope was stretched between her and the mole and everybody taken on board, after endless trips, by passing the boat along the rope.

Major John Nicholson RE, who was to become Colonel Dillon's right-hand man at Iyer Molek, was a little more organ-ized as he had sailed in local waters, but had as hard a time as any getting to the Indragiri. Given permission to escape with a Regimental party on the day of the surrender, he, with Captain

Geoffrey Hallowes, eventually secured a pram dinghy at the
Yacht Club, in which they started southwards at three am on
the 16th. After much hard rowing, during which six soldiers
were collected from St John's Island, they eventually reached
another in the Rhio Archipelago, to fall in with some officers
and men in the twenty-two-foot yacht *Columbine*. These agreed
to give the dinghy a tow and for several days the pair had a
trying but comparatively uneventful passage to Moro Island.
Trying because, as Nicholson soon found out, he had to take
charge; 'only two of the other fifteen had been in a sailing boat
before, so the aggregate inexperience of the crew was frightening;
however, most of them were too ignorant to realize it.'
   At Moro

> for the only time during my wanderings, the inhabitants were
> definitely hostile. They had only a little food and a few days
> earlier certain soldiers had threatened the natives with arms and
> had stolen food. . . . We learnt that there was a food dump and a
> camp of escapees . . . about four miles from the town across a strait.
> On the morning of the 19th there was no wind, so two of us with
> our Malay guide paddled over to the dump. There were about
> 100 troops there camping in the woods, waiting for a launch to
> take them to Sumatra. The food was packed in four-gallon petrol
> tins, each tin containing enough for six men for two days. . . . We
> took two tins from the officer who was in charge. . . . At the dump
> there were sailing instructions directing boats to Priggi Raja.

After days of various alarms, including the continual passage
of aircraft overhead, and a spell of bad weather, the end of the
long-suffering *Columbine* eventually came. She was badly holed
by rocks on a lee shore and then given the *coup de grâce* by a coral
reef. They floundered ashore in the dark through knee-deep mud
as Malays with torches came down to the beach to see what was
going on. Nicholson went off to contact the penghulu of the
adjacent kampong, and after further tribulations the party was
eventually taken by Malays up the Kateman River to Sungei
Guntoeng, where Major Leech and his Northumberland Fusiliers, intent on the same route, were encountered. Natives were
hired to row them up river. A jungle trek then brought them to

14. "Someone shouted 'Waterspout!' and there, sure enough, was our first sight of one, a few miles away" (p.85) (sketch by the author)

15. "At the same moment a merchant ship was seen coming straight for us" (p.89) – the *Anglo-Canadian*

16. "She had come to the aid of 18 desperate men
and brought them 1659 miles to safety" (p.89)

17. The crew of the *Sederhana Djohanis*.
Standing, left to right: Gorham, Broome, Brooke, Cox, Holwell, Spanton,
Campbell, Lyon, Davis, Rowley-Conwy, Fraser; *kneeling*: Davis,
Passmore, Lind, Jamal bin Daim, Waller, Lo Gnap Soon, Clarke

the big kampong of Maddat, the Emir of which arranged for a
motor boat towing a sampan to carry the combined parties to
Tembilahan. It was then 24 February. As we know, John Nicholson took too long to get to Padang to catch the last evacuation
ship and was desperately unlucky in the *Setia Berganti*.

Junks, especially big ones, were very difficult to control and not
everyone had Crawley's touch. To Lieutenant K. Bindoff RA

> it soon became evident that there was not going to be much to stay
> for, so we took advantage of the confusion of the first forty-eight
> hours of captivity to kill a guard and swim out to a junk in the
> harbour. Eighteen of us took part in the break-out, but as we were
> all brown types none of us knew much about sailing. We managed
> to clear the harbour in the darkness, which soon gave way to a
> crimson sea as we were illuminated by flames from burning oil
> tanks. It was very eerie and I have rarely been more frightened.
> Perhaps not surprisingly we hit something later in the night but
> were able to swim to an island, from which we were taken off
> the next day by some more army types and an RN petty officer
> whom we immediately promoted admiral. There were the usual
> problems with aircraft but we moved by night, hiding up in the
> shelter of islands most of the daylight. . . .
>
> During the night dash to the mouth of the Indragiri we hit one
> hell of a storm. The shallow draught *Sir Theodore Fraser* (a harbour
> tender) did everything except turn over. I asked the admiral how
> much more she could take and he said, 'If you know how to pray,
> pray now, and pray bloody hard.'

However, when it became light they were right in the middle of
the Indragiri estuary. (Bindoff got safely away from Padang.)

The largest of three Singapore water transport (river) boats, the
seventy-foot, four-knot *Sir Theodore Fraser* had been taken over by
Mechanist-Sergeant-Major F. F. T. MacLaren and a party from
RASC workshops, the Malay crew having deserted. After
landing and retrieving by night a raiding party of Argylls on
Pulau Ubin, she had been ordered on Black Friday to evacuate
Indian gunners from an island to the east of Singapore. There
MacLaren also picked up Captain Ernest Gordon, who had been
wounded. Return to Keppel Harbour was to find no instructions
and only masts and ships' bottoms showing above water, so, after

embarking one of his workshop crews whose ancient boat had run aground, he left. Next day, Gordon and MacLaren made contact with Ivan Lyon on Moro Island and picked up about eighty deserters and escapees collected there by the latter. Also Lieutenant Tom Rigden, whose minesweeper *Trang* had run aground, was rescued from a lifeboat together with his charts, which were invaluable in making the Indragiri. The *Sir Theodore Fraser* was abandoned at Rengat, among a lot of other 'one way' craft, after which the trio formed the river traffic team already alluded to.

The difficulties to be encountered do not seem to have loomed large for one group of civilians because their nonchalant accounts starts: 'We decided to close the offices and move to the Netherlands East Indies'. But it goes on to relate how they hired a thirty-five ton steam launch, the *Hong Chuang* on 11 February and departed. Laying up that night, they ran aground at dawn but reached Moro. Next day all the Chinese crew deserted, leaving them to tackle the boiler as best they could. On seeing a Japanese ship they turned round but eventually, after running aground three more times, got up the Djambi River; thence by lorry to Sawahlunto, train to Padang, ship to Tjilatjap (Java) and, it is thought, Australia.

The difficulties were only too apparent for a group of naval ratings a week later. The last remaining officers and men of the naval central pool had been evacuated on Black Friday in various ships, but a few missed the boat with a vengeance. Because communications had broken down in some places, they were being used as runners between Army units. One of these was Stoker G. T. Avery of the *Repulse*, who was still carrying messages between the Argylls and Australians on the 15th, when his Malay guide heard of the surrender. The latter took Avery and five other sailors to a fisherman friend; after pooling their resources they set sail in the latter's sampan and the small hours of the 16th saw the fires of Singapore dwindling astern. The sampan was among a lot of small islands that evening, when suddenly a submarine – she would appear to have been Dutch – loomed up and took them on board. Damaged, she could not dive, but made Batavia safely – whence the lucky sextet were sent to Australia.

Parties of soldiers, often from the same unit and with a fairly senior officer in charge, were of course better organized than most smaller groups. Colonel Dillon, a staff officer of the 18th Division, ordered to leave, embarked after dark on 14 February with a unit therefrom, and has left a vivid account, from which we have had extracts in an earlier chapter:

> Philip was at the top of the ladder which led down to the launch. 'All aboard except Tuf. He was here just now.' 'Where the hell is he?' I asked, and then shouted, 'Tuf!'. A voice answered from just behind my shoulder, 'D'you mind if I go with my own crowd?' 'No Tuf, of course not. Tell them from me: next stop Java! Good luck!'
>
> The G3 saluted and disappeared in the darkness. I did not know at that moment that all they had was a rowing boat. It was probably just as well for Tuf that I did not know: for he got out, fought through the war, and is now a Member of Parliament. *How invisible are the fine threads of fate.**
>
> A moment later we cast off, and the ancient motor launch, overloaded to within three or four inches of freeboard, nosed its way out of Singapore dock into the stream. It was like an old-fashioned battle picture – smoke and flames and flash of gun and shell. . . . Turning away from the wharves we made out into the darkness on a bearing taken off a chart ashore. For direction we had two field compasses lying on the dashboard. Every few minutes the engine misfired, the dynamo gave out blue sparks, the compass needles rocked violently in electric excitement and as often as not settled down pointing in considerably different directions.

The navigator had just said they 'ought to be near that buoy' when they hit it, providing the first laugh of a difficult day. Pilotage, over a minefield, was by courtesy of the unfortunate liner *Empress of Asia* which had been burning for weeks. At daylight the launch was found to be leaking badly, and when, with bombers streaming overhead, the engine began to miss, they headed for the nearest island, where a Malay in a kolek appeared

---

* Written in 1945. Author's italics.

with an invitation from the local Controleur. Dillon went with him, leaving the launch which was being repaired, to follow. The Controleur said that Singapore had fallen, Palembang was under attack and the way to Java therefore blocked. Having decided to make for Padang instead, Dillon strolled down to the water's edge to meet the approaching launch, in time to see it sink just off the jetty. However, the Controleur provided boats to take the party to Betoe, where they found 'junks, ships, lifeboats, small well-found motor launches, sailing canoes and even a Singapore one-design'. The Colonel's doings at Betoe and onward have already been chronicled.

'Tuf' of his opening remarks was another staff officer, Captain Tufton Beamish whose 'own crowd' was the Royal Northumberland Fusiliers party under Major Leech, mentioned above. Beamish procured an eighteen-foot rowing boat and a dinghy and in these the party pushed off in the early hours of the 15th, rowing from island to island until a Malay-speaking civilian passenger more than paid his way by organizing the purchase of a mast, sail, axe and cooking pot. Another important find was a school atlas. The *Pushme-Pullyou*, as the boat had been christened, had no keel or rudder, steering by broken oar over the stern. A day-by-day log noted: 'Although she will sail surprisingly near the wind, her progress is deceptive, and more sideways than forwards. Go about she will not. . . . However, with the enforcement of iron discipline by Major Leech, and great willingness on the part of the crew, things quickly improved.' After eight days' hard graft they arrived at Sungei Guntoeng, having sold the *Pushme-Pullyou* to an unreliable native guide who let them in for a jungle trek – 'Tumbles were frequent. Monkeys and parrots kept up a continuous cacophony of laughter' – the last stage being by hired sampan to Tembilahan with Nicholson and co. It only remains to record that at Iyer Molek Captain Beamish (who had been the navigator with an army compass, was to be my MP for 25 years and eventually ennobled as Lord Chelwood) 'let the party down by being unshaven on parade. It was a very handsome beard though!'

Both Dillon's original companions and the Northumberland

Fusiliers arrived at Padang whence they were lucky to be lifted to Colombo by the Navy. On the morning of 2 March the Fusiliers were reconciling themselves to a fight for Padang, but in the afternoon the small destroyers *Tenedos* and *Scout* fortuitously entered harbour looking for oil. Of course they found hundreds of men waiting and, literally loaded to the gunwhales (*Tenedos*'s captain was afraid she might capsize), ferried as many as possible to the Australian cruiser *Hobart* lying outside. Apparently the latter's CO knew his Army regulations, telling Tufton Beamish to shave off his beard ('Only Pioneer sergeants are allowed to wear beards')!

Another lot to be lifted from Padang safely – though not by the Navy this time – was mainly composed of FMS Volunteers under Lieutenant S. Y. Turner:

> At about 7 pm (15th) Major Stoke-Hughes spoke to the Volunteers and asked any who wanted to make a break for it to get ready to go down to the harbour and see if boats could be found. . . . Luck was with me as I saw two fairly good sampans moored about fifty yards out. It was as bright as daylight with the number of fires, godowns, oil tanks, etc. all blazing. . . . I swam out to the sampans and with the help of some of the others got one onto the beach. One lad I sent back to contact Major Stoke-Hughes' party and pilot them down. In the meantime, I went on the scrounge again. . . . At about midnight the party turned up - about fifty strong. A good many of them when they saw the boat decided the chances were too great and went back. We put our chances down at ten to one. Zero hour came and thirty-six men were on board. We hoisted the sail but with no success as the tide was going out; there was nothing for it but for all to get over into the water and wade her out. After about an hour we were in deep enough water and all scrambled aboard again covered in slime and oil, and feeling mighty cold. We then got a bit of breeze.

They sailed up the Johore channel and, having spent an aircraft-haunted day hidden among the islands, followed by an insect-ridden night on one, a Chinese fisherman was discovered and bribed to take them to Sumatra, setting out after dark.

Though propelled by a favourable wind all the rest of the night the sampan was still in the smoke off Singapore by morning, through which 'the sun shining gave an eerie light'.

They made for the more distant of two islands.

> This was nearly our undoing and after this we never sailed in daylight again. At about 8 am the wind started to die away, and we heard planes but could not see any. Every time we heard them we covered ourselves with mats made of palm leaves – kajangs they are called. At about 10 am 'Honourable Friend' came down and machine-gunned us. He made three runs. The first was about two yards wide; the second, he got two of us; I lost the heel of my boot so had to chuck them overboard and. use a pair of shoes I had fortunately brought with me; the third run by the plane would have put us all out, but his guns either jammed or he had run out of ammunition, the last bullet hitting the water no more than two yards away. He then made off and we saw him no more.

The sampan was becalmed near a Chinese village which had also been machine-gunned, but an evacuating Dutchman towed them in and sent them on an eight-mile trek to where they re-embarked in three boats, arranged by the Chinese towkay of the place. Turner was in charge of the first one, starting some time after midnight. The boat was well down in the water with nine of them and a Chinese. There was a strong wind and it went well, those in the bows getting thoroughly soaked by spray.

> We had been sailing for about three hours, with the wind getting stronger when just as we were entering the mouth of a river, a gust of wind got us and we went right over. As most were asleep, it was a rude awakening. I got all mixed up in the sail, but managed to break through, came up again, found the boat, and hung on. I tried counting heads – three were missing. It was bitterly cold with the wind blowing on wet clothes. We managed to grab one lad who had been missing, but never saw any sign of the other two. After holding us up for two and a half hours, our boat was sinking fast. Suddenly we saw a light and started shouting. It turned out to be some Australians. . . . They picked up one of our lads who had tried to swim for the shore and was done . . . the rest of us hung on to the side and were towed in. On landing we got a fire going, and stood around warming and drying ourselves, and pumping the drowned lad. After two hours we got him round.

They had lost everything but what they stood up in and Turner's legs were badly cut by barnacles on the upturned boat. The Australians took them up the river, which must have been one of the ones north of the Indragiri; a rowing boat was procured at a kampong and after some food they set off, dodging into the bank whenever aircraft appeared. It was necessary to cross from one river to another through a swamp, which was hard going and took till 3 am. No boats being visible, they slept, exhausted, until daylight which revealed a number of dugout koleks. A three-hour paddle brought them to a kampong, where a ten-mile trek ended at another river. This boasted a large scow – sort of flat-bottomed barge – in which they rowed all night, Turner's feet and legs giving him a lot of pain now. Next morning (20 February) they arrived at a small town 'consisting of one street of broken-down shops, two bungalows and a wharf' (see figure 7). It was Tembilahan on the Indragiri. In due course they reached Padang and the unfortunate Turner, hardly able to walk, embarked on the 900-ton *Palopo* (as did Colonel Cummins v c, Indian Army, hero of much fierce fighting, and Oswald Gilmour of Pompong). The ship arrived safely at Colombo on 11 March.

The last example here of the escape of an organized party is that of the 30th Battery 3rd H A A Regiment in a junk. The best organized and executed departure of all was unfortunately not rewarded with a similar degree of luck. As soon as he heard of the surrender on the 15th, the Commanding Officer, Major Geoffrey Rowley-Conwy (hereafter Rowley; later of *Djohanis*) sent an officer – the wounded Captain Kennard of the Argylls – to commandeer a junk and a launch. The entire Battery was got on board the *Hock Siew* (rechristened *Conwy Castle*) in the launch *Joan* and other small boats, as soon as the 'uncanny silence' that many have mentioned, descended with the sun on that momentous evening.

Rowley and another officer had dinghy sailing experience (the former's own dinghy features in another escape saga) and two gunners – one originally a Thames bargee – knew what they were doing. Good progress was made for the rest of the night. However, at dawn they ran aground almost irrevocably as far as *Conwy Castle* was concerned, near St John's Island and in full view of Singapore. *Joan*, still under Kennard, was refloated; with gunners in the water pushing, every effort was made to get the junk off, but to no avail. She was stuck fast and it would not be long before the enemy saw what was going on. The launch had been sent off to Sumatra when a kolek came alongside carrying the local Malay headman. He said he could provide boats, so Rowley, three NCOs and Fraser (a Malay-speaking Volunteer and eventually of *Djohanis* too) went ashore with him. The boats were considered too small and too few. Fraser returned to the junk while the rest continued to reconnoitre. For two highly uncomfortable days the 130 unfortunate men sweated in the smelly hold as Jap aircraft swooped low. A Malay came to help, kedging the anchor (dropping it to seaward for those on board to haul the junk up to) but it did not work and Fraser, with another officer, swam ashore in a last attempt to organize effective help. They were ferried from island to island over several days, until joining up with a launch party who took them to the Indragiri.

At Rengat, Fraser ran into Rowley; having progressed similarly, the latter had just procured a sizeable diesel launch called *Numbing* (subsequently exchanged for the *Plover*, a smaller and more reliable one) from the Dutch Controleur. The understanding was that Rowley would tour the islands and bring back not only his own men but anyone else he came across. This he and Fraser did, making two eventful trips in the *Numbing* and one in the *Plover* that picked up a large number of civilians – avoiding the bombs of a Japanese aircraft – and a boatload from the *Conwy Castle*.

Back on the *Conwy Castle* the situation had looked bleak. It was a case of every man for himself and Lance-Bombardier Grafton, with Gunners Parrot, Brewer and Sussex, dived over the side and swam ashore. Bob Grafton was to write a graphic account of his experiences, from which the following is taken. The shore was further than anticipated and they were in considerable difficulties when picked up by a native boat and landed on St John's Island, by no means its first visitors. Their rescuer made a speedy departure, explained by the arrival of a monk and several hideously deformed natives, the former saying 'My sons, you must leave here at one, this is a leper colony'. However, he gave them a boat. As many a would-be mariner was discovering in these waters, it had to be push-rowed and 'took a great deal of effort and swearing before we made any kind of headway. Ginger Sussex, always bad tempered, impatient and foul-mouthed, kept up a constant steam of criticism.'

Now in the open sea and heading for the next island, they were continually investigated by aircraft, surrounded by slowly circling sharks and increasingly tormented by thirst. On top of which Sussex, an old antagonist of Grafton's, was permanently disagreeable. Dragging their boat above the high-water mark of a small island, they searched some huts, but these only provided a little questionable water from latrines. Daybreak, after a night on the beach, revealed that their boat had gone. Some natives were to be seen loading oil drums on to a motorised sampan and it was made clear that the four would like to leave with them. The response was hostile to threatening, until the production of a hand-grenade acted as a boarding pass and two hours later they were landed on the other side of the island. Here an English-speaking Chinese gave them food and water. He said a Jap patrol had been there, was coming back, and he would provide a guide to take them to other British soldiers nearby. After dark a young Malay led them through insect-infested jungle, only to leave them on the outskirts of a kampong with a hurried 'Nippon here!' Wearily they retraced their steps, the headman giving them another guide. This one deserted too, but they persevered, following a recognizable path. Meanwhile, Brewer had become delirious, finally slipping into a near-coma. Sussex was for leaving him but the others would not have it. Eventually they came to a small kampong where the unfortunate and now unconscious Brewer had to be left in the care of some natives.

Stumbling on, they found themselves at a fishing village on the banks of an estuary and themselves surrounded by a crowd of sullen-looking Malays, wielding parangs and kerises. However, after much sign language and drawing in the sand, some rice and fish were produced; also, to their surprise, two British gunners who had arrived at Singapore in the *Empress of Asia* only two weeks before. These had heard of the escape route and food câche on Moro, also that by now Jap patrol boats were everywhere, looking for stranded escapees. They joined forces, all money was pooled and with the headman anxious to see their backs, a small sampan was bought for $35 and headed for Sumatra.

They were almost in the open sea when

> the unmistakable pop-pop of a diesel engine could be heard and we frantically started to propel ourselves towards the bank opposite the village. Fortunately we found a channel into the thick mangrove swamps only just in time, as round the bend from the direction of the open sea came a large motorised sampan full of heavily armed Japanese troops, standing alertly on deck, searching the horizon. As we were still visible we made our new companions crouch down as much as possible in the cramped conditions, to hide their whiteness. The next few minutes seemed like hours. . . . Either they really did not see us against the murky background, or they thought that we were natives and spared us no more than a glance as they slowly made their way towards the village we had just left. Once they were far enough away, the tension broke and in a few crazy minutes we had pulled and pushed our way into the swamp in case the natives told the Japs that we were about.

The sun went down and, because of the overhanging vegetation, was succeeded by utter darkness. Bitten by clouds of insects and surrounded by very unpleasant-looking water snakes, it took hours to retrace their steps but they were clear by daylight. Ginger Sussex had taken an instinctive dislike to one of the newcomers, an older man, and his continuous invective did not help matters. However, a curiously agreeable incident then occurred, though at first it did not look auspicious. A kolek came in sight and proceeded to overtake the sampan, manned by six Malays paddling in unison at great speed. A large white eye painted on the bow prompted thoughts of cannibals and headhunters. Frantic efforts on the part of the fugitives to outpace the kolek were unsuccessful, but to their astonishment, as it shot past them in a long sweeping curve, the Malays threw two or three packets into the bottom of the sampan and were on their way back without slackening pace. The packets contained meals of cooked rice and fish, neatly wrapped in large green leaves and as the recipients enjoyed them, they wondered what had prompted this kind and risky gesture.

In mid-afternoon they decided to stop for a rest and some fish or coconuts at an island where they could see attap huts, but

> we had hardly got through the first screen of powdery scrub when we were covered from head to foot with the most ferocious large red ants. The whole place was a gigantic ant hill, and the natives had been driven away long ago. Driven frantic by the stinging bites of thousands, we stumbled down the sandy beach. Contact with the salt water was a blessed relief, but it was only by removing our grubby shorts, that we finally rid ourselves of our tormentors.

The next drama, fortunately ending in farce, was caused by a sudden storm of frightening ferocity.

> At the time the older man had the oars and found difficulty in keeping the bows into the waves that were now threatening to swamp us. Sussex, sitting in the stern, issued a continuous stream of blasphemy and instructions, his face contorted and red with rage. Frantic efforts were made to change places with the rower and in a brief moment when the oars were out of the water, a large wave caught us broadside and overturned the boat. As I fell into the sea I thought of Dot, my girl, and had the sudden conviction that I would never see her again, for there was no doubt that these were to be my last moments. . . . However, when I managed to get my head above water, I was astonished to find that my feet touched bottom and the water was only chest high!

After most of their belongings had been recovered, they pulled the boat up a beach, near some empty huts which were raised a foot above the sand. The reason was soon apparent. Grafton cut coconuts from an uprooted tree and they settled down for the night, leaning against the huts, the interiors of which were uninviting. As darkness fell, pairs of tiny eyes began to advance towards them out of the jungle some 150 yards away. At the same time the sand by the sea came alive as hundreds of ugly land crabs crawled up the beach. The eyes belonged to large rats coming down to feed on them. Caught in the middle, the four musketeers took refuge on the raised floors of the huts.

They had better luck at the next stop where a Chinese produced ducks' eggs. He had a fair-sized motor launch which promoted a heated discussion. Sussex was for committing murder, if necessary, to obtain it, but examination revealed that the engine had been removed. The Chinese then offered to get one of his men to tow them to Moro; the next day brought not the expected motor boat, but a native craft smaller than their own, with a tiny triangular sail and a toothless Malay crouching sullenly in the stern, obviously press-ganged by his boss. However, they put out in a freshening wind and

were suddenly towed along at an amazing pace which seemed all the greater in the darkness and not being able to see where we were going. Ginger was beside himself with fury as he voiced his distrust and as usual blamed his misfortune on everyone else and in particular the older man. After some hours of hair-raising speed the Malay cast us off without warning, slewed round and made off into the darkness. Just ahead we could make out the outline of palms and hut roofs and we drifted onto the beach, arguing fiercely in whispers believing that we had been cast off into a nest of Japs.

Normally even-tempered, I suddenly felt overwhelmed by Ginger Sussex's unreasonable behaviour and rage poured over me like a hot shower. I told him in fierce whispers that as far as I was concerned one of us would not be leaving this beach. I could not believe what I was doing as I drew my bayonet and adopted a crouching position as Sussex did the same. The moon, with a fine sense of drama, came out at that moment and briefly illuminated the two of us circling each other on the sand, whilst the others were struggling to beach the boat. Recalling this moment later, it was the only time that I was ever out of control and I am sure that I could have killed him. Thankfully, before we could come to grips and inflict injury upon one another, a number of angry dogs appeared and began to bark furiously. Lights came on in some of the huts, fear drained the hot temper from us in the face of mutual danger and we all crouched down in the shadows of some large fishing boats.

We could now hear voices and, with bayonet still in hand, I

entered the space between the two rows of huts to be greeted by a Malay who after some parley made me understand that there were no Japs about. I called to the others and we were soon surrounded by Chinese, Malays and Indians. One of them, who spoke some English, took us to an empty hut built high on stilts on the foreshore and shortly they brought us a meal of freshly cooked rice and vegetables. On the floor of the hut I was astonished to find a very torn and grubby piece of old newsprint, which turned out to be the front page of the London Evening Standard dated 1938, the lunchtime edition announcing a record test score by either Sutcliffe or Hutton!

With full stomachs, they slept well for the first time in weeks, waking to entreaties that they should go over to another part of the island and join some British troops there. This they did, timing their arrival well as a mixed group of NCOs and ORs from various regiments were about to leave for Sumatra that very night in a fishing boat. This duly left at exhilarating speed in a near gale with heavy rain, but unfortunately the Malay skipper turned back after a time because of the alarming intake of water, and they transferred to another, similar craft. The wind then died and for two whole days they drifted, hiding under the sails whenever the many Jap planes came to look. Leaderless and suffering from the cramped conditions, tempers frayed, not allayed when the party landed at one fishing kampong to replenish water supplies. They were threatened by the inhabitants who produced a grinding wheel and ostentatiously sharpened weapons but 'to the relief of the faint hearts among us' a timely breeze arrived and they re-embarked. Two days later the steaming banks of the Indragiri were on either side, with crocodiles sunning themselves on the mud. They had joined the escape route and Grafton was not sorry to part company with his companions, joining up with some Australians. He had developed bad stomach trouble and they looked after him well, arriving at Padang on 10 March.
On the evening of the second day there, he was

relieved and delighted to be among friends again when the main party from the junk *Hock Siew* (alias *Conwy Castle*), having crossed Sumatra further north through much worse jungle than we had encountered. They had refloated the junk but had gone aground in the mouth of the River Kampa, which proved to be unnavigable, and had wasted two weeks of indecision and foraging, finally abandoning ship and walking some 90 miles through swamps and untracked jungle. [On the 17th] we woke at dawn to the sound of guttural voices outside the school, were paraded and there we saw our first Japs in close-up. They started pushing and manhandling us into line in front of several machine guns which were mounted on tripods and behind each gun squatted Japanese soldiers in shabby uniforms and wearing peculiar rubber and canvas boots which had a separate section for the big toe. Some of us were hit brutally with rifle butts and things began to look ugly. So our bid for freedom ended; we were prisoners of war in a strange land and far from home. As Sid, Ken and I made room for ourselves on the hard sleeping platform in the billet, my thoughts turned to home where I knew my family and Dot would be anxiously listening to the discouraging news from the East. . . . What I did not hear was a voice saying 'Son, if you think that was hard, you ain't seen nuthin' yet'. But that's another story.

*   *   *

Another link with one of my companions in the *Sederhana Djohanis*, this time Ivan Lyon, comes in an intriguing account by Lieutenant H. R. Oppenheim of the last days of the Light Battery, Artillery Section, FMSVF and the escape of some of its members, including Lieutenant H. R. Ross. The Australian Major-General Gordon Bennett, whose departure caused a great deal of controversy, also features.

Rumour has it that we capitulated at 16.30 but as it is now 19.30 and there is still firing the rumour must be false. The flag on Fort Canning is still flying and can be seen through the smoke very faintly. If the capitulation is true, Charles and I decide to make for Sumatra. Ross, Hay, Wilkes and Ross, H.R. come in from the guns and confirm the rumour. The guns have been smashed, Ingram killed and Ward wounded. A written order to surrender came to the CO but no one knew if it was authentic or not. Harley and Harvey decide to join us. We have food in the courtyard of the church and get sprayed with shrapnel. Hay and I go into town to find out the true position. We wave lighted cigs about to show we are not Japs. . . . I get shot at from over the river and turn out my torch in a hurry. Next we go to Clifford Pier and see troops (Gordons?) making a getaway. Some say the capitulation has been cancelled. Burning houses and lorries light the streets. Eventually we go to the Master Superintendent and ask his advice. He tells us that we officially capitulated at 20.30. He advised us to take a twakow [small junk] lying off Arab Street but says we must hurry as the tide turns at midnight. He takes us out on to the balcony of Fullerton Building and shows us Singapore burning. He warns us to take plenty of water and tells us the mines are four feet deep. . . .

Ackhurst half gives us his blessing and tells us officially we are asleep. We say farewell to the Battery and march to Arab Street. Although Harvey carries a suitcase we announce that we are out on patrol and so march through all guards, barbed wire etc and reach the sea just on midnight. Here we find a sampan in which are Major-General Gordon Bennett, his ADC Gordon Walker and the head of the Australian Broadcasting Company, Major Moses. They intended rowing to Malacca but decide to come with us. We eventually reach the twakow and I lose my haversack and all my worldly goods in getting on board from the sampan. After thirteen years in Malaya I leave it with one pair of trousers, a pair of shorts, a shirt, a pair of socks, boots and my life. [He had been a chartered accountant in Ipoh].

Another of the party, Lieutenant H. R. (Bobby) Ross wrote to his sister:

My battery surrendered by orders of the OC. . . . We were terribly distressed after a week's fighting during which we had supposed that the Japanese advance had at least been held. . . . Very few others escaped. Most of the battery were wholly pessimistic about our chances. I remember putting my head into the command post and saying goodbye. They wished me luck – one friend of mine said that he 'would love to come if only he wasn't a married man'. Most of them were tired of the failures of the high command and had no incentive to make the effort to escape. You must remember that we had witnessed the defeat of an army totally unprepared for the type of warfare, totally unsupported by aircraft, and misled into believing that Singapore Island was equipped with land defences, which of course was wholly untrue.

They boarded a sampan to get out to the larger craft. Oppenheim takes up the story:

There was complete chaos on the sampan. Charles announced we were rowing the wrong way, meaning the sampan was being rowed backwards but we thinking he meant being rowed in the wrong direction argue and shout at him. The General screams like a young girl and curses Gordon Walker who is standing up in the nude for being so, saying it would be scandalous if the Japs saw him like that. He was like that because he had swum out to collect the sampan. Charles tried rowing with a small oar while Moses tries a large one and the rest of us with bits of wood. Consequently the sampan spun round in circles and Moses kept hitting Charles on the head. Eventually we get under way and Gordon Bennett again suggests rowing to Malacca and Gordon Walker suggests making for an island and lying low. Luckily we strike the twakow and manage to board her. On board we find some other escapees who, not being able to persuade the taikong to sail, had gone below. Two of them decide to return to the shore and so dive overboard, but being tired are drowned or are taken by sharks – this stops the others following suit. We at last persuade the taikong to sail, it then being about 1.30 and he sails for an hour but on telling us he is drawing 7 ft and the mines being only 4 ft we hurriedly tell him to anchor. Eventually we find he is lying as the true draught is only $3\frac{1}{2}$ ft. We eventually anchor off Pulau Samboe which is blazing away gaily. Set sail again about 7.00 and messed about the islands trying to find a way to the open sea. About 11.00 we take on another Chinaman as pilot. Completely hopeless. Then two soldiers jump aboard and threaten to shoot us if we resist them. We don't. We have on board umpteen cases of A/A (Naval) shells which the taikong had been chartered to ship from Seletar to Singapore. We had to sleep on these cases. . . .

Everyone argued about the route to be taken. First Hay is put in command and then Wray takes over forcibly. It was he and Smeaton who jumped our boat, and he turned out to be a deserter who had been hiding in the islands. He was a Canadian. It was touch and go whether there would be a general shooting match on board as everyone was in a vile temper and on edge. The Chinaman wanted to go to Tanjong Pinang in Rhio but we believed the Japs were there. Bennett completely useless first crying and then imploring Moses and Walker to do something. Eventually we crash into some fishing stakes and anchor for the night.

Tues 17th. Most of the day we were becalmed. Several Jap planes fly over us throughout the day and we have to lie low under the tarpaulin covering the ammo.

Their slapstick progress – though it cannot have seemed funny at the time – continued, the Sumatran coast being reached on the evening of the 18th. With only a small school atlas they sailed southwards along the coast, making for the Indragiri. Several sailing and motor boats had been encountered, as well as Jap aircraft and at nightfall they anchored near a large junk full of soldiers (probably the *Hiap Hin*). Oppenheim again:

Set sail in the early hours. Very slow progress. At 10.30 a motor boat comes alongside and the General and his party jump on board and leave us without a word of thanks, but they do leave $100 towards the expenses of the twakow. Everyone cheers up after their departure. . . . After a lot of arguing with Hay I persuade them to take on board a Malay pilot. . . . This was lucky otherwise we would never have found the Indragiri which flows for several miles at right angles to the sea and hence the mouth is hard to see. The Malay pilot took us straight to it and we anchored there for the night.*

Bobby Ross, on this trip, must have passed close to Ivan Lyon at his outpost on Moro. Or if Ivan had been ashore in the Indragiri at the time, which he sometimes was, they would have been very near each other at some stage. The point is of more than passing interest. Sadly, both had 'a rendezvous with death at some disputed barricade' in that they were to be killed together – otherwise alone – on Sole Island, on their way to Marapas, in November, 1944. Ivan's second guerrilla operation (Rimau)† against Singapore shipping (see page 230) had failed and they were fighting a rear-guard action to cover the retreat of some of the party, accounting for upwards of twenty (reports

---

* Oppenheim and the others reached Colombo via Padang, General Bennett getting to Djambi, Padang and Java, when General Wavell sent him by air to Australia.
† Meaning 'Tiger', after a tiger tattooed on his chest.

vary) of the Japanese. After a two-hour fire-fight the latter had withdrawn, returning at midnight with 100 reinforcements, only to find that the gallant pair had died of their wounds. It is nice to know that after the war they were reburied, side by side, in Kranji military cemetery, Singapore.

*   *   *

A happier story, in fact containing an element of extreme good fortune, is that of Lieutenant K. Robinson, Singapore RA.

> We had been told by our section commander that now it was all over, we were free to escape if we wished . . . went down to the Yacht Club basin . . . saw Sam Pulleblank and another officer from the Loyals preparing a fourteen footer, which they sailed away. . . . All we could find was a small tug hard and fast aground.

Next morning, a large motor launch, *Sylvia*, anchored off and some soldiers came ashore from it to say they had left the previous night but the engine had broken down. Robinson offered to supply an engineer and navigator with charts if they would take him and friends along, to which they agreed. After being worked on all day – it was now 10.30 on the 17th – the *Sylvia* set off for Sumatra with twenty-seven on board. 'We had to risk passing over the minefield, but little things like that didn't matter any more.' An aircraft dived down to pass a few feet over their heads, but that was all and they sighted Sumatra at 5 pm, to carry on down the coast. When they got to Priggi Raja they found the instructions for onward travel. At Rengat Robinson went to the BAT agent to try and raise some money as the local shopkeepers would not accept Singapore dollars.

> He turned out to be an exceedingly nice Dutchman called de Jong, from the Barsemy Company, and he very kindly let me have 50 guilders. . . . De Jong took us round the local shops where he would not let us pay for a thing. He then sent us back to his bungalow where his boy kept us supplied with the most delicious iced beer in the world. . . . I shall never forget his kindness to us, and can only hope that I shall be able to repay him one day.

From Padang Robinson was taken to Tjilatjap, where he was transferred to the Dutch freighter *Zaandam*, sailing on 1 March for Fremantle, with the unfortunate destroyer *Stronghold*, whose story is to come. Next morning

> We picked up 33 survivors in a lifeboat from a small UPM boat which had been torpedoed 36 hours before. They had been forced to sail back towards Java, and were really very lucky to have been picked up. It was a nasty moment, stopping in mid-ocean, a sitting target for a submarine. . . .
>
> A most extraordinary coincidence occurred . . . we met a sailor who had been ordered to sabotage the *Sylvia* while she was in Singapore. He had already set to work and thrown all the plugs overboard and was just going to get to with a large hammer, when somebody called him away. Although he passed her several times after this, he never had time to finish the job, so she was left us. If that isn't providence what is?

Or 'how invisible are the fine threads of fate!'

The threads of fate were also concerned in at least two of the several escapes by dinghy. Sapper Lionel Morris of the 30th Fortress Company RE, from whose account the following is taken, was a keen sailing man, as was Lieutenant Bob Martin of the 9th Heavy Battery RA, but Major Gillie Campbell RA surprisingly was not. Intent on escape, the three met at the Changi Garrison Yacht Club 48 hours after the capitulation, their collective choice falling on *Goldeneye*, the sole survivor – the others had been destroyed – of 41 local class 12½ foot pram dinghies. (It happened that she belonged to Major Rowley-Conwy of the junk *Hock Siew*.) They spent two days collecting stores, including a chart, during which a Japanese party marched by within yards, before setting out on the night of 19 February. A current swept them close by a sentry and, after various other alarms, including a near-miss with a floating mine, they were clear and heading for the Rhio Strait. When Campbell, who had been told to sit still in the middle of the boat, said 'I think we should make it on this tack', it was reckoned he was learning fast! Hauling up on an island, they were surprised by three rough parang-toting Malays, but glared so fiercely through several days' growth of beard that these thought better of it. Good progress had been made when an enemy fighter, clearly suspicious, made several low passes, but they were wearing coolie hats and when Morris waved hopefully, the pilot returned the compliment and flew off.

Goldeneye was heading for the Indragiri when a violent storm took her past it and on 27 February she entered the Banka Strait, proceeding cautiously among the masts of sunken ships that stuck up everywhere. They then fell in successively with Malay and Chinese fishermen who fed them well. The latter hated the Japanese, one old man shocking them with a grisly mime of soldiers bayonetting prisoners in a pit from which there was no escape. The trio, having to leave hurriedly when an enemy destroyer and nine troopships loomed up, were lucky to slip through their lines in a rainstorm. Later, fishermen told them of a terrific battle, the sea strewn with dead sailors, debris and so much oil that there were no waves. (This was the battle of the Java Sea, where the scratch Dutch, British, American and Australian force was almost wiped out.) After another severe sumatra which nearly finished the enterprise, they found themselves on 5 March in the Sunda Strait with only one tin of peas, one of parsnips and half a pint of water left. By nightfall the island of Merak had been identified and there were high hopes of the morrow.

In the darkness they heard a ship's engines and a cruiser appeared. 'Looks like one of the County class', said Morris, then: 'We see a line of white-clad figures in peaked cloth caps. Suddenly Bob yells "They're bloody Japs" and he is all too perfectly right.' Incredulous that they had sailed 650 miles in 15 days – also that there was an Other Rank with the officers! – their captors in the *Asigara** treated them well before handing them over to the Japanese Army. Thus ended another heroic effort that had deserved to succeed.

All that is known of the other dinghy escape is that Basil

---

* Vanquisher of HMS *Exeter* in the recent battle, she was to be sunk by HMSM *Trenchard*.

Drakeford, a Straits Settlement Volunteer, sailed his international 14 foot dinghy right down to Batavia, picking up a naval officer on the way. Drakeford, suffering from exposure, was put straight into hospital. Tragically, he died. It is believed his passenger, identity unknown, got clean away.

VI

The Valley of Death

'Into the Valley of Death rode the six hundred.' The flood of little ships towards Batavia bears some comparison with the charge of the Light Brigade, in that (through no fault of the Admiral's) their orders were unrealistic and they had no chance.

It will be remembered that Admiral Spooner had sailed all the ships in Singapore, around forty of them, on Black Friday. They fell into three basic categories: a few *bona fide* merchant ships that happened still to be there; three ex-Yangtse gunboats and some large MLs that were purpose-built but not first line warships; and all the remainder. To describe the last it must be explained that Malaya being a backwater, at peace from the Admiralty's point of view, until the hardly expected attack at the end of 1941, it was an obvious, pragmatic ploy on the part of RA Malaya (who had little hope of augmentation of his mostly second-line warships) to 'take up from trade' a number of commercial vessels that could carry out many duties efficiently. These included minelaying, minesweeping, patrol, escort and the endless emergency calls to do this and that which at home would have fallen to destroyers, corvettes and the like. Thus a naval oddity peculiar to Malayan waters was the presence on RA Malaya's strength of this excessively large number of merchant vessels. They varied from sizeable ships like the *Kung Wo* to the Sultan of Johore's one time-motor yacht *Tengarroh*.

Their armament generally consisted of either one or two old four-inch or three-inch guns (dating from or before the First World War), sometimes a modern Bofors 40mm quick-firing, but short range, weapon and a couple of .303 Lewis light machine guns. None of these were of any use against high-flying bombers. The existing officers were given MRNVR (Malayan Royal Naval Volunteer Reserve) ranks, except of course when they were RNR already. Some RNVRs were sent out from England and a number of locally retired RN officers were recalled to the colours. One of these was Commander Hoffman of the gunboat *Grasshopper*. It is a fact that this stout-hearted old boy had such bad eyesight that on her last voyage Lieutenant Ian Forbes – recently joined from *Prince of Wales* – had to tell him when the aircraft were at the point of bomb release and which way to turn.

Coming back to the exodus, catastrophes were inevitable when Spooner's vessels, painted grey and flying the white ensign but invariably carrying hundreds of women and children as well as servicemen, met Ozawa's cruisers, destroyers and aircraft. One cannot blame the Japanese for attacking them. What else could they do? It is not easy, especially on a dark night, when a false move or ten seconds delay can mean a shell on your bridge. Even so, on some occasions they held off and acted with a commendable control and humanity, such as in dealing with the *Mata Hari* and the *Giang Bee*. RN ships are not permitted by King's/Queen's Regulations and Admiralty Instructions to surrender. However, these were not written with such vessels, crammed with non-combatants, in mind, and no sensible person would question their Commanding Officers' decisions to do so, painful though they must have been. By and large, most of the unfortunate reserve officers and ships' companies did well against hopeless odds. They fought their almost defenceless ships as best they could against highly trained, professional opponents and committed to a charge of the Light Brigade situation, it was no fault of theirs that so few ships came through. As will be seen, one of the Commanding Officers was awarded the VC, the only Naval one of the campaign.

A few sinkings have been covered already, but the best known is that of the *Vyner Brooke*, because of the horrendous behaviour of the Japanese soldiers concerned. Called after the Rajah of Sarawak of that name, she was a 300-ton patrol vessel with one gun. Her 200 passengers comprised civilians, including women and children, a few servicemen and sixty-four Australian nursing sisters. A Mrs Brown, who suffered from a bad heart, and her daughter Shelagh of about twenty-five were certainly not accustomed to the sort of embarkation that was their lot. The latter described it in her diary with telling brevity.

12 February, 1942. Daddy, Mother, Dorothy MacLeod and I had all spent the night in one room in Raffles Hotel. There were no boys in the morning and we got some food for ourselves. The ballroom was littered with troops – we spent most of the morning sitting in the air raid shelter, and someone from the RNVR came and opened cases of whisky and brandy etc, which flowed down the deep drains and Mother slept, exhausted and pleasantly intoxicated with the fumes. At 3.15 pm Willmott rings up and advises boats leaving. Mac arrived with passes and car. Daddy calls Bimbir (our syce). Mother dressed. Load cars. Set off. Terrible crowd of people leaving. Stop outside Mansfields. Unload, and lug cases through gates. Put Mother and Daddy on lorry with luggage. Get lift in car and pick up Mac and Dorothy. Drive to Laburnum Wharf (moved). AcAc guns go off close to. Dive into Godown. Wait turn on launch. Very crowded with Australian nurses. Get on. Luggage thrown on. Leave for unknown ship. *Vyner Brooke* – very small. (There is no mention here of the leaving on the wharf of Daddy and Mac – these moments cannot be described easily). As we boarded the *Vyner Brooke* we were issued with lifebelts by a kindly English sailor. No cabins. Take up a position on deck. When all on, find luggage and stack cases together beneath. For three of us four small suitcases. On deck with us one stretcher. Told no rations on board! Australian nurses share out theirs. Sail about dusk, 6.30–7 pm. Singapore is a sad sight – all fire and pall of smoke hangs over her. Sleep on deck. No washing next morning.
    13 February, 1942. Very little food. Just sit and lie all day. Ship stopped in amongst islands in daylight. Matron Paschke (just like Zaza Pitts) organizes 'Boat drill' – (she was superb and took command of feeding arrangements etc). Given half tin of Asp. Saus & Pot at night. Best meal so far! Shared it with Ina Murray, her sister Mrs Chambers and husband, and Mrs Parfait. Very exhausted after Singapore. Thankful for quiet day in spite of water and food shortage.

All concerned were trying to make the best of a bad job, though in the case of the nurses, after the hectic hospital hours they had been keeping, 'It was like an unexpected holiday' according to Sister Jessie Simons '. . . without any responsibility or nagging reminder of duties demanding attention'. Sister Betty Jeffrey found the heat and congestion below decks insufferable and with a sandy beach just opposite, the attraction of a swim was almost irresistible. Unfortunately a swim was only a few hours away.

The *Vyner Brooke* was attacked by dive bombers in the afternoon and went down in fifteen minutes. If some of the men from Down Under did not do much at the end of the campaign to add lustre to their name, the girls of the Australian Army Nursing Services more than made up for them. That morning their senior AANS Matron in Malaya, Matron Paschke, who must have been a wonderful woman, had called the sixty-four sisters together and detailed all their duties in the event of the ship being sunk. She herself could not swim and asked one of them jokingly to keep an eye on her.

Unusually for the enemy, many early bombs missed as the ship twisted and turned in frantic efforts to postpone her fate, but eventually there was a direct hit on the bridge, a bomb went right down the funnel to burst in the engine room and the gun with its crew was blown over the side. Betty Jeffrey's account goes:

Sister Ennis and I made a bee-line for the bridge. . . . Taking a child with us, we were the first out. We left the children with an Englishwoman and dashed towards the bridge, only to find it was an unrecognisable mess and burning fiercely. I grabbed a Malay sailor and put my inadequate field-dressing on his . . . leg.

Even this crucial time had its lighter moments . . . a woman's high-pitched voice called out above the din 'Everybody stand still!' It had an amazing effect. Immediately there was dead silence. . . . Then the same voice came again 'My husband has dropped his glasses'. This eased the situation and there were gales of laughter. . . .

We had been told to see that every civilian person was off the ship before leaving it ourselves. Believe me, we didn't waste time getting them overboard! . . . But the planes had not finished with us. Over they came again and machine-gunned the deck and all the lifeboats – rather effectively. The ropes holding the three lifeboats on our side were severed. Two dropped into the sea. One filled and sank, the other turned upside down and drifted away. The third was already manned by two Malay sailors and I'm sure they never anticipated such a quick trip down. . . .

Beth Cuthbertson searched the ship when it was at a very odd angle to make sure all wounded people had been taken off and that nobody remained while other nurses were busy getting people into the sea. At this stage there were quite a few people in the water . . . and the ship was listing heavily to starboard. The oldest people, the wounded, Matron Drummond and some of our girls with all the first-aid equipment, were put into the remaining lifeboats on the starboard side and lowered into the sea. Two boats got away safely. Greatcoats and rugs were thrown down into them and with brights calls of 'See you later' they rowed away. . . . The third boat was caught by the ship when she started to roll on her side and so had to be evacuated very smartly.

Matron Paschke set a superb example to us all by the calm way in which she organised the evacuation of the ship. As the Australian sisters went over the side she said, 'We'll all meet on the shore girls and get teed up again'.

Betty Jeffrey and Jessie Simons were eventually ordered to take their shoes off and go over. Another girl muttered, 'I'll drown anyway as I can't swim' and kept hers on, something she was going to thank her stars for for the next few years. Shelagh Brown and her mother had come up from below:

Fire on deck where we had been sitting that morning. Ship listing. One boat lowered. Told to go down rope ladder. Mummy descends. I luckily fall. (Forgot also to hold onto life belt but neck did not get broken.) (Mrs Mac goes down rope and takes the skin off her hands.) Swim away from ship – and the kindly English sailor sees me and tells me my Mother is searching for me. So I swim back towards her and find that her boat had capsized, being damaged and she is hanging on to mast with a Chinese boy and Olga Springer. Malay boy joins us and three Australian nurses. Have stretcher to hold on to too. Olga Springer very bad and drowning. Keep away from ship – ship rolls over – all in about under $1/4$ hour. Hot oil – raft. Have to pass through patch of oil and a sister produces some clean cotton wool from under the sea so that we can wipe our eyes! Join raft with a badly burnt sailor on it.

Betty slid down a rope so fast that she also took all the skin off her fingers. She swam away from the ship – which disappeared shortly afterwards – at the time enjoying the cool, calm water but then revolted as a gush of foul, clinging oil surfaced all round. Matron Paschke was located, with many others – including two small children – clinging on to a raft; everywhere were the heads of swimmers, some holding on to bits of wreckage but most relying on their lifebelts (a sight now beginning to proliferate for miles and miles around). Currents were strong and varying in direction, just as at Pompong, and the survivors were soon dispersed. Jessie went on swimming but Betty hung on to the raft which was being paddled, somewhat ineffectually with pieces of planking, until another sister, Iole Harper, climbed on board. 'Iole was wonderful; when not rowing she would get off, swim all round, count everybody and collect those who got tired of hanging on, making them use their feet properly to assist in pushing the thing along.'

Just before darkness fell they saw smoke on the horizon and hoped it was the Royal Navy. During the night the raft was swept in close to a pier, then out again; later they saw a bonfire on the shore and knew the two lifeboats had made it. They paddled furiously until they could see the girls, even hear them, but they themselves were not seen or heard due to an offshore squall which got up and blew the raft out to sea again. Coming close to a lighthouse they were again swept away. One of the ship's officers floated past on a piece of wreckage, shouting directions and wishing them luck. All of a sudden large rocks seemed to loom up. They were not rocks but ships! As the first went slowly past they had to fend it off with their feet. There was no sound and no lights. The third ship disgorged large motor boats, packed with troops. Some circled the raft, had a good look and then went off. The raft was in the midst of the Japanese invasion of Sumatra.

Their hands having become too painful to hold on, the two Sisters were swimming alongside when a current suddenly took the raft out of their reach. It disappeared in the darkness and they were alone. All those on the raft, including Matron Paschke, were never seen again.

Jessie, who had also seen the bonfire, was picked up – with a sailor from the *Prince of Wales* and a Malay seaman – by a Japanese motorboat, seemingly with only one man in it. He ran up on a beach covered in soldiers, landing craft, stores, and other impedimenta (including an AA gun which opened fire when British aircraft bombed them). A heated altercation ensued between their benefactor and what appeared to be an officer, who clearly wanted none of them; in fact it was also clear he wanted them executed (which they were to discover was not as far-fetched as it sounds). Eventually he relented and they were transported to a cinema in Muntok to join hundreds of shipwrecked survivors, including other nursing sisters, from twenty-eight of the ships sunk in the last few days.

Shelagh and her mother had a similar experience; 'Very difficult getting out of water into barge, especially for Mummy. . . . Japs cut open coconut and give us water from coconut – mouths very swollen and sore. Take us to shore. Lie down on sand. Many Japs crowd round and stare.' They were fairly well treated initially and later the diary notes ominously 'Now we know how fortunate we were in being picked up by launches that put us down on a part of the Island of Banka that the Japanese officers had made their HQ.'

Betty and Iole were not so lucky. The latter was a strong swimmer and some 400 yards in front as they neared land. It proved to be only mangrove, growing in water out of their depth, but they went to sleep floating, hanging on to the branches. Later they spent hours swimming up creeks and back again, as these all ended in jungle. Envious of curious fish that sped along the surface, upright on their tails, they saw crocodiles and, climbing into a low tree for the night, were battered in the face by huge birds that flew out. The tide was low when they started again, cutting themselves on sharp roots that stuck out of the mud. Very thirsty, they began to get light-headed. Betty, sinking in the ooze up to her thighs, distinctly saw her father asleep with a newspaper over his face and after dark Iole kept pointing down to the inky water and saying, 'There are the beds, why don't you get into one?' But this passed and they had a laugh when she suddenly said, 'By the way, what's your name?' They were swimming again and Betty was to write, 'So we paused, while we formally introduced ourselves . . . as we belonged to different units we had never met before. She was a little person, about five feet high, had short black curly hair and the smallest and prettiest hands I had ever seen.' Of course, most Australians swim like fishes but, pretty hands or no, Iole must have been a tough little cookie.

Swimming all that day, they at last came to a big river, continued up it until too tired to go any further and broke palm leaves with their arms for a bed, because their hands were too sore. Then wading through the mud, covered in mosquitoes and sandflies, they were very thirsty indeed but heard a dog bark, which was encouraging. Two natives passed in a kolek but took no notice. That night 'We heard some animal coming slowly towards us, snapping dead twigs as it came. We were scared stiff. Then two large eyes appeared above us; it sniffed us all over, and – thank Heavens, went away again.' The indomitable pair got back in the water and swam on up river yet again. Then the Malays returned, took them on board and eventually to their kampong, where they were well cared for. A Chinese appeared who spoke English ('He was a bit shattered to hear that we had been swimming since Saturday. It was now Tuesday.') He suggested that they give themselves up at Muntok. Betty ends their story:

In a little while a truck drove into the village. It seemed to be smothered with Japs, so we got up from the seat on which we were lying and walked out to meet them. Horror of horrors – they jumped off the truck and ran towards us, fixing their bayonets to their rifles as they came! We were too dazed to do anything but just stand there while these bayonets rested on our stomachs – actually on the button of my belt, which made the shank stick into me. It hurt quite a lot, so I moved the bayonet down a little.

We got on very well with these fellows; they spoke fluent Japanese and we spoke in our very best Australian, and after five minutes had not got anywhere. . . . After a lot of by-play they bundled us into their truck, allowed the Malays to give us some coconuts, and drove us off. Later we came to a queer-looking jail place and in we went. Two women dressed as Malays in sarongs were near the door. We were walking past them when one called to me 'Jeff!' To my surprise and relief I recognised two girls from my unit. . . . We went inside and were surrounded by other Australian Sisters. I walked past another Malay and to my amazement she said 'A bit haughty today, aren't you, old thing?' – another of the nurses I hadn't recognised. They were all so sunburnt.

Some of them had landed on Muntok pier, others on beaches several miles away. They were now in a native gaol.

A fortnight later another Sister arrived, by herself. She was Vivian Bulwinkel. They all hoped this meant there might be others still to come of the 24 missing from the original 64, but this was not to be the case. She came in holding a water-bottle against the front of her uniform, waist high. It covered a bullet hole and a grim story, though she kept this to herself as far as possible. Having jumped from the *Vyner Brooke* and reached an upturned boat, she had helped to paddle this to Muntok beach, near a fire lit by other survivors. There were eventually collected at this fire twenty-two Australian nurses, women and children, ship's officers and men, naval ratings, and also some forty British soldiers – some of whom were badly wounded – from ships sunk earlier. In stark contrast to the situation, their tropical surroundings were beautiful.

The Chief Officer of the *Vyner Brooke* with five *Prince of Wales* ratings and three women, including Vivian Bulwinkel, went inland to a kampong but its inhabitants declined to help for fear of retribution from the enemy. Thirty-six hours later they saw the Japanese invasion fleet land troops on Banka Island itself and of course their hearts fell. Though they had water from a spring, there was virtually nothing to eat, the elderly and children were becoming distressed and it was decided after a vote to give themselves up. Accordingly the Chief Officer, Sedgeman, and two ratings went off to contact the Japs. At this juncture Matron Drummond providentially decided that the civilian women and children should go too (they were taken prisoner) while the nurses, soldiers and few sailors sat on the beach and waited. One of the sailors was a naval stoker, Ernest Lloyd.

Sedgeman duly returned with a Japanese officer and a dozen men. The former indicated the party and that they wished to surrender, but the officer said something to his soldiers who then separated the men from the women and marched the men out of sight along the beach. When they came to a small bay the soldiers lined them up at the water's edge, facing out to sea. Until this point none had any idea what was going to happen, but then the Japanese officer told one of them to take off his shirt and tear it up into strips to put over their eyes. He refused at which the officer drew his sword and slashed him savagely across the face. 'We knew then all right what was going to happen,' Lloyd has written.

> The man next to me, who was a seaman I had known in Singapore – I think his name was Jock McGlurk – said 'This is where you get it Ernie, right in the back.' I said, 'Not for me, Jock,' and we both dived into the sea, with one other man, as the Japs opened fire with a machine-gun. They mowed down the others first and then turned the gun on the three of us. I was a powerful swimmer and was going well. Jock cried out, 'I'm hit, Ernie,' and both he and the other man sank out of sight. I then got the Japs' undivided attention – and they weren't going to leave anyone alive. I saw a bullet hit the water at my side and then felt a bullet hit my head and I thought it had gone right through; but in actual fact it only grazed my scalp. Then another bullet went right through my left shoulder and leg. I must have looked – and certainly felt – a dead man as I floated half submerged round the rocks, was washed up on a bit of sand, and lost consciousness.

Vivian Bulwinkel continues:

> The Japanese who had gone with the men came back wiping their bayonets. . . . We just looked at each other. We didn't have any emotion about it. I think by this time we'd had shock added to everything else. The Japanese came and stood in front of us and indicated that we should go into the sea. And we walked into the sea with our backs to them. We knew what was going to happen to us, but all I can remember thinking was, 'I am sorry Mother will never know what has happened to me but it will be nice to see

Dad again.' We didn't talk among ourselves. It was quite silent.
We were drained of emotion. There were no tears. Perhaps I was
thinking, 'How can anything as terrible as this be happening in
such a beautiful place?' I'm not sure I heard the shooting . . . yes,
I think I did hear a rat-tat-tat and I suppose it was a machine-gun.
I got hit. The force of the bullet, together with the waves, knocked
me off my feet. I just lay there, swallowing a tremendous amount
of salt water until I was violently ill. And, after a while it sort of
penetrated that I wasn't dying right there and then. I thought I'd
better stay low until I couldn't stay low any longer. The waves
brought me right into the shallow water. Finally, when I did sit up
and look around, there was nothing. The Japanese had gone and
none of the other girls were to be seen. Nothing. It's a bit hard to
say but I think it might have been just after midday. I started to
shiver and all I wanted to do was get up into that jungle and lie
down.

So I got up and walked across the beach and lay down just
off a track that led to the nearest village. Whether I passed
out or not, I don't know . . . but I know that I woke up on
one occasion and it was pitch dark. On the second occasion
it was daylight and I was hot and sticky and felt awful. All
I could think about was that I must get up and go down to
the spring at the beach and get a drink. But I couldn't be
bothered. So I lay down again, and for a while there wasn't
a sound. And suddenly, to my horrified gaze, I saw a line of
helmets and bayonets going down towards the beach. I don't
know how long I lay there flat, but eventually they came back
again and I swear I looked into every pair of eyes. If I'd gone
out for a drink when it was my first inclination, that would have
been the end.

Well, I finally got up enough courage to go down and have a
drink. Suddenly a voice from behind said, 'Where have you been,
nurse?'

It was Private Pat Kingsley who was the only soldier left alive.
He had had the top part of an arm blown off when his ship was
attacked and a bayonet wound in the side. Since the massacre
he had sheltered in a fisherman's hut, but they now went back
to the jungle. She filled water bottles from a beach spring,
wrapped some coconut fibre round his wounds and made him,
who 'wasn't in too good a state', as comfortable as possible. Her
own wound –

18. Some of the 24 surviving Australian Army Sisters from the 65 who set out in the *Vyner Brooke*, after liberation in 1945. Key: 1. Nesta James 2. Mavis Hannah 3. Jessie Simons (p.137) 4. Iole Harper (p.139) 5. Betty Jeffrey (p.137) 6. Jennie Ashton   Inset: Vivian Bulwinkel (p.142)

19. "I think I did hear a rat-tat-tat and I suppose it was a machine gun". The hole in Sister Bulwinkel's uniform (p.142)

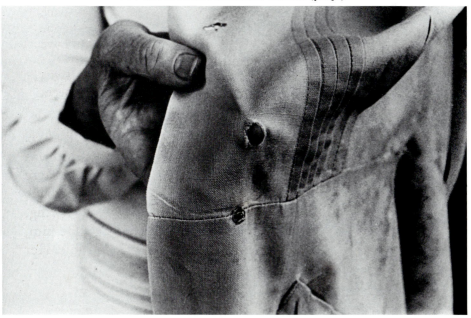

20. "The damaged ship was now approaching the *Li Wo*, still firing.
We had expended all our 4-inch ammunitions, so the C.O. decided to ram her"
(p.178)

wasn't too bad at all. I could tell from the holes in my uniform that the bullet had come out. I wondered how it had managed to miss my intestines, my liver and my stomach . . . although people have said since that it probably missed my intestines and stomach because they were so shrunk through lack of food . . . if I weren't so tall, of course, the bullet would have passed right through my heart. I didn't give my wound any attention at all and as the days passed, I felt myself getting stronger. Oh, I watched it in case of infection but I think the fact that I spent so many hours in the salt water had cleaned it out. Look, if I'd been near a hospital they'd probably have taken me in, opened it up and made it a lot worse, with their probing around!*

They stayed in the jungle together for a fortnight, she getting stronger but he not so. Twice they visited the kampong where the men would not help them but women met them with food on the way back. They had made a pact not to surrender but after a bit she said, 'We're taking a long time to die – perhaps we'd better do something,' to which he agreed, providing they waited for another two days. 'I'll be 39 tomorrow and I'd like to think I spent my birthday in freedom.' They finally walked into the kampong – where they heard that a prison camp had been set up, which included women wearing Red Cross armbands – and were put on the road to Muntok. It was decided they would say nothing about the massacre or the Japanese would certainly execute them there and then to cover themselves. On the way they were picked up by a Japanese naval officer in a car, Vivian being eventually deposited at the coolie lines camp while her companion was taken to the makeshift hospital.

Poor Kingsley died there a few days later, there being no means of draining the pus from his punctured lung. In the next bed was Ernest Lloyd, who agreed with Vivian, when she came to visit Kingsley, to keep mum.

It was dark and raining when Lloyd had come to, his head and shoulder throbbing. Next day he was able to explore and found

* See figure 19.

the spring and some coconuts. He lay quiet for a few days and then set out along the beach to see if any of the others had survived. 'It was quite horrible. All the male bodies had been piled on top of one another in one big heap. Then I went farther along and found the bodies of the Australian nurses and other women. They lay at intervals of a few yards – in different positions and in various stages of undress. They had been shot and then bayonetted. It was a shocking sight.'

Lloyd roamed about for several days and then walked towards Muntok to give himself up, being nearly shot by the Jap who captured him. There was also a fourth survivor, H. McDougall Junior, an American from Singapore. He had been shot and bayonetted and left for dead, but was to survive his years of captivity. Vivian went on post-war to high rank in her country's hospital service. They were a tough trio indeed, only the lack of normal medical facilities making it impossible to include the unfortunate Kingsley.

The Japanese officer responsible for the atrocities was traced to the Russian front at the end of the war but managed to commit suicide.

I feel the SS *Chilka*, en route, on 11 March, to succour those stranded at Padang, should be briefly saluted as an honourable fringe participant in Singapore's Dunkirk.

When only some 100 miles west of Pulau Nias, she was confronted by a 2-gun Japanese submarine on the surface. Both ships opened fire as Captain Bird turned away to keep his adversary right aft. Unfortunately the latter obtained an early hit that caused two ammunition lockers to explode, knocking out the one gun, causing severe casaulties and starting a fire. Though at first the *Chilka* outdistanced the submarine and hopes of escape were high, she continued to be hard hit, nine boats and much of the superstructure being carried away. The submarine was then seen to be gaining and as his ship continued to take punishment, Captain Bird realised that it was only a matter of time before her entire crew would be in jeopardy, together with any means of getting away.

Accordingly he hoisted 'I am about to abandon ship', at which the submarine ceased firing and stood by while the crew got into four boats with the wounded and left the ship's side. It called one of them over and gave the occupants water, biscuits and a course for the nearest land. The boats then lost contact with each other, Captain Bird's beaching on Pulau Nias on 16 March. It was an uncivilised locality where they could not make themselves understood and rowed up a creek for eight hours to a hospital that turned out to be a native rest house. However, after a long slog through jungle and swamps, carrying the wounded, they were able to deposit them at a mission hospital. Here the other boats' crews were met, having landed on different islands.

The Japanese were coming to take over; the stouthearted Bird did not intend to become a prisoner and having obtained a steel lifeboat from the helpful Controleur, set sail with a volunteer crew for Ceylon. After encountering the same 'adverse winds and calms' that were plaguing *Djohanis* and *Berganti* in the area, they were picked up off Madras on 4 May after 35 days. Captain Bird was awarded the OBE and an Indian cadet (who, though wounded, had tackled the fire with his bare hands) the BEM and Lloyd's War Medal.

Presumably the Controleur was attending to the rest of the *Chilka* men when Colonel Dillon was at Telok Island.

A happier story concerns Lieutenant Norman Bell RNVR and his triumph over rather less formidable odds. In command of an ex-customs motor launch, he had the unnerving experience of the desertion, the night before the surrender, of his entire Malay crew. However, two RASC sergeants and an Indian lorry driver having been impressed and the boat filled up with evacuating soldiers, he sailed as ordered. Manned entirely by the newcomers – except for Bell and his First Lieutenant – HMMF's only difficulties proved to be organizational. 'We would rave at them when a soldier put the helm over the wrong

way, though we realized it was no part of their job to know port
from starboard . . . and it simply never occurred to us to substitute
left and right. . . . There are some things you simply cannot do on
board a ship!'

The launch having been turned over to the Dutch, who were
pathetically grateful for its three-inch gun, in the upper reaches
of the Siak River, they made Padang, Tjilatjap and Australia.

*   *   *

Intended (and usually succeeding) to lift eyebrows, there is a
framed notice in my porch which says in large black letters
PLEASE DO NOT SPIT, followed by translations in Malay, Chinese
and Tamil. It was stolen, as a souvenir, off the bulkhead of the
Penang Harbour Board's ferry *Bagan*, which I found myself
running between Penang and Butterworth, forty-eight hours
after the sinking of my ship on 10 December. After the evacuation of Penang she was left at Port Swettenham; her eventual escape from Singapore was another of the few successful
ones.

Exactly three months later, the (Penang and Singapore)
Boards' chairman, Mr R. K. Rodgers, reached Australia
after many adventures and wrote an interesting report which
mentioned the *Bagan*. He had decided on information received,
to prepare for the evacuation of the Boards' staffs, so gave orders
for the ferry – by then at Singapore – to be fitted out for a
journey of 1,000 miles. 'On Wednesday 11th the battle front
had reached Pasir Panjang. . . . By 1 pm all were on board
and ready to leave when I made a final attempt to speak to
the Governor . . . to my surprise he not only knew nothing
of the situation at Pasir Panjang but informed me that the
General was also unaware of the position there . . . he gave
his consent to the whole of the staff leaving . . . provided
that someone stayed behind to look after the Asiatic staff. I
agreed to accept this duty.' On learning that he was staying
a dozen membes of Mr Rodgers' staff came ashore from the
Bagan, which sailed at 2.30 pm. Eventually all remaining
Harbour Board officers, except Mr Rodgers and his deputy

Mr J. R. Wiggs, were sent on board the *Mata Hari* which left next day, an unhappy switch as things turned out.

At 6 pm on the 13th Mr Wiggs and I [wrote Mr Rodgers] went to the *Laburnum* to see the position . . . godowns had just been bombed and were ablaze. The road in the vicinity of godown no 4 was impassable and we arrived to see the last tender leaving the wharf with evacuees for the *Kuala*. While we were discussing matters a heavy raid on Telok Ayer took place. Mr Wiggs and I had a very narrow escape and were badly shaken by blast. In our judgement the end of Singapore was close at hand, and we decided to accept an offer, made by the Naval Officers on the spot, to leave with them and boarded the *Tenggaroh*. This ship was built by the Harbour Board in 1929 as a yacht for the Sultan of Johore. She had a range of less than 300 miles . . . but we decided to accept the risks involved rather than fall into Japanese hands. . . .

The Japanese started to shell the Telok Ayer area. Arrangements had been made for all the remaining small naval craft to come alongside the wharf at dusk to embark the troops selected for evacuation, but the shelling not only caused large numbers of casualties, but disorganised the embarkation. The ships, however, came alongside in perfect order and left to a timetable carrying considerable numbers of troops. The *Tenggaroh* left at about 1 pm and returned a few minutes later to pick up a few troops who had run the gauntlet of the barrage. Mr Wiggs and I were the only civilians on board.

Captain Eddy of the *Bagan*, carrying approximately 150 European officers of the Boards and some women and children, took a course through the Bulan Strait to avoid enemy bombers, and arrived safely at Palembang at noon on, for them, not so Black Friday the 13th. Next morning the whole party (including Mrs de Malmanche's husband, Eric) were en route to the west coast of Java (and thence Colombo) even as enemy parachutists landed at Palembang. The faithful *Bagan* was left there, and I fear that 'Please do not spit' was added in Japanese to the notices in her saloon. The coxswain of the *Tenggaroh*, in which Mr Rodgers was a last-minute passenger, was Petty Officer L. V. Leather. An indefatigable character, he had been serving with Lieutenant-Commander Clark up country (for which he was eventually awarded the DSM: see page 186) and now takes up the story of the one-time yacht:

Self and AB Hartshorne had joined the *Tenggaroh* – not very large. The CO was Lieutenant Peter Whitworth RNVR, the son of the Admiral Whitworth who took the Fleet into the second battle of Narvik. The only other person on board was the engine-room man – a rather vintage Chinese gentleman. Our first passenger was Mr Rodgers of the Harbour Boards.

We ran civilians out to waiting ships. The women and children were arriving with stacks of gear – numerous suitcases etc but they were told to leave them and get on board. On one occasion a group came down, all well dressed men carrying huge suitcases, and I remember remarking to Lieutenant Whitworth 'They'll be lucky with all that gear'. However, they asked permission to come on board for a moment only so that they could throw the contents of these cases into the water, and proceeded to ditch what must have been hundreds and thousands of Singapore dollars all made up into bundles, into the sea. I've never got over it to this day.

Whilst alongside *Laburnum* jetty, looting was at its height, so I stacked the *Tenggaroh* with plenty of soft drinks, boxes and bars of chocolate and assorted tinned foods. I went on board *Dragonfly* on the Thursday evening (12 February) and PO Jones transferred a jar of rum to me. However shortly after I found myself giving this precious fluid to badly injured on the jetty – as the Japanese had dropped a few more bombs, hitting the AA guns not far from *Laburnum*. It was said that the Japanese mortars were now firing towards the harbour – I do know a couple of the large windows were shattered and I received a very nasty cut on my left hand. The only people we had taken on board up to this point was a rather motherly type matron with a Eurasian nurse who I had put down the after cabin. The matron bandaged my hand, having removed a long sliver of glass from it, and I spent most of the remaining time getting instructions from the CO who was showing me the chart passage out of the harbour, with a course set later for the Banka Strait, then through the Sunda Strait to get to the west side of Java.

At midnight we were still alongside, and things were beginning to get very frightening indeed, but Lieutenant Whitworth would not leave as he repeatedly said that he would collect a group before doing so. I had it in my mind that they could be some VIPs of course, but, about 0100 Saturday 14th, he finally said

'Let's go' after embarking about eighteen Indian troops with an
officer – who were in a terrible state. We cleared Keppel Harbour
about 0120, snatching a little sleep between us on the bridge, as
we pointed for the Berhala Strait. As light broke Jap aircraft
flew low near us, but they must have thought that we were too
small for them to worry about. As the forenoon wore on aircraft
came near on numerous occasions – but still they left us alone.
Towards the late forenoon we could see many ships lying low
in the water ahead of us, with Japanese aircraft flying around,
and when we finally reached the scene the waters around these
sinking ships were absolutely full – people swimming – in open
boats – hanging on to anything to keep afloat, and so began our
rescue attempt. I will always recollect this ship which was still
afloat with the decks awash – with personnel launching rafts,
floats etc over the side. We finally came to a situation where we
could not possibly take any more on board. All the women and
nurses had been put down the after cabin, where this matron
was able to care for them, and the upper deck was absolutely
packed.

This ship was the *Shu Kuang*, of which we have already heard
in connection with the *Tanjong Pinang* (page 45). Corporal V. Leah,
of Singapore Fortress Signals, was on board:

Survivors from *Prince of Wales* and *Repulse* formed the crew, who
shepherded us aboard as if we were passengers embarking for a
voyage on a liner! Politeness and jovial assurance . . . apparently
the engines were short of oil and men were detailed to pour water
into the bearings. . . . About 2 pm the air raid alert sounded
and those of us on deck lay in a heap . . . some steam pipes
were holed and the engines disabled. Several men were killed,
many wounded to greater or lesser degree . . . the order came
to abandon ship . . . let off steam which caused a roaring noise
that prompted one nervous soldier to jump overboard, but he
was fished out of the drink and told to abandon ship in a more
orderly fashion. One lifeboat was serviceable and the wounded
put into that. . . . I used a cabin door as a float, but parted
with it when a Chinese lad called to me, 'Please help me, I
can't swim'. He was holding on to a rope at the ship's side.
I showed him how to use the cabin door and paddle with his
feet and left him heading for Sumatra, where he claimed to have
relatives! (In charge of the lifeboat was Colonel Coates; see page
67).

Lieutenant Colonel T. F. Hartley R A, who had been ordered to evacuate ('I had raised that Battery, trained it, and been through two pretty unpleasant months with them; and now I was getting out and leaving them. . . . I have never felt so rotten in my life') was also on the *Shu Kuang*:

> The splinters killed 17 and wounded 35. One of my two fitters was among the killed. A depth charge saved me. I was sitting on the deck just behind it. A splinter, which would have hit me, ripped open its metal casing, exposing its yellow contents. . . . Two more planes arrived and finally dropped their bombs, this time holing us. The Captain, a silly old man, gave no orders, but someone started letting down two boats; a disgraceful scene followed, headed by some of our friends from 'down under'. Panic set in, and the majority took to the water. It was obvious she wasn't going down for many hours, and most of them came shame-facedly aboard again a bit later. Various small boats were around and the last of us was taken off about 6 pm.

A quick 'confab' between these small vessels (including the ill-fated *Tanjong Pinang* which was to go eventually to Pompong) resulted in their heading for the Indragiri. Arrived at Tembilahan, Lieutenant Whitworth's engine room staff reported the *Tenggaroh*'s machinery to be beyond further operation and when this had been confirmed by Mr Rodgers she was handed over to the Dutch. All concerned then joined the escape route. Mr Rodgers and P.O. Leather will be re-encountered shortly.

Also putting in to Tembilahan at this time was the small minesweeper *Malacca*, after an adventurous passage, as indicated in an account by her First Lieutenant, Lieutenant W. B. Bevis M R N V R. She had sailed late on the 13th with 62 Army officers and men (including Lieutenant-Colonels Phillips, Marsh, Kellet and Ashmore). Smoke from burning oil tanks having reduced visibility almost to nil, she was asked by HMS *Changtei* to help by showing a stern light. A Fairmile seemed to be heading for the rocks and they flashed U N C L E (You are standing into danger); this was probably ML 310, with Admiral Spooner embarked, her steering gear having broken down. *Malacca* was bombed while at anchor at False Durian Island next day, nine bombs falling within 20 yards and shaking her badly. That night: 'We heard shouts to starboard and picked up Signalman Finlay, who had been drifting for hours on an Oropesa float. He was from the *Changtei*, sunk by aircraft that afternoon. Hearing by W/T (Finlay on watch!) that Palembang was under attack, we decided to enter the Indragiri.' Having disembarked the troops, the *Malacca* loaded up with wounded from the various sunken ships and took them up to Rengat. Because of bomb damage (there were $2^{1}/_{2}$ feet of water in the hold), lack of coal and the way to Batavia being barred, she was scuttled, the ship's company getting to Padang, where they were put on board a cruiser. This was HMS *Danae*. It was 20 February when she put in to Emmahaven (Padang) where Major Swalwell (last heard of leaving the *Tanjong Pinang* at Tembilahan) had just arrived.

> The Docks were a short train ride and we arrived there in the afternoon – some 500 of us now. Almost as we de-trained a light grey shape slid into the harbour entrance . . . HMS *Danae*. Once again it was the Navy to the rescue and another illustration of that peculiar brotherhood relationship between the Navy and the Army which has endured since the 18th century. 'Blimey! Picking up the Brown jobs again?' 'Garn! Where have you been?' The *Danae* sidled up to the quayside. She did not actually tie up and kept her props turning slowly to keep her alongside – her nose was up against the corner of the quay. I understood that if there was any sign of aircraft she would push off at once. Embarkation was swift. I watched my party aboard and was one of the last to put foot on the welcome deck. I thought, at last we are out of it. Almost at once we were away. It was nearing the end of the day and Sumatra was a wonderful sight as we headed West. The evening sun was lighting up the mountains inland, nothing looked so peaceful. I went below. The lads were below with their matelot friends.

Also on board the crowded ship were Mr Rodgers and PO Leather. To the disgust of the latter ('A British cruiser had actually put us ashore – just to be taken prisoner by the Japanese') they were all landed at Tjilatjap, to kick their heels for several days.

However [he continues], a smartly dressed Captain of the RN walked down the jetty one particular day – had us all fallen in – and introduced himself as Captain Bell out of Singapore.* It was explained to him who and what we were – and he went off down the jetty with a couple of RNVR officers towards two old coasters laying at the end of the jetty. A couple of hours later the buzz got through that we had a chance of escape. All the stoker POs and engine-room ratings, Navy and Merchant Navy, went on board this coaster. Also Lieutenant Bevis of the *Malacca* and her crew. I found myself Master at Arms. PO Davies, as the senior gunnery rating, was collecting all arms and ammunition and setting up defences around the bridge. I put PO Watson (ex *Repulse*) in charge of the food and cooks looked at the cooking situation. Apparently Captain Bell had found a Dutch engineer with his wife and two children on board. The ship, called the *Khoen Hoea*, had been out of commission for quite some time, but the Captain was convinced she could be got under way.

He came along the jetty with a group of Australians who were soon placed in watches for moving coal from the bunkers and stoking the fires under senior engine-room bods. I cannot recall the time all this took, but engines were tested alongside and the whole party organized for watches, lookouts, manning the rifles and small arms around the ship. We left Tjilatjap at about 4 knots, with black smoke pouring out, but believe me we were a well-organized ship's company. Captain Bell warned us that we might run into trouble and slowly the thick black smoke was controlled to a hazy white, as it had been a good give-away, but the luck of the Irish was with us, we met nothing at all on our way south – a scare once of a sub periscope but no more – and after about two and a half days we arrived at Fremantle in Australia. [This story shows just what could have been achieved at Padang, given a free hand with the shipping there.]

An air attack being very much on the cards, there was in fact a general exodus from Tjilatjap, including the Dutch *Zaandam*, the *Wu Chang*, an old Yangtze steamer fortunate to escape from Singapore via the Banka Strait, and the ill-fated destroyer *Stronghold*. It seems that the only casualties were the latter and the inward bound *City of Manchester*, which was torpedoed

---

* Captain F. S. Bell, Chief Staff Officer to RA Malaya who had escaped from Singapore in a yacht. He had commanded *Exeter* at the Battle of the River Plate.

by submarine. The *Zaandam* and the *Wu Chang* were lucky as a round dozen ships were sunk by Japanese submarines in these waters at this time. The *Wu Chang*'s escape to Colombo was as fantastic as her escape from Singapore and not without a touch of farce, at least in retrospect. On board were Captain Barham Savory (previously encountered being ordered to leave Singapore), Major Swalwell who had transferred from the *Danae*, and his QMS Wiltshire. An absentee was a private of Savory's called Pitch. Apparently one who took life lightly, he was not on board when the ship cast off but appeared within seconds on the one that had been alongside. The quick-thinking Savory attached a rope to a lifebelt and threw it to Pitch, telling him to put it on, jump into the water and be pulled on board the *Wu Chang*. Though helpers put the lifebelt on to Pitch he would not jump and Savory had to let go the rope. Two hours later Pitch and others were being marched into years of captivity (which one is glad to say he survived; but after what a catastrophic hesitation!).

The *Wu Chang* had no other lifebelts and was virtually unarmed but Mr Wiltshire recorded:

> Some of our gunners had eased their boredom by rigging up a dummy gun on the upper deck; it consisted chiefly of a light wooden frame with a tarpaulin over it and a long spar thrust through a hole. They had developed a sort of Fred Karno gun drill, and gave a show of closing up and clearing for action.

This may have saved them all, as will be seen. Swalwell:

> After five or six days we had all come to believe it was only a matter of time before reaching Ceylon in safety. . . . With others I was in a bridge school to pass the time . . . I had just made a contract when an officer put his head into the saloon and said, 'Don't look now, but there is a sub surfacing on the starboard bow. He has already fired three torpedoes.' We said, 'Don't talk rubbish' – a pause – '*What* did you say?' We pushed over the table and cards (we never did find the whole pack again) and went to the rail. Sure enough there it was. Very close and submerging as it passed. My main recollection is seeing the conning tower going below the water and the periscope swivelling round peering at us. . . .

I was stupefied. I had read about submarines but never imagined I would see one submerging in real life – *and* in anger. . . . As I went below to see the troops I remember thinking, 'This is it', and in a sort of little prayer I said – aloud – 'Cheerio Pat (my wife); I will see you sometime' . . . I went below – actually on the Port side, and leaning over the rail were two of my lads, Lance-Bombardier Dare and Lance-Bombardier East. Dare was a pure cockney. . . . East was a Derbyshire lad. Quiet; slow (although he was an extremely fast bowler) and methodical. . . . I asked, 'What happened?' Dare said, 'Well, we were leaning on the rail chatting when we saw a streak passing under us and away to sea. I said, 'Blimey Bill, we are crossing the bleeding Equator'. I asked, 'Haven't you been to the other side and seen the sub?' They said 'No. We thought after all we have been through it is just our luck to meet a bleeding sub – sod him!'

Savory was writing a letter on the upper deck. It went: '2/3/42 At sea . . . I persuaded him . . . to change for me a traveller's cheque for £10 in spite of its being a bit bedraggled from its immersion.

Got to stop now. Submarine in sight, has fired two torpedoes and missed. . . .

Love to all and many thanks for everything.

Barham

6/3/42 Panic over. I am sorry for the somewhat alarming statement on the last page, but really thought I was done for that time, so gave this letter to a man in the battalion who was allotted a seat in the lifeboat. I was on deck the morning before yesterday when we noticed two streaks in the water . . . a periscope popped up followed by other posts and chains, all well within 100 yards of where I was standing. We all rushed round and collected water bottles etc and brought all the tables and chairs out on the deck so as to have something to float on . . . we expected him to pop up any moment and fire at us with his gun.

The submarine, having set its torpedoes to run too deep, had presumably expended its outfit and disliking gun engagements anyway, may have been taken in by the dummy gun. The *Wu Chang* arrived safely for the second time, to get her own back by being retained at Trincomalee naval base in Ceylon as a submarine depot ship (see figure 21).

The *Mata Hari** was not so lucky. Another of the small coastal steamers taken over by the Navy, she had left Singapore at 10 pm on 12 February with over 300 passengers, nearly all civilians. Just after weighing she was asked to take another 120, and did so, my guess being that they were the two boatloads of women and children that called at the *Kung Wo* but carried on when told of the bad state of our boats. As well as the Harbour Board officers there were, among the passengers: Mrs Russell-Roberts and Mrs Jennings (wives of the authors of *Spotlight on Singapore* and *An Ocean without Shores* respectively) neither of whom, tragically, were to survive imprisonment; Jack Barton, a planter cousin of mine serving in the Volunteers (he was to come home after the war but sadly did not live long, and Mr G. Haldane, a civilian stores officer from the Naval Base.

The *Mata Hari*, which had one four-inch gun, was jam-packed and her Captain, Lieutenant Carston, RNR, must have been very conscious of his responsibility for the near-defenceless cargo. At first all went well as they headed for Batavia under the standard instructions to make as much use as possible of island cover during daylight hours. A single aircraft bombed the ship next day but near-missed, gunflashes were seen after dark and on the 14th they watched apprehensively as enemy air fleets droned overhead. A few survivors from the gunboat *Scorpion*, sunk by Japanese warships, had been picked up in the early hours and Carston sensibly decided to hug the Sumatran coast and land his passengers as soon as practicable, rather than run the gauntlet to Batavia. At first light he anchored near the Moesi River, with the choice of either continuing up it, for which he had no pilot, that evening, or keeping along the coast in the hopes of escaping in the darkness to another sanctuary. He chose the latter and very nearly made it.

Searchlights were seen and gunfire heard in the Banka Strait ahead and as they proceeded, showing no chink of light of course, a chilly game of blindman's buff was played until 3 am when (Mr Haldane recorded):

A searchlight picked us out of the darkness and everyone on deck woke up. There was a flash and a bang and a shell whistled by.

* Malay for 'The Sun (eye of the day)'. Nothing to do with the spy!

Women and children started to panic but word went around that we had been stopped by a Dutch patrol ship. Signals flickered back and forth. At daybreak we saw a cruiser and a destroyer in the distance. Only when we looked up and saw flying from the masthead of our ship a string of signal flags and a white flag did we realise that the other ships were Japanese. We had lost the race by a short head.

The destroyer steamed towards us and when quite near circled slowly around, while a ship's boat with a boarding party pulled towards us. The ensign at its stern with its large crimson circle confirmed our fears and my heart, for one, went down to my shoes. Word came from the bridge warning us to be careful and to destroy all incriminating papers and revolvers, ammunition etc. We went to the other side of the ship and, like the other fellows, I threw overboard my revolver and ammunition, armband, tin helmet, Base passes, etc. Very soon the Japanese marines came on board and while they searched the ship, smashed the radio instruments, removed the breech blocks from the guns etc, we were lined up on deck with little yellow squirts guarding us with fixed bayonets. After about four hours they left, towing behind them all the ship's boats. The skipper was ordered to steam back to Banka Island and to anchor there. No lights were to be shown during the night or else shore batteries would fire on us.

Once, when we were lined up on deck, three of our bombers flew over and bombed a line of anchored Japanese transports, but, worse luck, they all missed the target. As the last bomber went by our ship a Jap scout seaplane dived out of the clouds on to its tail. We were holding our breath when there was a burst of firing from the bomber's tail; the Jap plane seemed to stall as if it had hit a brick wall – it dived, recovered, started to climb and then suddenly nose crashed into the sea. It was pretty to watch and we felt like cheering, but couldn't as the little yellow bellies had their bayonets half an inch from our tummies.

Another diversion occurred when a British 'Fairmile' ML suddenly appeared and went straight for the nearest destroyer, zigzagging about to try and avoid the fire of its much larger guns until in range. The massed watchers on the *Mata Hari* held their breath as the unequal contest went on for several minutes (described in Chapter VII) until the gallant ML was hard hit, stopped, and sank burning furiously.

The *Mata Hari* was ordered to Muntok, anchoring near its pier, already a mass of survivors and onto which all the new prisoners of war were landed. Haldane goes on:

> The pier was a quarter of a mile long and we remained there until seven o'clock next morning. Sleep was impossible as there was insufficient room to lie down and the night was very chilly. Before I left the ship I had managed to scrounge a new Army blanket, a dixie and a spoon, and these remained with me right to the end of our captivity. The blanket by that time would have almost stood on end for it was never possible to wash it.

Next morning the women and children were taken away in lorries to a prison camp and the men marched to some open ground en route to an airfield.

> By that time we were hungry and thirsty. One Air Force officer could speak Japanese but he could not persuade the Japs to give us anything. Another fellow, a civilian, who had lived for many years in Japan complained to the Jap officers and demanded better treatment according to the conventions. Later on he had another try and we could see and hear him laying down the law. He must have said too much for he was taken away and we never saw him again. There was just the sound of a shot. Believe me, we began to think!*

On arrival at the airfield all the new prisoners were put to hard manual labour clearing it, in company with 4,000 Chinese coolies imported from Hong Kong. They worked under guards with whips, sticks and machine guns, marching back to the native gaol at Muntock in the evening. There they all slept together on bare earth, with no lavatory facilities whatever until the new arrivals made ditches along the walls inside; even so, the coolies would not use them.

Poor Mr Haldane, my cousin Jack, and all the others. This was of course but the standard fare, meted out by the victors wherever they had prevailed in the far east.

The end of HMS *Giang Bee*, a 1200 ton auxiliary which also sailed on 12 February, was mentioned as another example of

---

* This was the elderly Mr V. G. Bowden, the Australian Government representative at Singapore.

Japanese forebearance. It was also to contain elements both of unfortunate misunderstanding and pure ill luck. She had about 300 service and civilian evacuees on board, including women and children. Two air attacks had caused superficial damage, with eight passengers killed and thirty wounded, but by the evening of the 13th it looked as if she might slip through the Banka Strait under cover of darkness. However, at dusk smoke on the horizon materialized into five warships – presumably Ozawa's two cruisers and three destroyers – closing fast. One fired a warning shot at which the *Giang Bee* stopped, her Captain ordered the women to show themselves on deck and lowered the white ensign.

A Japanese destroyer came close and began to flash unintelligible signals. The Captain kept replying that he wished to surrender, and eventually they appeared to understand, lowering a motor boat. Then bad luck struck. The boat was only 150 yards away when an RAF bomber appeared, circling the ships. They opened fire and the launch was recalled. It was now getting dark and a searchlight played up and down the crowded deck. After a strange period of inaction, the signal suddenly came 'One hour to get off', at which the ship's officers directed the women and children to the four serviceable boats. The damaged rope falls of one of them parted, spilling its occupants into the choppy sea, another, full of holes, foundered. With many still on board it was decided that the ship's 14-foot dinghy should go to the destroyer to ask for help for the women and children.*

Inexplicably the destroyer would have nothing to do with his dinghy, continually moving out of reach. The last boat was away from the *Giang Bee* when there was an explosion as one of the Japanese ships fired. Terrified figures could be seen jumping from the target's deck, soon ablaze from end to end. The moon was coming up as the enemy force disappeared into the darkness, the stern of the stricken ship rose up and she slid from view.

---

* In this boat was Rob Scott, Singapore's Director of Information (who was to suffer appalling torture at the hands of the Kempeitai, the Japanese secret police) but to see them off, just. He survived triumphantly to finish up as Sir Robert and Permanent Secretary to the MOD in the sixties.

The boats, including the dinghy which had picked up a few swimmers, duly made land. One finished up on the south-west corner of Sumatra, most of its occupants being rescued on the 15th by SS *Tapah*, herself captured in the Banka Strait two days later. Two hundred lives had been lost from the *Giang Bee*. Scott was convinced that the Japanese did not originally intend to sink her, or they would have done so at once; but everything went wrong.

*   *   *

Mr R. D. Rivett, an Australian of the Malayan Broadcasting Corporation, was sitting at his desk in the newsroom at Singapore when 'the phone rang and I heard Mr Davis's voice, hoarse with emotion, saying that he had been told by the military that we must close down at eleven o'clock since the transmitting plant had become untenable.' Rivett, through whose eyes we will see the rest of the action, was soon on board the *Siang Wo* ('It was a fateful decision. Other members of the staff got on another boat and have never been seen since'). HMS *Siang Wo*, yet another ex-Yangtse river boat sailed pm on 11 February to be heavily bombed next day off Banka Island, her steering gear being destroyed.

> Thanks to some merciful dispensation of providence, the enemy bombers had apparently decided that we were helpless and that they had better targets elsewhere because, after being hit, we remained unmolested. However, I subsequently learned in Batavia that, from half past two onwards, the Japanese concentrated on seven ships . . . which were then just at the other end of Banka Strait. Captain Daniels, a British MO, told me that from the deck of the smallest of these vessels he watched the Jap bombers sink or set on fire each of the other six ships within the space of an hour. It was impossible for his own ship to make any attempt to pick up the survivors struggling in the water, and in his belief very few, if any, from these six ships would have had a chance of getting ashore. His own vessel got through only because most of the bombers had used up their cargoes.

The women were put ashore, except for two who were taken off in an RAF yacht, the *White Swan*, after which the captain decreed that the ship was too crippled to have any chance of reaching Batavia. He ran her ashore a few hundred yards from Muntok pier, near two or three smaller victims which were already high and dry. It was soon found that as a result of a general exodus to Java and sabotage by natives, there was not a single navigable boat left at Muntok. After considerable confusion, Rivett found himself with most of the others in a local hotel, where he was woken at 3 am to hear that there was a large number of ships, including cruisers and destroyers, offshore and 'They're pulling towards the jetty now . . . thousands of 'em!' There was no doubt who 'they' were.

Commander Vickers, a passenger, took charge, sent the women to the Dutch hospital to be under the Red Cross and eventually agreed that it was every man for himself. Rivett, Carter (also of the MBC), Kinnear (the *Siang Wo*'s First Officer), and three MRNVR officers (including one Wade, who spoke Malay) got off on foot for Java. Unfortunately there is not space to chronicle all their struggles and jungle adventures ('suddenly there was a snarl, followed by hair-raising screams and a tremendous thrashing among the bushes on the bank of the stream. . . . In the morning we discovered a considerable quantity of blood and fur!'). Some natives encountered were friendly and gave them food, some not (they were directed towards a Japanese patrol, narrowly missed). Eventually, over a week after setting out, they exchanged a 17-foot rowing boat 'cumbrous and unwieldy and leaking in two or three places' for Rivett's watch. With his blanket acting as some sort of sail they set off in high spirits across the Banka Strait for Sumatra, not too easy with three oars to which recourse had to be had whenever the wind dropped. Kinnear had been elected skipper, but most of the rowing fell on Rivett and the much older Carter as the rest began to suffer from one ailment after another. After rowing without a break for nine hours they hit land in the form of a glutinous mangrove swamp and were skirting this when a Jap steamer appeared, fortunately taking no notice. A kampong then came in sight where Wade interrogated some natives. 'Christ Almighty!.

We're back on bloody Banka!' They had been round in a full circle.

Worse than this, Japanese troops were only a few hundred yards away and the natives could not get rid of our friends quick enough, though they did load the boat with coconuts. Minutes later a single-engined Jap plane, flying down the coast, circled them repeatedly at 200 feet, but, possibly out of ammunition, droned off without doing anything. An appalling sumatra then descended. The blanket was hardly down before it hit them; the boat's seams opened up with the constant buffeting, needing all spare hands to bale. After four hours the elements relented and they made Sumatra. 'The boat was too small to give us all lying space so we literally lay piled on top of each other, enormously grateful for the warmth which this gave to our frozen bodies.'

It was decided to keep rowing down the Sumatra coast until Dutchmen could be contacted. After a time they arrived at the huts of some fishermen who were friendly and fed them well. 'They seemed rather surprised that we had survived the previous night. These Malays were good friends to us in our hour of need, and, as they regarded Singapore dollars as quite useless, there was nothing with which we could repay them. . . . They appeared non-plussed at the turn of events which converted the 'tuans besar', or white bosses, into refugees seeking food and shelter.'

The indefatigable seven now entered upon

a period of toil which was not measured by hours or by day and night. Our hands blistered quickly, but with the aid of salt water they also calloused rapidly and our main discomfort was caused by the hardness of the ribs and thwarts on the softest parts of our anatomies. We usually rowed in hour-long shifts, but since Marr was never strong at the best of times and Kinnear had developed dysentery, I felt that, being the youngest and in many ways the fittest, I should do most of their work at the oars. We adopted the system of rowing as much as possible during the night and resting in the heat of the day. I found that, provided I got at least two meals a day, seven or eight hours at the oars were quite possible. Things were not so good when, as sometimes happened, we went twenty-four hours without food, during which time we had to battle against storms or currents for long hours without being relieved at the rowing seat.

A major anxiety, apart from the storms, was the morning and evening air reconnaissance, from which they had to hide. Quite by chance, six refugees like themselves were encountered ashore (including a Colonel, and a Stoker from the *Repulse* who had been sunk on three other occasions) all at their last gasp. After repairing leaks with clay they relaunched the boat, now with thirteen on board, and headed for a tall, purple mountain in the distance that they knew was Java. It was the thirteenth day since setting out from Banka.

Suddenly, rounding a point, they found themselves being swept by a current towards a convoy of troopships, soon recognised as Jap. All, except the most sunburnt three, lay under palm leaves in the bottom of the boat, as it passed within 100 yards of one ship and 60 of another. Every second they expected a shot or a challenge, as men were at the rails of both, watching them idly, but the oarsmen were rowing native fashion and presumably were taken for fishermen. Half a mile past the last ship they ran ashore and held a conference. Though the current had carried the boat down the coast away from Batavia it was now obvious that a large Japanese force was in command of the whole area; the boat was leaking worse than ever and it did not look as if she could carry thirteen of them much further. Two of the original party elected to make for Batavia on foot, and set off, but the rest decided to row on, in the hopes of finding a larger boat in which to reach Allied occupied territory, or even Australia.

In sight of a patrolling cruiser, a halt was made for coconuts somewhere near Labuan, where it was learnt that the Japanese were just down the road and that the Dutch had retreated a long way inland. Later they came to a creek where a number of Javanese in prauws were fishing, and ran the boat ashore to be surrounded by a clamorous crowd of natives. These, though friendly, were anxious that they keep going as the Japanese were expected at any time. But the boat badly needed repairs and another storm was blowing up, so they sheltered in a large cave until it was over. Their Malay speaker, not a reliable fellow, came back from visiting the kampong to say that the natives had become very hostile – he had presumably rubbed them up the wrong way – and a few minutes later the party was surrounded by a horde of yelling Javanese, brandishing parangs and long knives, and waving Japanese flags.

They started to launch the boat, but the crowd, now about 80, seized it and attacked them. Quite defenceless, utterly worn out and with three sick there was no point in resisting and in no time they were helplessly trussed. It was Saturday, 7 March. For twenty-four hours they were marched along rough tracks to a main road, along which an army truck full of yellow soldiers appeared and that was the end of their tremendous effort.

Later they were questioned by a Japanese officer who was courteous and immensely impressed that they had rowed from Banka to Java (350 miles as the seagull flies). Another said 'You are very brave men; we would like to do all that we can for you.' This they did, before handing them over to the POW organization, 'the first and last occasion,' wrote Rivett, 'when I was treated with consideration by the Japanese.'

*   *   *

A very personal story is that of an RAF telegraphist, R. A. Fryer. It concerns the cargo boat SS *Derrymore*. One of a party of about 200 from all three services, he had a lucky escape, followed by a fine display of initiative, the whole linked to a strange old tradition of the sea.

As the ship sailed on Black Friday and made for the open sea, its passengers watched sharks around her with some interest.

It was around 7 pm, just dark when the torpedo struck us. We were near the Banka Strait carrying gelignite, but the torpedo struck in the hold carrying food. The ship was alight and heeling over and before we could realize what had happened the Captain deserted his ship and, with a few crew and others, was away in a small boat. The first mate took charge. We were told to jump over the side and, unable to swim a stroke, I went over thinking that's the end of me! As I came up for the last time my head hit a piece of wood and getting my arm around it I tried to get away from the side of the ship. To my horror the wood was tied to the rail but fortunately a figure about to jump saw my predicament – a knife flashed and I drifted away. I was about 20 yards from the ship when she sank, which pulled me down and down and just when I felt this was the end I was on the surface again; the wood had pulled me up.

Soon after, a searchlight beamed across the sea and we thought rescue had arrived, but alas it was the Jap submarine surfacing. I saw it very close to me; it stayed there for a short while, then submerged and I heard its engines as it passed beneath me. I remained in the sea all that night and most of the next day. One fellow near me was pulled under after giving a scream – presumably a shark. After 22 hours, around 5pm a ship appeared on the horizon and eventually, only half-conscious, I was dragged aboard. It was an Australian corvette called the *Ballarat*. I was told I was delirious all night, but reaching Batavia the next morning I thought I had gone blind – I could barely distinguish anything, presumably sun-stroke. I was carried off on a stretcher and finished up at a hospital on Java. Singapore fell the next day.

Eventually I heard that the Japs had landed on Java and as there seemed to be no one around who could speak English, I walked out of the hospital wearing only a pair of pyjamas which the hospital had supplied and by various means got to the docks at Batavia. The last boat to leave was about to sail, the *Orcades*, full of Australian troops who were too late to land. I had no papers, no identity, the only thing I possessed were the pyjamas and I had great difficulty in satisfying the officers on the gang plank that I was British and RAF. Fortunately someone up at the rail who had travelled out from England with me, spotted me and vouched for my identity.

We subsequently reached Ceylon. I still cannot swim a stroke!

Postscript

There is a legend that anyone born with a 'caul' over their face will never die from drowning. Sailors years ago would pay large sums for one to take to sea with them. I was born with a caul over my face!

The *Derrymore* is the only ship I have heard of to be sunk by torpedoes on the East side of Sumatra. There were a dozen on

the Indian Ocean side. On the *Orcades* were other survivors from
the *Derrymore* and also Mrs Reilly, the Governor's cypher officer.

Sergeant-Major E. C. Hosking RAOC was in a party of two
officers and twenty-three other ranks ordered to embark in the
minesweeper *Jarak* on 12 February. They were to form a Base
Workshop in Java. The 300-ton ex-coaster sailed in the late
afternoon and next day laid up in a channel between two islands.
Continuing at dusk, they tuned into the BBC – 'Churchill's
speech likening the heroes of Singapore to those of Dunkirk,
Crete and Greece, rather surprised us, we thought Singapore
was holding well and waiting for reinforcements of planes and
men. During the night saw searchlight in distance . . . flashes from
Connaught Battery were visible as the old 9.2s did their stuff.'

Sergeant-Major Hosking was to be taken prisoner and to
interest himself – and posterity – by recording a number of
personal accounts of the campaign, now in the Imperial War
Museum. One of these is a vivid description of the end of the little
Jarak by an unnamed member of his party, probably a private:

All went well till about three in the afternoon when we spotted
a plane heading towards us. We stood by the guns. We had two
Lewis guns and one twelve-pounder and hoped for the best. He
came low and circled around twice to examine us . . . and off he
went the way we had come. Well, for myself I did not feel at
all easy. I had a feeling something was about to happen and in
half an hour it did. On the horizon four specks appeared and did
they grow quick. . . . At about seven miles they turned broadside
and signalled. What they said I do not know, but the skipper
answered back and we still kept on. Well, the signals stopped and
the leading cruisers, there were three cruisers and one destroyer,
not forgetting the sea-plane, opened fire. I saw the flash of flame
and smoke and there seemed an awful long wait, till soon it
started, the scream of shells. Well, my poor tummy turned.
I thought, well, I have gone all through Singapore, bombed,
machine-gunned, shot at, and now it looks as if I am due to
be done in by shells. Well, the first hit about a hundred yards
from the ship. I could actually see it hit the water. It burst and
the pieces kept richocheting off the waves just like when I was a
boy and used to skim stones on the water. I lost count of how

many were fired, but we seemed to bear a charmed life. Then
the sea-plane came in, but we gave him two and a half drums
from the Lewises and a couple of twelve pounders to occupy his
mind. He dropped two bombs, one to starboard and the other
missed the ship and dropped on the port side. . . . By now the
destroyer was coming up fast. The cruisers were still firing but
as yet we had not been hit. We could not do a thing in defence
as a twelve-pounder has no range at all. We were just a sitting
target wondering if the next moment would be our last, and it
nearly was. The destroyer let fly next. I heard his shots coming
and dropped flat on the deck and the next time I looked up the
side of the ship was missing. I got up but had to drop again as
another lot came over. I dropped by the mast. The next thing I
heard was a terrific crash as he took the top of our mast off and
half the bridge with it. It was a steel mast and the ring nearly
deafened me. I heard the shrapnel whizzing. Some hit my steel
hat and I had one small cut on my back . . . I heard the ship's
siren blow and someone yelling, 'Take to the boats', so I made my
way over the wreckage towards one. We only had two and luckily
neither had been touched. When I reached the side the boat was
away and packed to the limit so I made for the other side and
found this one away and full too. I thought, well, I cannot stop
here, so here goes . . . I dived overboard and swam for the boat.
It is a good job it was not the cold Atlantic or we would have
died that night.

Hosking's own, rather more factual description goes

Seaman P. O. Tucker (ex *Repulse*) manned the twelve pounder
alone, the Malay gunners would not go out to it, and he fired two
rounds of shrapnel, fuse set at the minimum. . . . Simultaneously
our Lewis Guns and rifles cracked away on our deck. The plane
also machine-gunned us as it dived. The bomb just passed over
our twelve pounder and made a large splash just off our starboard
bow. . . . The spray from these bombs seemed to rain down for
several seconds on the ship, but no damage was sustained. Staff
Sergeant Ambrose was flicked across the bridge of his nose by a
m.g. bullet as he stood by his Lewis Gun, but this just grooved
under his skin. . . . The destroyer had moved away from the
line, and appeared to be coming straight for us at full speed.
Our captain ordered that a moveable chest containing codes
etc. be thrown overboard, and Captain Coulthard threw our
confidential rolls and documents over also.

The destroyer . . . opened fire with about a four-inch salvo. Immediately the muzzle flashes were observed we started turning the steering wheel. . . . One hit the bridge on the port side three or four feet from me and a splinter of about forefinger size entered my left thigh, about nine inches above the knee. Other shells struck the forward hold (magazine) and the starboard side plating. As we were now in a hopeless position, Mr Hooper telephoned to the engine room personnel to come up and ordered 'Abandon ship'. . . . I was able to make my way by hopping and climbing with my hands to the starboard boat and crawl into it before it was lowered, but in great pain. Both boats were successfully lowered, Mr Hooper being last off his ship although he had several small splinter wounds in his leg. Shells continued to rain on and all around the ship during this proceeding. One shell burst near the other boat and wounded Staff Sergeant Shazell in the small of the back.

Sitting up in the boat I was able to apply a 'Shell Dressing' to my wound but through loss of blood could feel myself becoming unconscious so purposely fell into the bottom of the boat and used my steel helmet as a pillow. . . . Later we rigged a sail using an oar as a mast and as I was the only yachtsman in the company, I had to give instructions from my 'bed' . . . the sea became much rougher and was pouring over the sides, I had to be lifted out of the bottom and sat on the seat at the stern. I started to shiver with cold and a young sailor kept me alive by pressing his jacket around me and pressing his face into my neck. We arrived at the main island, about midnight and went ashore on the rocks.

At daylight the *Jarak* could be seen still afloat, at which the First Lieutenant (Huntley) took a party of Naval ratings on board. After pumping out the engine room and raising steam, using any wood they could find, he brought the ship back to the island. Shortly after which a Japanese seaplane came down and machine-gunned her and the jungle behind the beach, but without causing casualties. Quarter-Master Sergeant Sigee got the wireless going to learn that both Singapore and Palembang had fallen, deciding the Captain to make for Rengat.

After everyone had returned on board in the evening, the *Jarak* set off at best possible speed, in order to try and make Sumatra by dawn. Unfortunately the engine bearings gave out and she had to be run ashore on the south coast of Singkep. After stores had been landed the *Jarak* was taken into deep water and scuttled, Harper being the last to leave his ship for the second time.

Huntley contacted the nearest kampong and the shipwrecked mariners were taken in sailing koleks and a lorry to Dabo, where they found some 300 in a similar state (under, it will be remembered, Commander Alexander). Hosking's wound was by this time 'very dirty and smelling foully' and his imagination 'ran riot with thoughts of some native sawing off my leg without an anaesthetic'. It was therefore a great relief to find that 'a real doctor had turned up – Captain Kirkwood IAMC' who dealt with his wounds. 'The nurses and patients were all survivors from the *Kuala, Dragonfly* and *Grasshopper*. . . . Captain Kirkwood worked day and night amputating gangrene limbs and was a pillar of strength; he did a grand job of work in Dabo.'

Lieutenant Hooper and all the fit men from *Jarak* left for the Indragiri, he to become Colonel Dillon's prauw skipper.

On 25 February the Singapore water-boat *Heather*, fitted out as a hospital launch, which had evacuated a party to the Djambi River, arrived at Dabo and removed Hosking and 50 other patients to a Dutch military hospital at Djambi. On 1 March they heard that the Japanese were closing in. With Dutch help, Hosking hired a small bus, which, with a party that included two nurses, headed for Padang. After covering 140 miles and crossing two rivers they came to a ferry that had been destroyed and had no option but to return to Djambi. On 4 March the Japanese arrived and took them prisoner.

*   *   *

Commander Alexander had reached Dabo via the minesweeper *Trang* and a week's rowing. Her First Lieutenant was Richard Cox and one of her many passengers (mostly RAF radar personnel) was Lieutenant Holwell; both ended up in *Sederhana Djohanis* with me and the following comes from an account of 'Holly's'. The *Trang* sailed at 10 pm on the 13th but in the awkward conditions of oil fires, dense smoke and absence of navigational marks, ran aground on a falling tide. They were able to disembark the RAF party into two ships that stopped (except for a Flying Officer Dodd who wished to stay). Holwell had come from the Fort Canning HQ and each time the searchlights from Blakang Mati swept across the sea he, knowing how jittery the Fixed Defence people were, expected a deluge of nine point two or six-inch shells, but their luck held. Daylight, with the *Trang* high and dry, brought the inevitable aircraft. Each time one came to look, they did all they could to give the appearance of an abandoned hulk, which seemed to work. With high tide, vehement protests from the overworked engines and much bumping, she floated off to lie up and wait for darkness by St John's Island, meanwhile regaled with a grandstand view of the inferno of Singapore. This culminated in a shattering roar and terrific burst of flame from Blakang Mati as Connaught Battery and magazine went up.

The next shock was that the far from expert engine-room staff could not get any more water into the boiler, though no damage was apparent. They worked like beavers but to no avail. Japanese disinterest could not go on much longer and the decision was made to destroy the ship and take to the two boats. After *Trang* had been set on fire and scuttled, Alexander and Cox shoved off with eighteen in their boat, Holwell having ten in his smaller one. It was now the early hours of Sunday the 15th. (The Captain, Lieutenant Rigden, was to follow in a motor dinghy with the remaining six, but it failed to start and they had to paddle with coaling shovels until picked up by the *Sir Theodore Fraser*). The two boats rowed westward into the black smoke from Dutch oil installations at Samboe Island, which became so thick that they had to secure a line between them to maintain contact. With the help of a strong flood tide, dawn found them South of Raffles Light, at which Alexander made sail and headed South; Holly, having to make do with an oar and boathook as jury mast and gaff, followed some distance astern. Enemy aircraft were continually overhead, one jettisoning its entire bomb-load – presumably the plane was in trouble – rather too near. Contact having been regained, the two boats, under oars whenever the wind was unfavourable, continued southward for several days, their goal being Muntok Island. When currents became too strong they either anchored by an island or pulled inshore to await a change of tide.

The longest 'hop' was some seventy miles to Lingga Island. Having not shaved for ten days they had difficulty in persuading its natives of peaceful intentions, but eventually learnt of the Dutch controleur in nearby Singkep. It was decided to go there – a fortunate change of plan – and on arrival on 22 February, Commander Alexander, finding many rudderless escapees, stayed to take charge, telling Cox and Holwell to carry on to Sumatra. After battling with very bad weather they duly reached the Indragiri. Flying Officer Dodd, who was taken prisoner at Padang, kept a lively diary in captivity. Sadly, he died on the way home after release.

*   *   *

Major J. W. P. Marsh RAOC – a prominent Shanghai businessman of fifty plus who had stoutly joined up at Singapore as a Second-Lieutenant when war in the Far East threatened – was OC the MT Base Ordnance Workshop at Anson Road. He was ordered without warning on 13 February to get down to the docks with his men to evacuate. Some went in unnamed ships, he boarding at 130-ton river patrol launch, the *Paula Suegi*, with the remaining seventy odd, including a Private Arthurs, who later described his experiences to Sergeant-Major Hosking. Grossly overcrowded, the launch sailed shortly after dark. The following day enemy aircraft scored hits on ships nearly, but the *Suegi* only came in for one bomb which failed to explode.

On the 15th there were various alarms – a huge air fleet flew over on its way to Sumatra and a Japanese cruiser squadron forced the *Suegi* to run for cover – but as night fell they were entering the Banka Strait. Marsh recalls:

> I lay down on the top deck near the smoke stack and as I was absolutely played out, having had no sleep worth while for nearly a week, I was able to sleep. The very next thing I knew was being awakened by an explosion and the ship was in a blaze of light; the explosion was the first shell which hit the ship exactly the opposite side of the smoke stack less than a couple of yards away; to say the least I was a bit shook.

Private Arthurs told Hosking that a terrific explosion took place underneath him and he was partly lifted and thrown by the blast on to the hatchway beneath and fell on the lads who had been sleeping there, but had now jumped up, wondering what was happening. Another salvo hit the ship forward and Arthurs rolled off the hatchway and managed to get between the hatchway top and the engine room plating and in this position was sheltered on two sides. At this stage Major Marsh shouted an order: 'Over the side and every man for himself', but as he shouted, Arthurs saw another set of flashes, so stayed under cover, and this salvo whistled over the ship and fell 'plus'. He managed to find a steel helmet nearby and put this on and waited for some time, it seemed like hours to him, and lay watching the gun flashes every few seconds, and the shells would either hit the ship or go overhead and explode in the water. Arthurs felt a bit 'shaky' but felt safer in his position on the ship than being in the sea, although he was surrounded by men moaning and groaning, and to hear the screams of some of the wounded was a ghastly experience.

There was a short pause in the shooting, so thinking the shelling had finished, Arthurs decided to go over the side. Just as he stood up another salvo hit the ship, and he seemed to be in the midst of hot wires and sparks flying all around him, and suddenly his left ankle felt as if someone had stuck a lot of red hot needles into it, then his right leg similarly, then something hit the side of the engine room plating, then his steel helmet. Arthurs dropped to the deck quickly and as he went to put his helmet back into position on his head, he burnt four fingers. Examining his steel helmet later he found a shell splinter about four inches long had stuck into the helmet and had penetrated about half an inch. After this experience Arthurs waited again to ensure that firing had ceased – the pain in his legs was making him feel sick. He heard someone call out to see if there was anybody all right on the ship and Arthurs stood up and called back. By this time the ship was blazing furiously and small arms and Bofors ammunition started to explode through the heat. The man who had shouted came up and asked Arthurs if he could help with some of the wounded. They went up on deck but one lifeboat

was away and the other had a shell hole in it. They then went
down below and found a stock of lifebelts, which they put on
the wounded and threw the latter over the side. This was a very
unpleasant job as most of Arthurs' friends were badly wounded
by shrapnel and blast, and he found his own injuries were very
slight compared to theirs. The ship was listing badly by this
time; they decided to leave before it was too late and going
up on deck, saw a man staggering around the Bofors gun; in
the light from the fire, Arthurs recognised him as Private Jack
Fleming from Anson Road workshop, who explained that he was
going to sit on the bench in the dark, pointing out over the water.
Arthurs realised that he was mentally affected by blast etc and
the three of them went over the side together, making their way
to a raft about a hundred yards away. This was a Carley float
designed for eight men and there were thirty hanging on to it,
those outside holding the shoulders of those holding the raft.
The sea was very rough and beating onto their faces with some
force. Two men could be heard shouting for help in the distance
and Major Marsh asked for any strong swimmers to volunteer
to go to their assistance. Arthurs and another man eventually
set off, guided by the shouts and found Privates Jock Kinney
and Reggie Ballard, the latter being dangerously close to the
blazing ship which was about to founder; Arthurs was conscious
of the danger of the suction taking him down with the ship. They
returned to the raft successfully. Land appeared to be only about
five miles away and Major Marsh suggested that good swimmers
should leave the raft to the weaker and non-swimmers; at which
several men including Marsh set off independently, all wearing
life jackets.

Marsh, who had jumped into the sea at the outset, continues:

Soon after the attack there were numerous screams from men
in the water – I am afraid they were caused by sharks . . . I
came up with a raft with about 20 men around it . . . we could
see high land looming up in the distance. [He tried to organize
the fit men to paddle the raft towards it but this did not work
and so he led a do-it-yourself movement of those who could,
and was soon alone.] I saw all through the night our late ship

blazing away in the distance with explosions from time to time. The night was apparently endless but at long last dawn arrived ... I was very nearly all in. ... During the whole time I was in the water on my own I had no worries about anything, I was so terribly tired and only wanted to rest; I had a pocket knife in my pocket and made up my mind to cut my wrist arteries if things got too difficult.

With daylight I could see the shore and there were a number of ships anchored ... made little headway and was being taken mainly by the tide towards them ... the one nearest seemed to have a number of people on board; afterwards I learnt that this was the *Mata Hari* full of Singapore evacuees, mainly women and children.

Towards midday he drifted towards a large ship with landing barges round it and managed to hold on to one of these. 'Japanese faces by the thousand' were looking down at him and shortly a voice asked in English who he was. A boat was sent round for him and he was carried up on deck. The voice belonged to the ship's doctor. 'He came and asked me if I liked whisky (did I?) and produced a bottle of Johnnie Walker and poured out half a tumbler which I drank and promptly passed out for a while!' He was then well treated, as Margot Turner was to be; my guess is that it was the same ship, noted by Marsh as the *Kwei Maru*. Later an RAF rescue launch with Commander Philip Reid in command, under a Jap escort, came alongside, full of survivors, and took him off. They went to the anchored *Mata Hari* and the launch transferred all her people to the pier at Muntok.

Meanwhile, Private Arthurs' account goes:

During the morning a Japanese cruiser circled me twice and I could distinctly see the crew looking at me and laughing but they never picked me up. ... Once or twice I got hold of the identity discs round my neck to try and strangle myself but I thought when there's life there's still hope so I carried on. Every few seconds I had to keep putting my hand on the muscles of my legs and other soft parts of my body to pull or scrape the water bugs off which were very troublesome. ... The heat of the sun gave me a terrific headache in the afternoon but I still kept on swimming. It grew dark once more and I was still a good distance from land but the sea grew more calm and I made more headway.

It was just breaking daylight when I managed to pull myself ashore on Banka Island. I could not stand or walk so I crawled a little way up the beach to rest . . . must have dropped off to sleep when I felt someone prod me with a stick; when I looked up I saw two Japs looking down at me . . . as their eyes caught the ring and watch, one of them took the watch off and put it into his pocket. The ring which took me a minute or two to get off at normal times, they pulled and tugged in turn and I thought they were going to break my finger. After that they kicked me and made me get up on my feet and walk. My legs kept on sagging but they kept me going by hitting me with their rifle butts and kicking me. I was then shoved into a small motor boat and taken round the other side of the island to a long jetty. I could see a lot of people on it . . . they started hitting again to make me climb up but I had not the strength so started pulling myself hand over hand. An RAF officer who was on the jetty came down and carried me when he saw what was happening and put me down amongst the Red Cross nurses, who immediately laid me on a blanket and got busy massaging my legs and arms.

The nurses provided drink and food, but Arthurs' lips and tongue were too swollen to eat. 'The RAF officer, who I found later to be Air-Commodore Modin saw how things were and he fetched three large tins of Ideal milk. I drank two with hot water and he told me to use the other when I felt like it.' It was Air-Commodore Modin who had collected Mrs Reilly from her home in Singapore and put her on board the *Kedah*. He subsequently ran 'the star turn of camps in Palembang' according to Marsh.

Arthurs was delighted to meet Major Marsh at the Police Barracks, which was being used as a hospital. 'There were many people much worse than myself,' said the former, 'women and children who had been on rafts . . . for three and four days with the boiling hot sun . . . and it almost made one cry to see them.' A civilian doctor from Penang and a Naval Medical Officer, Dr Reid, 'worked on the wounded and although they had little equipment and no anaesthetics they made up for this by their kindness and were loved by all the patients.' A satisfactory postscript is that nineteen men who had stayed

21. The 3200-ton Yangtze steamer *Wu Chang*,
missed by three torpedoes on her way to Colombo (p.155)

22. "Of seventeen attacks, eleven concentrated on the *Durban*," (p.183)

23. "Hit after hit was registered in quick succession . . .
after which HMS *Stronghold* finally stopped and was abandoned" (p.202)

24. HMS *Scorpion* "purpose-built for showing the flag
up and down the River Yangtze" (p.186)

on the *Paula Suegi*'s raft were picked up by an RAF launch (probably Commander Philip Reid again) and brought in to Muntok. Reid was to command a prison camp in Sumatra and became a byword for standing up for his men, often getting the beatings intended for them.

*   *   *

It happens that I have dealt with ships normally manned by Naval Reserve officers and men in one chapter and those by regulars in another. It is fitting to end this record of the former with the valiant episode of HMS *Li Wo*. She was a Yangtse river passenger steamship like the *Kung Wo*, but considerably smaller at 1000 tons. Her total armament was one old four-inch gun, two Lewis machine guns, a depth charge thrower and an Asdic set. For some reason there were only thirteen shells for the four-inch, some of them 'practice', i.e. solid shot and of little use. Her Commanding Officer was Temporary Lieutenant Thomas ('Tam') Wilkinson RNR. Though he came from a seagoing family, had served in the Merchant Navy during the First World War and knocked about the China Coast for the twenty years following it, he had never had a day's naval training.

On Black Friday the *Li Wo* was sailed for Batavia as one of RA Malaya's fleet of exodus ships, having just landed her native crew and taken on board eighty-four officers and men of all three services. These were detailed for duties by CPO C. H. Rogers (ex-*Repulse*). It is from his and the account of Leading Seaman T. H. Parsons (ex-*Prince of Wales*, where he and I had the same action station) that the following is taken.

The next afternoon the ship survived four air attacks, before anchoring for the night under the lee of an island. Rogers wrote:

The next morning we were bombed again but escaped being hit. The planes were very low which gave us the chance to retaliate with machine-gun fire. The Captain then decided we would make a dash through 'bomb alley', the Banka Strait. Whilst proceeding we sighted a convoy of about thirty ships on the horizon off our starboard bow, heading in the direction of Banka Island, but were unable to identify them until we had closed to about 16,000 yards.

Suddenly, on the horizon, dead ahead, we sighted the tops of three funnels, which turned out to be a cruiser. We also sighted off our port bow a destroyer heading the convoy which was in sections of four and six ships.

Lieutenant Wilkinson sent for Parsons, who was gunlayer of the four-inch and had recently served on the China station, to confirm that they were Japanese, asking if he had any doubt. 'None whatever,' replied Parsons.

Wilkinson then told his scratch crew, 'A Jap convoy is ahead. I am going to attack it. We shall take as many as possible of those Jap bastards with us.' This was clearly a suicide course, but 'drew resolute support from the whole ship's company'. The *Li Wo*, though small, was very manoeuvrable (with twin rudders) and Wilkinson was a superb ship handler as well as natural leader.

Rogers continues:

> Word rapidly passed that we were going into action, and that the leading ship in the nearest section would be our target. Battle ensigns were hoisted, one on gaff and one at masthead as we closed rapidly with the four-inch gun ready. With no sign of enemy activity we closed to 2000 yards before the order was given to open fire. The first salvo short, the second crossed the bow, the third and others scored direct hits just under the bridge. She appeared to be on fire and turned to port. The other ships turned to starboard and commenced firing at us with small calibre guns. The damaged ship was now approaching the *Li Wo*, still firing. We had expended all our four-inch ammunition, so the CO decided to ram her. We hit her at top speed amidships and became interlocked, our bows being buckled back – we were now really at close quarters.

A machine-gun duel took place which was fast and furious, with many men being killed or wounded. The *Li Wo* machine gunners, including an unknown Flight Sergeant who was deadly accurate, eventually wiped out two four-man Japanese guns which caused the enemy to abandon ship; by this time she was well on fire.

> Whilst all this was happening, the Japanese cruiser had circled around behind and was heading for us at high speed. We eventually became disentangled from the crippled ship and set course

away from the cruiser. She opened fire at a range of 18,000 yards and we then noticed that the enemy destroyer, that had been heading for us from the opposite direction, was turning away. No doubt she knew that we were at the mercy of the cruiser.

We zigzagged as the salvos fell – we had a very poor opinion of the Japanese gunners as her six-inch shells were falling wide, sometimes 300 yards or more off target. However, gradually they came nearer and nearer and shrapnel was now hitting us, causing many casualties. I personally was hit with three pieces of shrapnel in the leg, but not seriously. Parsons was hit in the chest. After about the ninth salvo we were told to abandon ship, so all who were able to jumped overboard. Very soon after, the cordite locker amidships went up. The last sight I had of the *Li Wo* as she started on her last voyage to the bottom was something I shall never forget – her ensigns were still flying and the Captain was standing on the bridge; although listing to port, she was still under way. Then, suddenly, she disappeared.

After swimming for some time, CPO Rogers saw a lifeboat as it rose with the swell.

Leading Seaman Thompson and myself struck out towards it, but as we were approaching, we noticed a troopship from the convoy coming towards us. We swam away as fast as possible and, in glancing back, saw the ship ram the lifeboat. Around this area were about thirty men struggling for their lives, little realizing that the worst was yet to come. The Japanese were not content to leave us to our fate, but circled around and opened up a murderous attack with machine guns, hand grenades, coal and wood. It was just plain 'cold-blooded-murder'. Amidst the hell, men could be heard crying out for mercy, but still the Japanese continued their 'sport'. I lay on my back with my arms outstretched and luckily no more shot came in my direction. Eventually the ship moved off, leaving only eight men alive to try and get into the lifeboat. Lieutenant Stanton (the First Lieutenant) had a bullet hole through the back of his head, another officer was wounded in the stomach and had part of his hand shot away. Petty Officer Huntley had his foot blown off and was in a very bad way. We helped each other into the lifeboat which was now submerged to the gunwhale, and tried to make the best of a bad situation.

Without oars, food or medical supplies, they could do nothing, though encouraged by the sight of the ship the *Li Wo* had crippled, still drifting and on fire. As dawn broke after a cold, miserable night, an officer whom Rogers had been holding in his arms, died of his wounds and was lowered into the water.

Two days later distant land was visible. Though in bad shape and ignoring the sharks that swam round continuously, but did not interfere, they tried swimming and towing the boat, but to no avail. An enemy destroyer loomed up, gave them 'a cursory glance' and sheered off. The boat was now waterlogged and expected to sink at at any moment. Lieutenant Stanton and another officer tried to swim to the damaged Jap ship but, beaten by the tide, were lucky to be picked up and taken prisoners. That left five. Petty Officer Huntley died, a soldier was lost overboard, and a Leading-Seaman Spenser set off to swim ashore, also being picked up exhausted. The remainder chose to let the tide take them where it would. Fortunately a naval whaler drifted towards them just before dark; swimming over they found it badly split but boasting oars and a sail. This rigged, they had just set course for the land when shouts heralded two rafts; there were three on one and Leading Seaman Parsons alone on the other. He had riches, a tin of biscuits. Helped by a strong wind, Rogers took the rafts in tow, with those in the whaler now sitting in the water.

During the night a Japanese patrol boat shone her searchlights on the whaler, but they dropped over its far side and were not detected. Six fit men were then put on the oars and rowed hard for the land. It was Banka Island, reached at the same time as a Japanese invasion party who took no notice initially, but made them prisoners later. And that, as for so many of these accounts, is another story. Leading Seaman Parsons escaped from their camp at Muntok, but was betrayed by Javanese natives and recaptured, as described on page 238.

After the war, when this was all made known, Lieutenant Wilkinson was awarded the Victoria Cross, posthumously.

In addition, Lieutenant R. R. G. Stanton received the DSO, Leading Seaman A. W. Thompson the CGM, Leading Seaman W. Spenser and Able Seaman Spendlove the DSM: and two officers and four ratings were Mentioned in Despatches, including Chief Petty Officer Charles Rogers. (It is very hard to see why Leading Seaman Parsons was not also recognized).

This action, born of a deliberate decision to sell his life and his ship dearly and then carried out with the utmost dash and skill by an officer with no relevant experience, must rank as high as any in the annals of the Navy.

VII

Some Regular Naval Occasions

As was demonstrated by the sinking of the *Prince of Wales* and *Repulse*, ships without air support cannot last long when in range of enemy airfields. Hence the eight-inch cruiser *Exeter*, which had arrived at the outbreak of war with Japan, the few elderly six-inch cruisers, and some of the destroyers based on Singapore were sent down to Java to place themselves under the Dutch Admiral Doorman, to bolster him somewhat for the clash with the Japanese Navy that was surely coming. This left only two or three destroyers, three gunboats, some M Ls and the auxiliaries described earlier.

HMS *Durban*, one of the cruisers sent away, was recalled on 10 February, with the destroyers *Jupiter* and *Stronghold* and the patrol vessel *Kedah*. As a result of instructions given by General Wavell on a visit to Singapore that day, they were to embark key personnel at Singapore and escort the liner *Empire Star* and the SS *Gorgan* back to Batavia. On arrival *Jupiter* took on 122 passengers, *Stronghold* fifty, *Durban* (to Captain Peter Cazalet's surprise) only sixty; *Kedah* embarked over 300 (Army, R A F and civilian) including Mrs Reilly, last heard of waiting six hours at the docks without being allowed to say goodbye to her husband.*

The convoy sailed in the early hours of the 12th. It seems a shame the first three ships could not have taken more, bearing in mind the scenes at the docks the following day, but there was

---

* He was taken prisoner but she got away to Australia; they were reunited at Singapore after the war, to take up where they had left off.

just nobody there. The Black Friday evacuation, occasioned, it will be remembered, by Admiral Spooner taking matters into his own hands, was not to be organized until the next morning and it would have been suicidal for the ships to wait around. Due to the thick smoke from the city drifting over the water, all had difficulty locating a buoy that marked the end of a minefield and had to anchor until dawn. They were forming up when a heavy air attack developed; the *Empire Star* was hit twice, but shot down a low flier.

For another five hours the convoy was attacked, mostly by high level bombers, without respite. Of seventeen attacks, eleven concentrated on the *Durban*, the Captain's report stating:

> No bomb is estimated to have fallen further than 300 yards from the ship and the majority were within 100 yards. In nearly every attack the bombs dropped in the position the ship would have been if no avoiding action had been taken . . . a number of near-misses did considerable superficial damage. The ship's side in the Wardroom and in several cabins aft was punctured in many places. About five officer passengers were in the Wardroom at the time, but they were all lying on the deck and only one RAF officer was seriously injured by a ricochet.

I have always found it intriguing that sailors – speaking particularly for myself – find enemy action ashore thoroughly unnerving and that soldiers find the same at sea. Major Angus Rose, that considerable fighter of the Argylls, (and author of *Who Dies Fighting*, from which the following is taken) who had been ordered away from Singapore and was one of the five, appears to have subscribed to this.

> In the next attack there was a sickening thump which vibrated through the whole ship. . . . Iain* and I, considering discretion the better part of valour, eased under the Wardroom table . . . then suddenly there was God's own crash and a blinding flash. . . . I couldn't quite understand why I was still alive . . . the ship's side was one mass of ugly gashes and the pungent fumes

* Lt-Col I. MacA. Stewart DSO, OBE, MC and bar, then OC 2nd Battalion Argyll and Sutherland Highlanders and architect of their proficiency.

of cordite permeated the whole room. We had merely taken a
near-miss to port. . . . Someone called out, 'Fire aft in Number one
hatch'. Seamen moved down the passage outside the Wardroom,
running out a hose . . . it was splendid to watch the quick and
silent deliberation of the ship's company. There was no shouting,
no wild rushing about, no blinding or swearing. The fire was very
close to the wardroom and the prospects of being burnt alive were
more than unpleasant; they were frankly frightening. If a fairy god-
mother had appeared and asked me whether I would take a free
ride back to Singapore, I think I would have accepted the offer.

Though the last remark should be taken with a pinch of salt, his
preference for terra firma can be understood.

Mrs Reilly in the *Kedah* had been told to 'get under the dining
room table and stay there'. 'There followed the most fearsome
five hours I have ever experienced . . . we sustained three hits and
thirteen near-misses and every time the *Kedah* just jumped out of
the water like a fish and settled down with an awful jar.' Her Captain, Commander J. L. Sinclair, DSO, RD, RNR, impressed
everyone with his cool efficiency in dodging the bombs. Cigar in
mouth, he watched and waited until the right moment and then
with a 'Here they come, gentlemen, it is time to lie down', ordered
maximum helm. The *Gorgan*, with 300 passengers instead of her
normal eighty, was not so hard pressed, but narrowly missed.

The little convoy made Tanjong Priok, the port for Batavia,
safely, but was more than lucky as the Banka Strait must have
been sealed by Ozawa's force not long after it passed. The *Empire
Star* – hit again, but fortunate to have a total of only fourteen fatal
casualties – had over 2000 passengers, 135 of them Australian
deserters who had forced their way on board. Captain Cazalet
was signalled that the unit told off to greet this party was
unreliable and that he was requested to deal with it. This was a
tall order for a light cruiser with a small complement, but was
successfully accomplished in a novel way. He called for thirty
volunteers, and when the *Empire Star* berthed, sent them on
board under the First Lieutenant, all unarmed and dressed in
anything but naval uniform. 'Number One' ordered the deserters
to hand over their weapons and fall in. Taken by surprise, they
complied, their weapons were collected by the 'funny party' and

the deserters filed ashore into the arms of the *Durban*'s Royal Marine detachment, who, ready for anything, had been kept out of sight until that moment.

The Captain's handling of his ship during the air attacks had been more than appreciated by her company and Angus Rose adds a pleasant postscript to what must have been a difficult day. 'As we stood on the quayside Captain Cazalet came ashore, unostentatiously, in the dark, to inspect some damage forward. He was spotted and someone called for three cheers. The whole ship's company crashed out in splendid unison.'

As we know, of the ships following behind the convoy, only a handful got through. One of these was a tug towing half a dozen small craft, including a brand new Harbour Defence Launch with no engines, commanded by Sub Lieutenant Tony Sheldon, (who, ex-*Repulse*, had been with me at Penang, running a sister ferry to the *Bagan*.) Threading its way through a forest of bomb bursts in the Strait as ships around were sent to the bottom or set on fire, the tug providentially escaped attack. However, it was running out of fuel and Tony received the unwelcome order to sink his ship. Subsequent entry into the Palembang River coincided with the descent of hundreds of Japanese parachutists. The refinery at Palembang was on fire when they arrived, to be told to sink the tug and sabotage cranes etc. before catching the last train to Oasthaven on the SE coast. The faithful *Kedah* was there, which took them to Batavia, whence another ship got them safely to Ceylon. (There is a nice postscript on the *Kedah*: she was to end her war in style, the Navy according her the honour of leading the Fleet into Singapore in August, 1945.)

* * *

On leaving Singapore the *Durban* had exchanged signals with a small ship 'apparently HMS *Scorpion*'. She had asked for instructions, saying there were women and children on board. Cazalet told her to proceed at once to Batavia. The *Scorpion* was one of three gunboats normally based at Hong Kong but withdrawn to Singapore at the outbreak of war with Japan and we will now follow the fortunes of this unlucky trio.

Purpose-built for showing the flag up and down the great

Chinese River Yangtze, with its fast current, bends and treacherous shoals, the little *Grasshopper*, *Dragonfly* and *Scorpion* were of 540-650 tons, with flat bottoms, triple rudders and large upperworks for their length (see figure 24). They had a reasonable surface armament of two either six-inch or four-inch guns, but for anti-aircraft purposes only three machine guns. Asdics (now called Sonar) and depth charges completed the picture. They only drew seven feet and though their maximum speed was twelve knots they were in fact well suited to the mainly clandestine operations on which they now found themselves engaged. One particular exploit concerning *Dragonfly* and *Scorpion* cheered us all, thoroughly depressed by the constant bad news. Lieutenant-Commander Victor Clark (ex-*Repulse*) took them up the coast with several motor launches to rescue an entire brigade cut off at Batu Pahat. Four nights running the boats crept up a shallow creek, Clark and his men sometimes swimming alongside them, the best method of propulsion as the Japanese were within earshot! Altogether 2000 exhausted soldiers were ferried down to the gunboats, just offshore.

Commander J. S. Hoffman of *Grasshopper* was put in command of the 'Dunkirk' operation that everyone expected would be necessary when the Army retired across the causeway on to the Island. Presumably the Japs would follow up closely and there would come a time when the inner bridgehead (of Argylls) would be sitting targets as they dashed across; that is if the causeway had not been made impassable by bombs. So ropes and ladders were hung from the jetties on each side, down to waiting boats. I was beachmaster for the east side, Lieutenant Ian Forbes (a *Prince of Wales* shipmate) for the west side. The beachmasters would be the last to leave and we did not rate our chances highly. However, against all previous experience, the enemy did not follow up this particular retreat and the whole thing went off without the loss of a man. The jovial Hoffman, inclining to *embonpoint*, waved us away and returned to his *Grasshopper*. Our future was now obscure to say the least and it was with considerable envy that I learnt that Forbes had received an appointment to her. I was not to know that fate would be kinder to me than to him.

Fate was not kind at all to the brave little ships from the Yangtze. They were put to death in the open sea in conditions quite alien to those they were designed for, like three small country girls suddenly enveloped in the blitz. The first to go was the *Scorpion* (Lieutenant-Commander G. C. Ashworth RNVR). Reports of her end vary somewhat; she left Singapore for Batavia on 10 February, making even less speed than usual because of recent bomb damage. One account goes 'Scorpion passed through the Berhala Strait, nearly seventy miles south of Singapore. Off Berhala Island a Japanese cruiser and two destroyers were sighted and all four ships opened fire immediately. The relatively tiny gunboat had no chance. Out of control, blazing from stern to stern, she was abandoned. Moments later the *Scorpion* went down. Only three carley floats could be launched, and there were twenty survivors, all picked up by the Japanese.' An invaluable record of the fates of ships out of Singapore was compiled in Changi gaol from imprisoned survivors' accounts by Captain David Nelson. This says the *Scorpion* was sunk by one or two destroyers and was carrying thirty-eight communications ratings as passengers. 'Eight survivors were picked up by a Japanese destroyer, their subsequent fate unknown.' Lastly, Mr L. G. Haldane in the *Mata Hari* recorded that on the night of the 13th the ship was hailed by swimmers, a boat lowered and two officers and four ratings from the *Scorpion* picked up. They had been in the water six hours, which put the sinking at about sunset. Since she took three days to cover seventy miles it looks as if she stopped *en route*, like the *Kuala* and *Tien Kuang*. As we now know, the sands of both Mr Haldane's and their own hard-won freedom were running out.

The two gunboats eyed enviously by Captain Swallwell 'humming away at the quayside' as he boarded the even smaller *Tanjong Pinang* at Clifford Pier on Black Friday evening were the *Dragonfly* and the *Grasshopper*. They had been ordered to embark certain army units, civilian men, nurses and in the case of the *Grasshopper* half-a-dozen Japanese prisoners (under Clarke, the Intelligence Officer, whom we have already met) and some women and children. Able Seaman W. J. ('Taff') Long, one of the *Dragonfly*'s Asdic ratings, has described for me with vivid Welsh flair what happened to his ship:

Singapore was now a very unhealthy place. Smoke and flames were to be seen in all directions. Fighting was taking place in the city. Shells were falling in and around the harbour and small arms fire was to be heard in all directions. Oil from the massive installations on the island of Pulau Samboe had been released into the sea and was now on fire; from it arose great columns of thick, dense, acrid smoke which billowed hundreds of feet into the sky to cast an oily, sooty residue wherever it settled.

Dragonfly's ships company, weary from days and nights at sea, constantly at action stations, had arrived at a point where sleep was taken when possible; food and drink at one's post. In spite of this, morale was good, especially as rumour had it that Australia was our eventual destination. It was dark when the gunboat made fast at one of the jetties, except for the areas where burning buildings cast their orange light and falling shells lit momentarily their point of impact. No organised party of men appeared. Stragglers there were in twos and threes but these were denied access because they were men seeking to leave unofficially.

At approximately 2200 I was detailed with four other seamen under the command of a Petty Officer to contact the men who were to be evacuated. We were issued with rifles and bayonets and climbed on to the jetty. Bullets were striking the galvanised sides of warehouses, whether fired by friend or foe we had no idea. It was eerie with the numerous fires casting flickering shadows everywhere. Pungent smoke rose and wafted in dense pockets and visibility was such that imagination made one see an enemy that wasn't there – or were they? Confusion reigned supreme, and I remember thinking, 'This is what Hell must be like,' unknowing that in the future a great deal worse was to be experienced.

We made our way along the jetty, hugging the warehouse sides for cover and running across the gaps between each pair of 'godowns'. Suddenly a group of men appeared and 'Do you know where the *Dragonfly* is?' was audible above the general racket. These were our men led by an army captain called Brown, I think. Apparently the remainder had been split up into sections to lessen the risk of casualteis if they were fired upon.

Some of us remained at that point while the rest led the soldiers back to the *'Fly*. About another fifteen men appeared and while the PO remained in position my 'oppo' and I took these – running – taking cover – hell-bent for the ship. About this time mortar shells began exploding in and around the godowns, smacking down on the jetty surface and scattering shrapnel in all directions. . . . I dived into a doorway and landed right on top of a Tommy who had done likewise. He told me in a Welsh accent and British Army language to go and find my own b– doorway. . . . 'Where are you from Taff?' I said. 'Pontypridd'. 'I'm from Porth. What are you doing here?' He said he was looking for the *Dragonfly*. On arriving alongside everyone in the party threw their weapons over the guard rail and clambered aboard with a few chosen words of relief.

In our absence others had come aboard. The gangplank had been stowed away, when yet another party, led by the Petty Officer, dashed up and threw themselves any way they could on to the ship's deck. . . . They must have been spotted because mortar bombs began expoding all round us. The Captain on the bridge shouted 'We can't wait any longer. Cast off forrard. Cast off aft' and the bow swung away from the jetty. For some reason we did not cast off aft but proceeded out to sea snapping the spring with a loud 'twang'.

Of the army contingent now on board, totalling sixty-three offic- ers and men, it is known that two officers (Lieutenants Quinn and Mitford) and twenty-four other ranks were from the 1st Manchester Regiment. The original total number of troops to be embarked was 250, but it was just as well for those left behind that they were. Taff Long continues:

It was now approximately two am and with the morning watch to keep I found myself a corner to sleep. . . . By four am we were well out to sea – running at full speed, the engines throbbing with power and taking us further away from that ill-fated island. I took over the Asdic and my 'oppo' said that the *Grasshopper*, somewhere off our port beam, was to accompany us wherever we were going.

Dawn broke (it was St Valentine's Day); behind us lay Malaya, and ahead we thought, Java and possibly Australia. It was a bright, clear dawn, the tropical sky cloudless and the sea like a huge burnished lake with hardly a ripple to break the surface. Off our beam was the *Grasshopper* and both of us throwing up bow waves as we steamed ahead at full power. The *Dragonfly* was grossly overloaded, our small galley quite inadequate but tea and cocoa were handed round. Most, however, preferred to sleep; exhausted, dirty and unshaven they lay in all manner of places, wardroom flat, alongside the wheelhouse, on top of the 'spud' locker – anywhere they could lay their heads.

Shortly before 0800 an aircraft was sighted flying low down on the horizon and as we hadn't seen a friendly aircraft for weeks it was assumed to be hostile. . . . Doubtless it was a spotter plane reporting ships' positions. . . . Our captain, Lieutenant Iley, gave orders that all men not on watch were to go below to the mess deck, and that all guns were to be closed up at Action Stations. My relief took over the Asdic and I went to breakfast. I couldn't get down to the mess deck as it was choc-a-block, but managed to get a tin of peaches from the storekeeper. . . . At about 10 o'clock someone shouted 'bloody Hell!! Look astern at that lot', and there in the distance was a host of aircraft. They were flying in their usual vee formations of nines – twenty-seven–fifty-four and so on to a total of 180 or more. They droned on way up in the blue, to fly right over the top of us and vanished, to the relief of all. On their way to Java perhaps?

HMS *Dragonfly* was off Posik Island, one of the many in the Lingga Group. All troops had been issued with life-belts and those not on aircraft look-out duty were below in the aft mess decks, the officers being in the cabin flat, when sixty-three Japanese bombers appeared, flying in seven flights of nine, and attacked the two ships. Taff Long again:

Suddenly there was a shout 'Aircraft off the port beam'. Heading for us at low level were nine twin-engined Jap bombers. The multiple 0.5 machine guns and twin guns opened fire. The bombers dived down and all hell was let loose. There was a terrific explosion – the ship shuddered and stopped as if she had hit a concrete wall. I looked aft from the wheelhouse and saw flames and smoke from amidships and potatoes rolling all over the place. The force of the explosion had burst open the 'spud' locker. I heard the quartermaster report to the bridge 'Steering wheel jammed. Telegraph U/S'.

The *Dragonfly* was already down by the stern as the Captain shouted 'Abandon ship'. I ran down the ladder to the upper deck and looked into the boiler room to see more flames and smoke. There was the hiss of escaping steam and two or three stokers there with the skin hanging off them in bits and pieces . . . (engine room personnel in the tropics wore nothing but shorts and slippers and therefore they had no protection whatsoever from the scalding, boiling steam). The whaler was being lowered and was level with the upper deck. I helped some of them into the whaler when there was a shout 'What about the engine room?' Two or three of us ran to the engine room casing. What a sight – flames, smoke but no sound of wounded men; just the hissing of escaping steam – great clouds of it being forced out at high pressure. It was impossible to get down there. The mess deck must also have been a shambles. All those men crammed into a restricted area had received a direct hit as also had the engine room. The force of the explosions had blown the bulkheads between the boiler room, the engine room and the mess decks. We were now well down by the stern, the upper deck being level with the sea.

I made towards the whaler. On my way I saw a stoker standing in the gangway. He had been hit in the throat and blood was coming from his mouth. He couldn't talk and he couldn't see as his eyes had been caught by the steam. I led him to the whaler which by now was loaded beyond capacity with wounded and unconscious men. The stoker was helped aboard but when I was about to get in a PO named Brennan shouted 'Sorry Taff, we've too many now'. There was no panic – just common sense and endeavour. I turned away, blew up my lifejacket, kicked off my sandals, ran to the other side of the ship to be out of reach of the suction when she sank, and jumped in. I was not an excellent swimmer – competent yes, and I did have a lifebelt. After a few minutes I turned and looked at the *Dragonfly*. She was down by the stern with about 15 feet of bow sticking out of the water. Hanging on to the bullring was a seaman called Finch who came from Canvey Island, and who I knew couldn't swim. As I looked the ship sank gradually lower and with a final shudder and a hissing of steam – a maelstrom of bubbles on turbulent water – she slid below the sea, carrying with her the bulk of the ship's company and nearly all the odds and bods we had picked up in Singapore. This all happened in about ten minutes.

About a mile away the *Grasshopper* was now being attacked and was taking evasive action. Bombs hit the water sending up great spouts of spray and shortly afterwards I could feel the shock waves shuddering into my body. I looked around. The sea was calm except for ripples caused by the latest bombs. Our whaler was now a few hundred yards away with some men in the vicinity swimming in its direction. In my immediate area there were eight or nine, some of whom I recognised. We shouted to each other to try to get together so that we could all swim to an island that lay in the distance. I then noticed nine aeroplanes flying in line astern at a very low level. They were coming in at an angle from the *Grasshopper*. Suddenly they opened fire with machine guns from their rear turrets. First they fired on the whaler and then at the men in the water near it. Before we could do anything they opened fire on us. I could distinctly see the canopies of the rear turrets slid back, the twin barrels of the machine guns poking over the side and the figures of the enemy gunners. I also saw a fusillade of bullets lashing the water all around, and heard the awful cries of men being hit – some of whom were already wounded. The planes circled around and I had a premonition that the same thing was about to happen again. I took off my lifebelt and trod water with it tucked under my arm. Suddenly the planes turned and came in. I let go of my lifebelt and dived as deep as possible. As God is my witness – I could hear the bullets hitting the water with a zip zip zip, and I could see the bubbles rising as they penetrated beneath. If I ever prayed I prayed then. How long did it last? Seconds, I suppose, but it seemed to be the longest time of my life. I shot up to the surface and looked around – the planes were climbing to vanish into the distance. My lifebelt was floating a short distance away and mercifully it was undamaged. I fastened it around me and looked about for signs of life, but tragically, all I could see were the bodies of six or seven men lying lifeless in the water. Of the two or three others there was no sign. I was alone with no help at hand. The whaler was now a speck in the distance, heading for one of the small islands that abound in these parts. I was not to know until later that men had been killed and wounded in the boat; what kind of people were these? Who could do this thing to fellow human beings? I was to find out in the days and months and years that lay ahead.

The *Grasshopper*, which had suffered damage and was on fire, was also making her way to the island. I gathered my wits together and decided I had no alternative but to follow suit. How far was it? Five, six miles? I also thought about sharks, but with the bombing and machine gunning any sharks should be miles away by now. We had had a rough time in the last few weeks; I thought that it would be a mistake to strike out strongly and that I should try and conserve what strength I had left and swim in a leisurely manner. So I swam and rested and swam again.

By late afternoon I had made some progress and was now possibly two miles from land. I was finding things more difficult with thirst the main trouble. I found that when I rested, depending on my lifebelt to keep me afloat, I was falling asleep due to exhaustion and the sun beating down. I was beginning to get lightheaded and confused and the hours of darkness that followed were a complete nightmare. I remembered retching and vomiting on numerous occasions, I must have been falling asleep, my head dropping into the water which I was then swallowing, and this in turn causing me to vomit. I had now been in the water since 11 am the previous day in the direct glare of the tropical sun and with very little sleep or regular food for days past. I also remember during these confused hours watching the sky lit up by streaks of fire and sparks like the old Crystal Palace fireworks.

I later realized this must have been the *Grasshopper*'s magazine exploding. When I finally came to my senses it was daylight. It was a beautiful tropical morning and I was in a small bay still supported by my lifebelt. I must in my semi-conscious state, have been carried by the tide. . . .When I finally got inshore and my feet touched the bottom it was amongst the mangrove. I made my way out again, and skirting the edge of the mangrove, found a narrow short strip of sandy beach. Darkness was descending. Exhausted and racked by thirst, I threw myself down on the sand and slept – the sleep of utter exhaustion. I had been approximately thirty-two hours in the water, and from the time we had been machine-gunned I had seen no living creature. When I finally awoke I had a raging thirst and must have been a little lightheaded. My back was on fire (the shoulder muscles had been rubbed raw by the strings of the lifebelt) and my lips were cracked and bleeding. Despondency overtook me. I distinctly remember thinking 'What the hell am I doing here? A Welsh Robinson Crusoe, cast away on a tropical island, while only a few short years ago I was working in the mines in the Rhondda Valley.' But I possessed four things, a pair of white, soiled naval shorts, a seaman's regular issue jack knife, my lifebelt, and above all, my life!

On the edge of the jungle a few short yards away stood several coconut palms and I decided to attempt to climb the shortest one in order to obtain some of the nuts because I realised that my thirst had to be quenched. The effort that I had to put into climbing that tree is beyond description. I would succeed in climbing a few feet only to slide down again, removing patches of skin from my thighs and arms in the process. Finally I made it and threw some coconuts down. When endeavouring to remove the husk the blade of my knife snapped, but with much effort, and what remained of the blade and the splicing spike I finally removed the husk and penetrated the nut. I drank the life-saving liquid, broke the nut open and ate some of the white flesh. After resting for a while I began to make my way along the beach. The sand was very hot as

I walked in my bare feet. My back was now very painful and the sun's rays didn't help. Suddenly, as I was approaching the corner of the bay, I heard voices but couldn't distinguish whether they were English or Japanese. Had this island already been occupied? I dived into the bush with my heart thumping like a kettledrum. As I listened I realized it was English. Coming towards me out of the jungle were two of the *Grasshopper*'s ship's company. One of them was a New Zealander called Pardoe. They were looking for a native village or whatever. (It finally turned out that the island was uninhabited.) Apparently other survivors from both the *Grasshopper* and *Dragonfly* were some way along the beach and there were quite a few serious casualties among them. They asked me what I was doing there. I almost told them I was waiting for a bus to Cardiff Arms Park!

Round the corner of the bay I came on the survivors from the *Grasshopper*. What a shambles! Wounded people were lying everywhere. There was no medical supplies – there was no food and precious little water. What water they had had been found by Judy, the Pointer bitch that had been the *Grasshopper*'s mascot. I was greeted by several of my shipmates who told me that our skipper had gone down with his ship. Our Sub-Lieutenants had also perished and nearly all our engine room branch gone. Very few of the seamen had survived – some were badly burned and some had machine-gun bullets in them. There were half-a-dozen dead who had been laid some distance away as there were no tools with which to bury them. It had been decided to throw them in the sea and hope that the tide would take them out. There were half-a-dozen or so Australian nurses who were busy attending to the wounded, both male and female. One of them looked at my back but having no medical supplies of any description it was a case of carry on and fend for yourself. I was given a little water to drink but this was rationed and the wounded quite rightly were given priority. I found myself a space in the sand and settled down for the night.

Sub-Lieutenant Victor Ash was a *Dragonfly* passenger who had been in hospital with pneumonia until the last moment. He got away in the whaler – eventually to India – that Long had so narrowly missed (the fine threads of fate with a vengeance):

On reaching the upper deck I saw it was nearly awash and that we were sinking fast. I also noticed they had lowered one whaler which was a few yards from the ship. I was so weak I knew I would not have been able to stay afloat long in the water, so I jumped in and managed to swim the short distance to the whaler. After they had pulled me in I noticed the boat was full up and the First Lieutenant was in the water hanging on, at the same time calling out 'No more in the boat'. Shortly afterwards nine Jap planes swooped down and machine-gunned us at point-blank range, only a few feet above us. Many in the boat were killed outright and several others badly wounded. The whaler was beginning to fill up with water due to holes made by the bullets, so I ordered the men with tin helmets to bale, and also ordered the dead to be thrown overboard. Our only means of survival was to keep the boat afloat. . . .

I saw one poor fellow sitting on the middle thwart, with a gaping hole in his thigh, huddled over, and, pointing to him, I shouted, 'Is he dead?' The man opened his eyes immediately and called out 'No, I'm not dead'. He died very soon afterwards and was put over the side. Twice more the planes swooped down shooting up all of us in the boat, and also those in the water hanging on to rafts or any woodwork floating. I remember well praying hard with my eyes shut that He would protect me, and He did. To this day I know it was a miraculous escape.

Another fragment is from an unknown soldier in the lonely, desperate boat:

The planes returned and machine-gunned us. It was a matter of a few seconds. The man next to me was killed and three others killed. The others dived overboard and as I cannot swim I huddled myself together dressed in uniform and tin hat. The swine had passed but had left their mark. I can never describe the sight of the wounded and the stench of blood in that lifeboat and the cries of the wounded. However, after saying my prayers as I definitely thought it was the end, the raiders passed over.

The First Lieutenant (Lieutenant Shellard) was hit in the shoulder when alongside the whaler. Hauled into it after the disposal of dead bodies, he kept his hand over a bullet hole to minimise leakage. Ash again:

Slowly we made for what turned out to be an uninhabited island . . . had great difficulty in pulling the boat up in one foot of water. At high tide there was only about three yards of dry sand, and then just dense jungle which we found too thick to penetrate. . . . Two poor stokers died in two days. Both had been blinded by one of the bombs and their hands and arms were red raw. They must have suffered agony and were continually crying out for water of which we had none. We scooped a hole for them in the sand with our hands some distance away and buried them. Two of our survivors were Malay ratings who were able to climb a palm tree and throw down some coconuts.

Ash had landed near Posik Island. Of the unfortunate army personnel, only two officers and six other ranks were still alive and of the latter four died in the next twenty-four hours. There were no medical stores and no water, only the men's water bottles and coconuts. They set off for Sumatra after a rest, making the Djambi River where they were put on a bus to Padang, whence the Australian cruiser *Hobart* took them (except Shellard who joined Dillon's prauw) to Colombo. The rest of the now combined *Dragonflies* and *Grasshoppers* were not so lucky. But first let us go back to the beginning of the *Grasshopper*'s story.

When they were first attacked, both Commander Hoffman and Lieutenant Forbes were slightly wounded:

I began to realize [said the latter] that I had a charmed life. For some reason I changed my position at the last minute a couple of paces to port. The bomb dropped. Where I had just been was riddled with large holes. I only got a slight graze on my right forearm – Hoffman was nicked in the leg by a piece and bled profusely. This little episode decided *Dragonfly* to make for the nearest land to hide. I knew it was too late. . . . The ship wriggled and squirmed, gradually making towards the beach. Survivors of the tug *St Breock* were ashore on one of the islands and told me later that they watched the *Grasshopper*'s last fight for two hours with bated breath. Each stick exploding completely enveloped the little ship in great curtains of water. But each time she popped out again with her 0.5 guns rattling away. Eventually a bomb hit us aft. . . . It was obvious that the after magazine should be flooded at once, but where the flooding valve should have been there was a gaping hole. . . .

The ship was beached and the wounded were ferried ashore in the whaler. The Japanese prisoners were magnificent. All pretence at guarding them was dropped and they went around calmly and efficiently helping the wounded. Two more waves of bombers came over but by some chance missed; when everyone was ashore the aircraft came back for a last fling with machine guns.

John Duke, a civilian passenger, was hit by shrapnel and, jumping into the water some way back, had a long swim to the island. He was to write to his wife (from India):

> There were about 100 people ashore, mixed bag, including a Brigadier, Naval ratings, Flying, Naval and Military officers, about six women, six Japanese pilots who had been brought down . . . funny looking blokes, their straight black hair was uncut and stuck out all round like gollywogs. . . . Sir John Bagnall was there . . . wandering around in his shirt only. He was luckier than I, he did have a shirt. I hadn't even a shirt at that time, only a lifebelt. We couldn't light a fire as the smoke would attract further bombing. Bill Steel was good to me. He was fully clothed as he had stuck to the ship. . . . To sleep on the hard ground at any time to one who is not used to it, who is over 50 years of age, is an ordeal, but to one who is wounded as well was an agony which I do not believe I shall ever forget. The succeeding four nights were bad. . . . Later that night someone took compassion on me and gave me a shirt and later I got a dead man's shorts. . . . During the night Bill and I wrapped ourselves round each other for warmth. I think this must have saved my life.

Two of the women passengers gave birth on the beach, their babies being safely delivered by the ship's cox'n – PO G. L. White (they were duly christened George and Leonard!)

The Brigadier had wisely told Hoffman to carry on in command and the latter's first order was to Ian Forbes, just – 'Go and get help!' Accordingly, he selected an army officer who could speak Malay, another who knew Japanese and Chinese (a Malay sailor also volunteered) and off they went on foot, soon coming across 'an exhausted sailor from the *Dragonfly*. He had had a long swim,' who was probably Long. The island proved to be uninhabited and when they were having a breather before the two-mile swim to the next one, Forbes recalls:

> We suddenly realized we had not been introduced, so this little British formality was properly observed. The Japanese interpreter was called Macfarlane. 'Oh, what part of Scotland do you come from?' It might have been a cocktail party. We then undertook the swim and arrived cold and cramped at the other side on a dry patch amongst the mangrove swamps. Some natives approached us in a canoe; they appeared rather hostile. However, Macfarlane and my Malay sailor (who was splendid throughout) haggled with them and quietened them down a bit. They agreed to go and fetch their chief.
>
> This venerable old boy arrived in a large dugout boat with a gang of thugs armed with bared *parangs*. They stood in a semi-circle around him and he squatted in the middle; we four faced him. Macfarlane did very well and converted them from their murderous intentions to complete co-operation. They supplied me with a boat to take me to yet a third island with a proper native village on it. They left us on the beach there with many 'Salamats'. The inhabitants of this village, seeing us coming, took to the jungle and we had to sit quietly on the beach for some time, knowing that black eyes were watching us, so as to entice them out. The first to come was the Chinese store-keeper. He sold us three bottles of beer. I was staggered . . . desert islands . . . shipwrecked mariners . . . and BEER. But then the Chinese are a wonderful race.
>
> The high priest then contacted us. He was the leader of the community and later proved of great value to me. He promised to arrange for boats to collect the survivors from island number one, bring them to his village and tend them, and also to send me to the island of Singkep, where there was a Dutch resident, to carry on with my order 'Go and get help'.

Forbes reported progress to Hoffman and lay down for a few hours 'listening to the groans of the wounded and the ship blowing herself to bits' before setting out again, this time in the whaler. After battling through a severe storm, contact was eventually re-established with the high priest. Though agreeing to his mosque being used as a hospital, this worthy was terrified of the Japanese and now took a great deal of persuasion to stick to his word. Eventually, however:

The high priest and his son manned the boat and I and my two interpreters were laid in the bilges and covered with sacking. I bade farewell to my Malay sailor, who said he would prefer to remain amongst his own people. . . . He was very moving in the genuineness of his attachment to the Royal Navy and wished us every possible good fortune.

A favourable wind sped them to Singkep, where they joined forces with survivors from the *St Breock*. Next morning (16 February) saw them sailing across a bay to a landing stage (I expect the one I was to use in a few days time) and then on by bus to the Controleur at Dabo. They were probably his first British refugee customers and, magnificently as he was to rise to occasions later, the Controleur, having destroyed his radio transmitter (how often this was done prematurely!) was initially despondent. However, under Ian Forbes' energetic prodding he undertook to bring all the gunboat survivors to Singkep and put deserted European houses at their disposal (which he did).

Taff Long, back on the island, now takes up the story:

The wounded were pitiful to see and suffered greatly. We spent four more days on the beach sustained mainly by coconuts and then a large motor launch in charge of a Dutch civilian and manned by natives came searching for us. Told that we were in a desperate situation, they had put off looking for us until nightfall for fear of being spotted by enemy aircraft. They made several trips that night and transported us all to the island of Singkep, where we were directed to the Dutch clubhouse. The majority of the wounded were taken to the native hospital – to lie on bamboo slats. The Dutch medical staff had been evacuated but our Australian nurses took over the organizing of the hospital.

One of the wounded was a stoker from the *Dragonfly* called Farley. He pleaded with us not to let him go with the other wounded but to keep him with us and he would take the consequences. The sailors amongst us decided that we would look after him ourselves. He was a mass of raw flesh after being scalded in the 'Fly' and he had been shot twice when he was in the whaler – but his resolve and courage were magnificent.

About this time a Lieutenant-Commander Eustace MRNVR (a New Zealander who could speak Malay and Chinese) managed to persuade the owner of a Chinese junk at the jetty to take some of us sailors, and anyone else who was prepared to come, to Sumatra.

We embarked a lot of women and children and set off in the heat of one morning with everyone below – not an inch to spare – except Eustace, two sailors and the Chinese. Sometime in the afternoon came the dreaded words 'Aircraft approaching!' A lot of large banana plant leaves had been brought aboard and we held these over our heads. As the planes circled low many a prayer was said and every heart missed a beat, but eventually they flew off. After anchoring for the night we went up the Indragiri to Rengat, where we were told that an escape route led to Padang.

*   *   *

The hospital at Dabo was actually taken over by Captain Kirkwood RIAMC, as mentioned previously, who had escaped from Blakang Mati with his staff in the launch *Nightingale*. Most of the gunboat survivors were on Singkep for ten days, before leaving in various different batches. Hoffman and a party got to Padang on 22 February, via the Indragiri, as did Forbes with another party via the Djambi.*

We will now go back to Ian Forbes on his arrival at Dabo. At a discussion with the Controleur as to how he could get away to wireless for help, the former said that the remaining Dutch residents were just about to leave for Sumatra in a small ship. This was good news but at that very moment a Jap plane appeared and sank the ship. 'Give me a motor boat and I will get your people to Sumatra,' said Forbes and at midnight – having visited a crashed Hurricane to avail himself of its compass – he sailed with twelve Dutchmen 'wearing his flag' in a motor sampan with a small launch, the *Landjoot*, in company. They moved only by night, on the second of which the sampan broke down so that all had to squeeze into the *Landjoot*.

There followed a nightmare seventy-mile trip to the Djambi River, the nearest to Singkep and about that distance south of the Indragiri. The sea became very rough. Forbes was fearful of being swamped, though he kept this from his passengers, all of whom were too seasick to take a spell on the tiller. He himself

---

* That day I was at Commander Alexander's conference at Dabo. Also present was *Grasshopper*'s First Lieutenant, Lieutenant D. R. Campbell. He was to get safely to India, but the other two had no such luck.

was exhausted by now, but held on until the coast was raised just before dawn, after which the ubiquitous Jap aircraft could be expected. The carburettor then failed. The float had to be removed and petrol poured straight in from the drums; with spray flying there was grave danger of mixing it with water but their luck held and at 9 am on Friday the 18th a native policeman was embarked at a fishing kampong who could steer them to the town of Djambi, nearly 100 miles up river. There was a Dutch motor vessel at the village and this Forbes despatched to Singkep to evacuate the gunboat survivors.

The Controleur at Djambi had also destroyed his w/t set, but a convoy of Dutch soldiers was due to leave for Muaratebo (on the way to Padang) and he sent the party off with them. On arrival Forbes was able to signal the Allied HQ at Bandoeng, Java, for further help to be sent to Singkep. Brigadier Archie Paris (who had succeeded Major-General Murray-Lyon as GOC 11th Indian Division) was there. Forbes goes on: 'After lunch a large car drew up and in stepped Paris and his staff, and off to the coast. That got my mettle up, and I determined that my little band should not be far behind him.' The Controleur produced 400 guilders and the hire of a small bus with native driver.

> I sat beside the driver and wouldn't let him slow down or stop once. He wanted to sleep during the night, but I wouldn't have it. By pressing on, we passed the Brigadier's car parked outside a Rest House. [After various vicissitudes, including running out of petrol, they reached Solok fifteen minutes before the daily train left for Padang. Arriving that evening, they found that the Brigadier had just beaten them to it.] He met me and we had a laugh over the race. That was the evening of 21 February. One week only after I left Singapore. It seemed a hundred years.
>
> Hoffman and St Aubyn* turned up the next day. They had had many adventures since I last saw them and had found their ways by various routes to Padang, where we awaited British ships. But none came. On the evening of the 23rd a small Dutch steamer, *Dumeyer van Twist*, arrived in the harbour. She was bound for Java and Paris was of no mind to go that way. He wanted to go to India.

---

* Commander E. K. H. St Aubyn, originally Staff Officer (Operations) at the Naval Base.

The Navy, now about sixty strong, reckoned this was better than nothing so Paris sent us off in her.

The passage down was painfully slow, when the Japanese advance was so swift. Happily it was uneventful. We sailed into Tjilatjap harbour during the morning of the first of March. . . . Alongside the quay was that ever-heartening sight to a sailor, the White Ensign. HMS *Stronghold* was to sail that night for Australia and Hoffman, St Aubyn and I with thirty of our sailors were embarked for passage. The remainder we put on board the Dutch liner *Zaandam*, also sailing for Australia that night. She got there.

Duncan Macfarlane, who had stayed with me throughout, was turned off *Stronghold* as they were expecting to go into action and did not want any non-Naval passengers. He was sitting disconsolately on a bollard ashore when someone asked who he was, and eventually got him on board the *Zaandam*.

Stronghold sailed at 6pm. At 9am on 2 March, we were sighted by a Japanese reconnaissance plane and stood by for the rest of the day awaiting the bombers. By tea time nothing had arrived and we considered ourselves out of danger. Half past five found all the officers sitting on the quarter-deck, thinking about the bar opening and our general good fortune.

At ten to six someone sighted a ship on our starboard quarter. We increased to full speed, just in case. St Aubyn turned to me and said, 'It is probably a Yankee cruiser.' No sooner were the words out of his mouth when vivid orange flashes appeared on the distant ship. 'No, it's not,' we both exclaimed at once and, although the gravity of the situation was quite apparent to both of us, we laughed. The Japanese cruiser *Maia* and two modern destroyers. What a jolly prospect. She was far faster than us and wriggle and speed as we did, she inexorably crept up on us, but it was not till she was fairly close that she started to score any hits. When she did we knew all about it. Hit after hit was registered in quick succession. The forward tubes were hit, the ship was slowed down considerably and a terrible carnage began on the decks. Then she lost speed alarmingly – I believe there was a fire in the engine room – ready use ammunition was used up and it seemed damage prevented hoisting more. The two undamaged torpedoes were fired, to no effect, when the *Maia* was lying a mile or two on our starboard bow. The Captain (Lieutenant-Commander G. R. Pretor-Pinney) was severely wounded and the last words I heard him say were 'Pass the word for Commander St. Aubyn'. After which the ship finally stopped and was abandoned.

CPO Verrion (Chief Gunner's Mate at the Naval Base, evacuated in the *St Breock* and then a valued ally of Forbes since Dabo) was in a Carley float in the dark and, recognizing the latter's voice, pulled him out of the water, saving his life. Ian Forbes, who was awarded the DSC after the war, was the only officer survivor. Rescued by the *Maia*, he and fifty ratings were imprisoned in Celebes.

It remains but to clear up the grim saga of the gunboats by returning to AB Long's party at Rengat:

'The Indragiri escape organization was closing down by the time we arrived and after a while Lieutenant-Commander Eustace explained that it seemed no help of any kind was available; it was every man for himself.' So, having decided to make for the railhead at Sawahlunto, Long and fourteen naval ratings set out for a town that was roughly 170 miles away with jungle, swamps, mountains and valleys in between, not forgetting the heat and humidity of the equator.

Our wounded stoker [Farley] was now in a parlous condition and had to be left behind with the nurses. I never saw him again and many times wondered what happened to him, until in 1983 I attended one of the FEPOW reunions at Scarborough. Who do you think I bumped into? Yes, it was him. Still with the indomitable spirit which he showed on our journey from Singkep to Rengat. What a reunion we had! He was taken prisoner, of course.*

What a sight we must have been leaving Rengat. Some with no shoes – ragged, filthy shorts, some with native clip-clops – bits and pieces handed to us by Australians who were also making for Padang. By now we had arms, discarded by soldiers who also took pity on us in our plight. We had no money – no soap – no provisions. We lived either off the land on bananas, pineapples etc when we came upon them, or went hungry. When we reached a native village we either depended on their generosity for a meagre gift of rice or, failing co-operation, took food by other methods.

* When being transhipped, still very ill, from Medan to Singapore in the notorious *Van Warveijk* which was torpedoed with the loss of hundreds, Farley's life was saved by a fellow prisoner, none other than Sjovald Cunyngham-Brown, who jumped with him and supported him until help arrived. The semi-conscious Farley did not know this until I told him 46 years later!

We were desperate men. We climbed and descended mountains, waded through swamps and small rivers and finally reached the railhead at Sawahlunto in a sorry state, but overjoyed to be informed that a train could take us to Padang that very afternoon. After several hours' slow journey we saw, through a gap in the mountains, the Indian Ocean. What a sight! The first ray of hope for nearly a month. But when we arrived at Padang it was to be told that the last ship had left several days ago, and that the Netherlands East Indies had unconditionally surrendered. The Dutch had declared Padang an open town and the Japs were expected to occupy it at any time. Despondency and despair descended on all.

It will be recalled that shortly after this the Japanese arrived and they were all taken prisoner.

One of the most poignant documents I came across in the course of research for this book was a scribble in green ink on two sheets torn from a naval signal pad. Admirals write official communications in green (except Commanders-in-Chief who use red) to catch the eye, and this was a personal note from RA Malaya, Rear Admiral Spooner, to the Commanding Officer of the *Durban*, dated 10/2/42. It read:

My Dear Cazalet

Singapore will probably be captured tonight or tomorrow. The story of ineptitude, bad generalship, etc. is drawing to a close. I am sending with this three trunks (tin) and one suitcase of mine and my wife's. Please take to Batavia and turn over to Collins or to my wife who is staying with Lady Sansome at Bandoeng.

My wife left here in *Scout* last night. I am getting away all the sailors and soldiers I can in the various patrol boats and intend to follow myself in an ML at the last – not to be captured if I can avoid it.

The present state of affairs was started by the AIF who just turned tail, became a rabble and let the Japs walk in unopposed. My marines have been cut up. The young N. Officers in MLs and Fairmiles have been splendid.

A certain number of officers and sailors may come with you. As they come in from various boats and jobs all over Island am sorting them out as boats' crews and getting surplus away. I do not intend that any be taken prisoner if I can help it.

You must go by midnight. All good luck and tell my wife I'll follow soon.
Yours
    E. J. Spooner

It will be remembered that at a few minutes to midnight on 12 February, my ship, the *Kung Wo*, which had signalled to the HQ ship *Laburnum* for instructions, was answered by Lieutenant Pool RN in ML 310. Dickie Pool, who had been my opposite number ('Sub'. of the Gunroom) in the *Repulse*, was now Senior Officer of the ML flotilla (the CO of ML 310 was Lieutenant J. Bull RNZVR) and he said he was waiting to embark RA Malaya. The next day was a hectic one as we know and Admiral Spooner, accompanied by the Air Officer Commanding, Air Vice-Marshall C. W. H. Pulford, did not arrive until the evening. The total number on board was forty-five: six Naval Officers, one Army Officer (Lieutenant Ian Stonor, Argyll & Sutherland Highlanders, ADC to General Percival), two RAF Officers, nineteen Naval ratings, six Royal Marines, eight Army and two RAF Other Ranks, and one Chinese cook.

For the full tragic story of this party the reader is referred to *Course for Disaster* by Commander R. A. W. Pool, the senior survivor (Leo Cooper, 1987). Suffice it to say that from the first few minutes after casting off from the Telok Ayer Wharf just before midnight on the 13th, nothing went right. ML 310's steering gear failed, causing her to sheer off course and run aground. Pool jumped in to ascertain the extent of damage to her screws, slipped while getting back on board and had the fingers of one hand crushed. The ML was refloated at daylight and continued to lay up by an island for the rest of the day but Pool's hand was so bad – he had become feverish – that the Admiral decided he must be got to medical attention as soon as possible. Accordingly course was set for Muntok on Banka Island.

Passing between Tjebia and another island of the Tuju group, they steered for a kolek carrying two natives, one of whom was trying to attract attention by waving a letter. This proved to be from the Commandant of a Dutch lookout post, warning of the presence of a large number of warships (and other ships). Commander Pool has written that the Admiral was not inclined to attach much importance to the news. He said that since there had been many such scares in the past few weeks, which in each case had been untrue, he proposed to ignore this one. Course was resumed. From this it is clear that Admiral Spooner had previously received no firm enemy report from the Dutch. (It was after the next, surprising development that he complained, in the hearing of Lieutenant Pool, that he had given no instructions for the demise of the code books.)

Approaching Banka Island they were suddenly aware of the masts and funnels of three Japanese cruisers and two destroyers. The M L swung straight round but had been seen; a shell landed in her wake, a seaplane was launched to attack her – its bombs narrowly missed – and a destroyer set off in pursuit. M L 310 ran down the far side of Tjebia but went aground on coral, as it turned out – for good. All waded ashore to hide in the jungle, except for Bull and his crew, rejoined shortly by Pool and Wing-Commander Atkins. The destroyer arrived, fired a few rounds and launched a motor boat whose boarding party, under a Midshipman, demobilised the M L and lined up the four officers (the ratings had been sent ashore) in front of a firing party. At the last moment the Midshipman, who had explained he could not take prisoners, suddenly relented and told them to pull ashore in their dinghy. Still expecting to be shot – 'less messy this way' muttered the Wing-Commander – they were, however, not molested and the motor boat returned to the destroyer, which made off.

The native fishermen of the island decamped overnight, leaving only empty huts and two derelict prauws, the only other inhabitants being a Javanese officer and a few men manning a hill-top lookout post. They had just destroyed their radio set on the approach of the Japanese! One of the prauws was shortly repaired, Bull setting off in her for Java with two ratings, the Javanese officer and two of his men. He was to succeed in reaching Merak, North-West Java, encountering six Allied ships. After the war the Dutch Admiral Helfrich, in his unpublished notes, commented that at the time they didn't know anything about the stranded party, but 'if I had known, it would have been easy to rescue them by sending a submarine. The *K14* was near the place'. Again nothing had gone right, but this was not all.

Somebody did do something about them because the American submarine *S-39*, in the vicinity of the island, was ordered by her Senior Officer to rescue the British party and (according to her log) manoeuvred close inshore and flashed lights off Tjebia on 27 February and the next day, landing a party on the third. These found only smashed pots and pans, huts and footprints. Surprised by a destroyer, the submarine then departed. Dickie Pool points out there is a mystery about this because the unfortunates on Tjebia kept a keen and constant lookout all round and they never saw a destroyer. Moreover, there were no smashed huts on the island; those they used were still standing when a War Graves party visited the place after the war. It would seem that if *S-39* went to any island, it was the wrong one; yet the position in her log tallies with that of Tjebia.

Though hopes of rescue were at first quite high it only remains to record that the forty-five (augmented by three castaways) were now relegated to three months slow but sure deterioration of body and mind. 'Monarchs of all they surveyed', a real Robinson Crusoe existence ensued. There were springs of water and a finite supply of tinned food and rice, plus some fruit and vegetables that were just eatable; but ill health began to manifest itself, at first insiduously and then with increasing effect until the strongest would be struck down without warning. The main trouble was malaria of a particularly vicious and possibly cerebral strain (the Javanese officer had said that Tjebia was known as 'malaria island'). Also, as prospects of delivery faded, so did morale, with many just giving up. The first to go was a Naval officer, followed steadily by eighteen others, including the Admiral and Air Marshal.

After nine weeks it became obvious that something must be done if they were not all to perish of disease or starvation and a concerted effort made to virtually rebuild the least derelict prauw. Eventually it set off with Pool, Stonor, Atkins and two others; after a hazardous sail they were rescued by a fisherman who took them to Dabo. Those still on Tjebia were sent for and the whole party handed over to the Japanese, for return to Singapore (and slavery on the Burma Railway) over three months after setting out.

This traumatic story, of which several twists have been omitted, is yet another echoing 'the fine threads of fate'.

The following extracts from the official 'Report of Proceedings' by Lieutenant-Commander V. C. F. Clark DSC (a decoration earned at Narvik; he was to be awarded a Bar for rescuing the cut-off brigade at Batu Pahat) RN, to the Captain, Coastal Forces, East Indies, gives the bare bones of the action witnessed by those on board the *Mata Hari* as they stood facing the bayonets of Japanese marines. Submission of the Report was perforce delayed until Clark was released from captivity.

Singapore
9 September, 1945.

REPORT OF PROCEEDINGS OF HMML 311 AFTER DEPARTURE FROM SINGAPORE FEBRUARY 1942.

Sir,

I have the honour to submit the following report of the passage of HMML 311 from Singapore to Banka Straits and sinking there by enemy action. This report is forwarded by me, as Senior Naval Officer on board, in the absence of her Commanding Officer, Lieutenant E. J. H. Christmas, RANVR, whose subsequent fate is unknown.

2. I embarked in HMMML 311 pm 13 February 1942 as passenger.

3. Orders were later received from RAMY, through Commander Alexander, RN, to embark about fifty-five Army personnel after dark, then proceed to Batavia via Durian Straits. . . .

6. At daylight (15th) we sighted what appeared to be a warship from two to three miles distant, almost dead ahead, in the swept channel, at a fine inclination, stern towards us and to all appearances almost stopped. We maintained our course, being under the impression that this was probably a Dutch destroyer. When about a mile away the destroyer altered course to port and was immediately recognisable by its distinctive stem as a Japanese

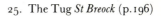
25. The Tug *St Breock* (p.196)

26. The Naval 'Fairmile' *HMML 311*
was sunk by a Japanese destroyer on
15 February, 1942. See 'Report of
Proceedings' by Lieutenant-Commander
V.C.F. Clarke on pp.208–10.

27. Doris Lim: "Her story . . . is the most horrific
of all those I have come across" (p.216)

28. "The *Rooseboom* went down in minutes" (p.219)

destroyer of a large type. At Lieutenant Christmas' request I took command of the ship, and increased to eighteen knots, maintaining my course, to close within effective range.

7. The enemy opened fire and, with the first salvo, scored two direct hits, one of which penetrated the forecastle deck, laying out the gun's crew, putting the gun out of action (not immediately realised) and killing the helmsman. Lieutenant Christmas took the wheel, I increased to full speed (approx twenty knots) and made a four-point alteration of course to starboard to open 'A' arcs for the Lewis guns, now within extreme range. This brought me on a course roughly parallel and opposite to the enemy and closing the Sumatra shore, which, in the almost certain event of being sunk, should enable the crew and the troops to swim to the mainland. On my enquiring, after this alteration, why the 3-pounder was not firing, I was informed that it was out of action. By constant zig-zagging further direct hits were avoided for a short time, during which the LGs continued to engage the enemy.

8. The enemy, however, having circled round astern of me, was closing and soon shrapnel and direct hits began to take their toll both above and below decks. The petrol tanks were on fire, blazing amidships, and there was a fire on the messdecks. The engine room casing was blown up and two out of the three ER personnel had been killed, whilst the third, a stoker, was wounded in the leg. The port engine was put out of action. The ER services as a whole, however, were maintained throughout the action. Finally, Lieutenant Christmas at the helm reported the steering broken down with the rudder jammed to starboard. We began circling at a range of about 1000 yards. Further offensive or defensive action being impossible, all guns being out of action and the ship ablaze amidships, I stopped engines and ordered 'abandon ship'.

9. Casualties were heavy. I estimate that barely twenty men, including wounded, took to the water. The Japanese destroyer lay off and, although the White Ensign remained flying, ceased fire but made no attempt to pick up survivors. I advised men to make for the mainland shore but a number are believed to have made for the middle of the strait in the hope of being picked up. The action lasted about ten minutes. The Captain of the *Mata Hari* (Lieutenant Carson, T 124), who witnessed the action, states that the Japanese ship fired fourteen six-gun salvoes. There were four, or possibly five, direct hits, and, in addition to the damage from these, most regrettable carnage was caused on the closely stowed upper deck by bursts from several 'shorts'. The ship sank not long after being abandoned, burning furiously. . . .

11. In accordance with KR&AI recommendation for award is attached herewith.

(The recommendation was for the DSM to Stoker P. H. H. Donne. Though wounded – the other Engine Room ratings were killed – he kept the ER in action to the last, in spite of blazing petrol tanks and adjacent Lewis gun ammunition. At the order to abandon ship he assisted with the seriously wounded and was one of the last three to leave the ship.) I wrote and asked Commander Clark if he could add to the above and also what happened to him subsequently. He replied:

After a salvo at approx 400 yards from the Jap destroyer the ML (100ft Fairmile), of which I had on request taken command, was reduced to a shambles – fire in the fo'c'sle – fire in the engine room, gun knocked off its mounting, rudder jammed hard-astarboard and boat slowly turning in a circle and sinking. No further action was taken by Japs. Upper deck, on which were sixty key Army personnel, was a bloody shambles, deck and scuppers running with blood and a horrible gory sight. My left arm was broken at the wrist.

Those of us capable of doing so lashed helpless survivors hopefully to planks etc. and the unwounded (about a dozen soldiers including a Colonel and a young acting Petty Officer) told to swim towards the shore (mangrove). This party found an abandoned Dutch lifeboat and the young PO (trained by me at Shotley!) discovering mast, sails, compass, charts and provisions on board, took charge of the party (including the Colonel!) and sailed them for thirteen days and nights through Banka Straits and down towards Batavia. Within short distance of Batavia they were caught by a junk full of Japs and became POWs. Rotten luck!

I found myself alone and proceeded to swim slowly towards a 'hull-down' lighthouse, with an empty wooden ammunition box under my broken arm (time 7 am approx.) At dusk, about twelve hours later I scrambled up into a fishing pagar for the night. At daylight I started swimming again towards the lighthouse. About mid-day I spotted another pagar with a man in it (a British major). After a short confab we swam ashore and tramped for six hours through mangrove swamps (agony!), arriving at a river. After about three-quarters of a mile down the river we saw a native village, so we swam down to it, got a not very friendly reception and took up abode in an empty house (all houses on stilts). We were joined by another Army major. During the night we decided to escape in one of the canoes which were moored under the house. By this time were also joined by an Army private. So we quietly slid out and started paddling up this jungle river. I think we were paddling for six or eight days, by day, lying up by night. The weather alternated between tropical downpours when we got soaked, and boiling sun against which we had little protection. One Army officer was in a coma most of the time. My wounded arm had reached the size of a bolster (no sign of any elbow!) and I was wondering whether I would end up as a one arm Nelson or just dead, when the Yorkshire private said, 'When I had anything septic, Sir, my granny always put on a soap and sugar poultice' – which struck me as rather funny in the middle of the jungle. But we came to a clearing with four or five huts and to my amazement the private procured some sugar and soap and some hot 'porridge' rice, and proceeded to make a poultice in my grubby handkerchief, wrapping it round with one of my stockings. At the same time we occupied an empty hut. Within thirty-six hours my arm was down to normal and within forty-eight hours shrapnel was being sucked out of the wrist.

The private and one fit Army officer proceeded up river, leaving me and the sick Army officer in the hut. I put a wooden splint on my arm and within (I think) two weeks the bone had joined and flesh was returning. I think we were in the hut about six weeks, eating rubber nuts and a handful of green beans provided by the natives. They then told us (lying!) that the Australians had driven the Japs out of Palembang and offered to take us upstream and to P. where we could get clothes and hospital treatment. We were a bit weak by then, but they started us off, eventually leaving us to follow directions and we spent one interesting night making our way through the rimba (deep jungle) the only 'path' being along felled tree trunks. Fortunately bright moonlight. At the far end we were met by other natives, who took us to their village and eventually to the river and across to Palembang. There we got into a tiny bus and (trusting that they were helping us) were driven to a barrier guarded by armed Japs. We were POWs (40 guilders a head) together with a considerable number of others, mostly British, already POWs in an old school.

Not a very heroic story, I'm afraid, but I did at least make as big a nuisance of myself as I could for the next 3½ years!

In concluding this chapter on some of the RN's doings at

Singapore's Dunkirk I venture to record that the officers and men of the *Prince of Wales* and *Repulse* did not let down their comrades who had died in the sinkings. Several accounts speak highly of ratings from the two ships (Petty Officer Leather was awarded the DSM) and of two Lieutenant-Commanders (one from each) and four Lieutenants (three from the *Prince of Wales*): both Lieutenant-Commanders earned DSCs, one being killed and the other taken prisoner; two Lieutenants earned DSCs, both being taken prisoner, and of the remaining two one was killed and the other was the only one to escape, undecorated. I can mention all this because the latter was me!

VIII

Gallant Losers and Outright Winners

The stories in this chapter are a mixed bag concerning 'second lap' escapes of individuals who had already reached Sumatra and one from mainland Malaya. Escapes from prison camps are also touched on.

Captain Mick Jennings RE (he had been Municipal Engineer at Kuala Lumpur) had boarded Crawley's junk at Singapore. Having heard nothing about his wife's *Mata Hari* he was a worried man, had never done any sailing before, and was a poor swimmer; but when, at Padang on 14 March, Captain J. Thorlby RE invited him to join a getaway boat he had procured, Jennings agreed with alacrity.

It proved to be a dugout sailing kolek, twenty-six feet by only two, one glimpse of which was enough to make three (including MSM MacLaren of the *Sir Theodore Fraser*) turn back. However, the remaining seven in Jennings' words 'turned our faces resolutely from the shore' and set course ostensibly for India. Unfortunately the navigator, a padre, failed to come to terms with a pocket compass and several further mishaps led to general bad feeling; with the result that on reaching Sikiakap on Pagi North Island (about 175 miles due south of Padang) the party split up, Jennings, with Privates Hall and Green, transferring to a small but well-found dinghy. Clinker-built – that is with overlapping strakes – she was only seventeen feet long and went by the name of *Gilca*. After she had been strengthened by a native shipwright, and stores, including a chart from an abandoned merchant ship taken on board, they sailed (as did the other boat) on the inauspicious 1 April. A Dutch officer had told them it was a fair wind to Australia, for which both parties now aimed. Enganno Island (due east of the south tip of Sumatra) was 220 miles and Australia 1800!

In spite of bad weather that caused the ditching of fifty coconuts, good progress had been made by *Gilca* when, on the seventh morning, Jennings found Green asleep at the tiller, not apparently for the first time, and, completely lost, they had to go back for three days to obtain a sight of recognizable land. Arrival at Enganno was to find the place under a Jap-controlled native agent. Thorlby had left five days before, so it was a surprise when he returned, with the agent, Marinas, to whom he had surrendered. Their boat had leaked, as Jennings had foreseen. Green then announced that he was rejoining Thorlby, at which Marinas approached Jennings about surrendering too. He was told not to interfere or the world would be short of one Marinas. Given a sheet for use as a foresail 'enabling us to sail closer to the wind, whatever that meant' and reloading fifty coconuts in lieu of Green, they set off again. It was 1 May. Comparing the very short line on the chart which represented their progress so far, with the 'great blank space of paper' which was the ocean yet to be traversed, Jennings quickly put away the chart!

Troubles soon came thick and fast. First, all the jars of fried chicken were found to have gone bad, reducing their store of preserved food to some tins of cooked porridge. Then a shark, of which they could see several, came up and crushed the rudder pintles – adequately repaired by Hall – and lastly, a full gale blew up to last seven days, and leave them exhausted (and now tormented by leg sores). During their first fifty days the wind was favourable for only two, needing endless tacking. Then real disaster struck. The tinned porridge was found to be bad too. The fresh produce was finished and starvation stared them in the face. The chart was produced and Jennings asked, 'Do you think we can sail twenty-five miles a day?' and 'Do you think you can last twenty days without food?' The answers to both were a courageous yes and they shook hands on 'Australia or sink'.

There was sufficient water and after a few days the complete lack of food did not worry them as much as feared. However, energy decreased to an alarming extent, underlined when they decided to cut a few feet off the mast to facilitate tending the sail. However hard they tried they just could not step the mast again. After a time Hall, who was not at all religious, said, 'Why not say a prayer, Skipper?' So Jennings said, 'Almighty God, help us and give us strength to restep the mast; we've done all we can, and now we ask for Divine assistance, for Jesus Christ's sake, Amen.' They then stepped the mast with no trouble, Jennings recording: 'Hall's red beard opened in an unbelieving smile and my grey one followed suit as we turned to mutter our very grateful thanks.' The only reading matter on board was a Bible and after this incident they obtained much solace in reading a chapter aloud every day.

Both were pitifully thin. Then a miracle came to their aid. A seagull landed on the bowsprit and Jennings, taking half an hour to obtain and point his revolver, shot it. The bird was bled, skinned and eaten raw, Jennings breaking two teeth in chewing the bones. In the next thirty days they got three more gulls. Though these indicated land Jennings realised they were completely lost and they agreed to sail west for what they expected would be the southern tip of Java. The wind dropped, returning only fitfully. Though more seagulls were caught – using a specially prepared 'hunting position' from which these were grabbed – 'The awful gnawing of our vitals was almost beyond bearing'. A hurricane force gale descended on them in the second half of July, when all their meagre energies had to be concentrated on baling.

Then one sunrise brought a tremendous thrill – a sail. After which a mountain was discerned. They set course towards it and at midday overhauled a fishing boat whose two occupants gave them bananas and a small fish. A town was now visible and they asked what it was. The reply 'Bencoolen', was a dreadful shock. Bencoolen was only 120 miles from Enganno, whence they had set out on 1 May, 127 days before.

It only remains to record that they landed on a breaker-lashed shore, the gallant *Gilca* being completely broken up. A native indicated a nearby kampong to which they progressed in short stages, to be taken prisoner and incarcerated in Palembang. Thus ended the saga of two stout hearts who defied the sea for four months without any relevant experience. Surely they deserved better.

*   *   *

For forty-five years after the events of the *Kung Wo* and Benku Island I had from time to time wondered what had happened to the pretty little Chinese girl, Doris Lim, who had captivated us all by her combination of *sang froid* and high spirits in unpromising situations. Then, researching this book, I suddenly found out and was pitched into gloom, even after all this time. Her story, which is also that of Sergeant Walter Gibson of the Argylls – it came to be told by him – is the most horrific of all those I have come across.

When Gibson's regiment was overrun at the battle of Slim River, small parties of survivors struggled through the jungle behind the enemy lines, he and a handful reaching the coast a month later as the Japanese launched their attack on Singapore Island. Gibson and two others sailed across to Sumatra in a fishing boat, eventually reaching Padang, where on 20 February he was detailed to board the small Dutch steamer *Rooseboom*; it had called at Padang on its way from Batavia to Colombo.

Doris Lim looked younger, but must have been in her late twenties. It transpires that, born in Shanghai, her parents had died and she was brought up in an American convent, speaking little Chinese; she had in fact a slight American accent. Since 1933 – the early days of Japanese aggression – she had worked for both British and Chinese intelligence, escaping only just in time successively from Tientsin, Shanghai and Singapore. She was on board the *Rooseboom* when it put in to Padang, having earlier left Padang for Java in the destroyer *Encounter* (with the rest of the media party) only to be transferred there and find herself back again.

The *Rooseboom* sailed with over 500 passengers in all. The Senior Officer was Brigadier Paris, fresh from beating Ian Forbes in the race across Sumatra. There was also Group Captain Nunn of Pompong, with his wife, having obtained preferential road transport because he said he was carrying despatches from General Percival, a statement which Colonel Dillon for one did not believe. One of the luckiest people ever was a Major who was about to board the *Rooseboom* when Brigadier Paris barred the way, saying, 'Sorry, full up'. I was also fortunate as it looks as if the *Kung Wo* party that left our island with Doris Lim also boarded the *Rooseboom*.

A Jap reconnaissance aircraft had been over Padang before she sailed but after two nights her Captain announced that they were out of bombing range and the Brigadier gave the toast 'Safe arrival at Colombo'. A few hours later, just before midnight, a torpedo struck the 1000-ton ship.

Immediately there was pandemonium. The *Rooseboom* went down in minutes. From all around came screams and shouts to the background of escaping steam, inrushing water and the bellowing of a bullock that was to have provided meat. Sergeant Gibson, through whose eyes we shall follow the unfolding tragedy, shared a baulk of timber with a police officer for an hour, before swimming to a lifeboat which he discerned in the moonlight. Dawn revealed eighty in this, the only one, designed to hold twenty-eight, with fifty in the water clinging onto rope lifelines. In the stern were Brigadier Paris, the Captain, his Chief Officer and Chief Engineer, Mrs Nunn (her husband had drowned after pushing her through a porthole) the Chief Officer's wife and Doris Lim. There were forty-eight tins of bully beef, two of fried rice, forty-eight of condensed milk and six bottles of fresh water. Colonel Ackworth took charge of rationing and ordered that every fit man was to do a spell of four hours per day in the water. That night they had to doze upright; to slip down into the bilge water was to drown or suffocate.

A raft was constructed and towed astern with twenty on it semi-submerged; men slipped off to vanish, until after three days there were none left. Many hanging onto the lifelines also drifted away. Numbers in the boat dwindled too. The three women among a mass of sweating, groaning men, reclined together; when nature called Brigadier Paris would order, 'Everyone look to the bows'. If Mr Nunn did behave improperly crossing Sumatra, his wife made up for him in her last hours, moving about the boat in a motherly fashion, encouraging and alleviating pain. Doris Lim sat impassive, gazing ahead, seemingly resigned, with the stoic fatalism of her race. 'She looked very young and very pretty,' Gibson was to write, 'even by European standards. Her complexion was particularly noticeable – with a fresh bloom to it, unusual in a Chinese girl.' Gradually the spirit of comradeship evaporated. A particularly suspicious group consisted of five disaffected men, all from the same regiment, who sat huddled together near the bows, occasionally looking round furtively. More people just disappeared in the night. No one asked any questions; there was always the thought that every man fewer meant greater hope for the others. A storm blew up after dark one night; the boat shipped a lot of water, everyone baled frantically and there was a good deal of panic, with screams and shouts. When daylight came twenty people were seen to be missing. It was then realised what the group in the bows were up to. They were a murder gang.

One by one people would go mad or just give up. The blond First Officer, who was in a coma, head in his wife's lap, suddenly broke away and, shouting 'Going for help', sprang over the side and swam away. His wife just sat for a day and then followed him. At the end of a week, Brigadier Paris sank into a torpor, weakening by the hour, looked after by a young Captain Blackwood. The older man suddenly turned to him, 'I say, let's go along to the club for a drink,' to which Blackwood replied evenly, 'Better make it later, Sir'. Soon the Brigadier was struggling with Blackwood and Gibson, his mind completely gone. He then fell into a coma and died. Blackwood survived him by only one day, slipping unconscious into the bottom of the boat to drown in the six inches of bilge water. The next to go was the Dutch Captain. He was dozing at the tiller when one of his engineer officers leapt at him with a shout and buried a knife in his ribs. Trying to grab the rations, the man was forestalled and leapt over the side. Mrs Nunn bathed the Captain's wounds with salt water but he died with his head in her lap. Colonel Ackworth vanished one night. Colonel Palmer was in charge when Mrs Nunn said she would like to conduct a service. This she did; they sang 'The Lord is my shepherd' and 'Abide with me' and felt the better for it. Then Palmer died, at which time there were fifty or sixty left, much less than half. Mrs Nunn then slipped quietly away, with Doris Lim, naked now, bathing her lips with salt water.

Gibson was to write rather obliquely, 'I knew the dreadful things that had been happening to others who had died and whose bodies had remained in the boat and I said to Doris Lim, "Get her over the side quickly".' He was referring of course, to cannibalism, and soon realised that if any discipline was to be maintained, it was up to him. The crux was not long in coming.

While everyone watched, helpless and apathetic, they jumped from behind on a young QMS of the 18th Division and drew a jugged bully beef tin across his throat: 'They had, as we knew, tried to drink the blood of people who had died, and had found it impossible. Now they were trying butchery.' The poor fellow tore himself free and, after staggering aft for protection, lay dying slowly and painfully. 'For God's sake put him overboard,' said Gibson and they did. He and another then organized a team of volunteers who rushed the gang in the bows and after a fierce struggle pitched them over the side (a sad casualty was Drummer Hardy of the Argylls, a great character who had been Colonel Stewart's drummer. I remember the two of them marching across the Causeway from Johore to the skirl of pipes).

All the survivors were now naked, the sun having rotted their clothes. To the good there was a violent rainstorm, which produced a quantity of water and, as with Jennings and Hall, some seagulls arrived out of the blue and settled on the boat. Seven were caught and wolfed raw. Then for a long time nothing happened until the day when Gibson realized with a shock that he and a big gunner were the only two white people left alive. Up in the bows sat the last four Javanese seamen. Suddenly the gunner cried out for help. Two of the Javanese were battering his head with rowlocks, the blood running down all over him. When he ceased to struggle a third started tearing at the body with a blade made out of a tin. They could hear the grating of metal against bone. The man 'plunged his hand into the wound

... and pulled out something dripping with blood, into which he dug his teeth like a dog ... the other two ceased to hammer the gunner's head and grabbed greedily at the wound. They were unquestionably mad. Blood dripped from their faces as, still chewing, they grinned horribly at us. One of them shouted and proffered something he held in his hands. All we could do was shake our heads.' This one vile meal seemed enough for them; as soon as it was finished they pushed the body overboard. Their serang died soon after, his companions chanting an incantation in the dark, while Gibson crawled forward and threw the rowlocks over the side. From then on he and the girl tried not to take their eyes off the new group of murderers in the bows.

But one night Gibson was awoken by a touch. It was one of the Javanese, who pointed repeatedly into the darkness. All five peered in the direction where there seemed to be a shadow and in a while they could hear surf breaking over coral. Then there was a jolt, a grating sound and the boat had grounded, to turn broadside on and tilt over. They all scrambled out; Gibson grabbed Doris Lim's hand and together they staggered, fell and crawled through the surf. On the beach at last they tried to stand up but collapsed, then crawled a safe distance from the water and, clasped in each others arms, fell into an exhausted sleep. The boat had taken a month to drift 1000 miles.

Found by natives they were taken to Sipoera Island and eventually turned over to the Japanese, who separated them. Gibson was tortured, being perpetually told to admit that he and Doris had come to ferment insurrection against the Japs. At that time he knew nothing of her past and they, eventually believing him, discharged him to a prison camp. He was told and for a long time believed that the Japanese shot Doris, but in fact she was released to work in a cement factory in Sumatra. There she met a Singapore Chinese nurse, Janet Lim (no relation) who had also been released. The two went to work for a Chinese farmer whom Doris married. Janet had returned to Padang when she was called as a witness in a murder trial. Doris had been stabbed to death by her husband.

*   *   *

At Padang on 16 March – the Japanese arrived on the 17th – a scratch party of two officers, nine other ranks and a Malay serang clubbed together and went twenty miles south to the seaside village of Sungei Penang, where they were able to buy a boat. She was twenty-seven by six feet, drew 2 feet with a freeboard of eighteen inches and had an 8-foot outrigger on each side; very similar to the craft Thorlby had procured not far away. There was a 30-foot mast, a mainsail with dipping lug – the sheets of which went to a small capstan – and foresail coming down to a bowsprit. Normally open, some canvas was obtained for coverage amidships.

The enterprise received a body blow when just before sailing on the night of the 17th, Ibrahim the serang was dissuaded from going by the local priest, leaving only one of the party who had done any sailing before; but they set off in good spirits.

The crew of the newly christened *Venture* consisted of (with the nicknames soon bestowed and to be used hereafter): Major H. M. Kilgour MBE, RAMC (Doc), Flight-Lieutenant F. Dykes RAF (Dickie), Sergeant Beaumont HK/S RA (Snowy), LAC D. Bowler RAF (Tom), Conductor F. Daintee IAOC (Tiny), Sergeant D. Eastgate AIF (Lofty), Sergeant E. Forty AIF (Ernie), Sergeant D. Gavin East Surreys (Gabby), Private U. Hudson AIF (Titch), Sub-Conductor S. Lissenberg IAOC (Lissy) and Bombadier Rawson HK/S RA (Bosun). Lofty and Gabby have left vivid accounts, not always agreeing chronologically with Dickie's precise, brief record, which has been taken as the basis. As is not unknown when an isolated group is really up against it, the strongest personality – the Admirable Crichton – whatever his rank, rises to the top. Here, it appeared very soon that the six-foot-four-inch Tiny was that man, a giant in more ways than one. I can confirm that *Venture* was not short of big men because Bosun (Bombadier Rawson) was the same large, fair-haired 'Bosun' of Crawley's *Hiap Hin*, who had handled her hawsers on our way up the Indragiri.

Tiny was voted skipper and another vote was taken as to whether it should be India or Australia. India won and course was therefore set NW for Siberoet. For navigation, which was Dickie's responsibility, there were two pocket compasses, one of them luminous 'for a while', a Chinese map and a school atlas. They soon found, as had all the rest of us by now spread out fanwise from Padang, that having no keel the boat would not sail close to the wind, and that her sails were rotten. A squall blew up and probably caught them unawares, Gabby recording: 'There was a whip-like crack as the back of the boom was broken and then the white sail was flapping and sagging like a broken wing. . . . It seeemed as if fate, even now, would turn us back to Sumatra but every heart aboard was against retracing one single foot of the way. The oars came out while Dickie Dykes came to the rescue on the boom.' Very seasick, sailing and rowing in turn, they duly arrived at Siberoet where invaluable help was received from the Dutch Controleur and his son, David and Immanuel Loembantobing, who roofed in the boat, strengthened the rigging, gave them a small kolek and provided provisions and good advice.

Snowy and Lofty shortly went down with malaria, though the latter recovered fairly quickly. Reaching Pulau Nias in rough weather, they sailed up its west coast to Seramboe. Food was bought, in the course of which it was learnt from Malays that some Germans had taken control after the Dutch had withdrawn to Sumatra, and it would be better if *Venture* left immediately. 'Left immediately' was easier said than done, with the boat facing a strong onshore wind and sea. With some on the oars, some hauling on the anchor rope as Tiny roared encouragement, they fought to pull the boat up to her anchor, but the capstan broke and she was hurled back onto the beach. Tiny was already in action as they picked themselves up, but it was evident that help was at hand; scores of watching villagers, impressed, had suddenly become a cheering, helping mob as they shoved the boat out, and the battle was on again. 'Get the foresail up, Bosun!' yelled Tiny. 'Come on, Gabby, pull, PULL!' Suddenly a shift in the wind filled the sail and sent them riding forward, free. 'You're a bastard, Tiny,' said Gabby later and Bosun added, 'Captain Bligh would learn from you, Tiny!' But the latter only grinned.

The weather was squally all next day, rising to a crescendo after dark when a vicious sumatra tore into *Venture*, so that, crashing down like a stricken forest giant, the mast took everything before it. In a moment the boat was filling up, with the mast lying on the port outrigger and pulling it down so that the starboard one pointed to the sky. For the rest of the night they hacked with parangs at the side-straps and finally got the mast on board. Dickie noted laconically, 'All hands completely exhausted. Drifted all night.'

In the morning they rowed to a small island just off the north coast of Nias, where Tiny swam ashore near two empty huts. *Venture* was in a terrible state and there was a lot to be done, including sails to be sewn and the mast renewed. Tiny, Dickie and Gabby set to, chopping at the sizeable mast with blunt parangs. When the job was finished they found themselves too weak to lift and step it (even as Jennings and Hall would shortly do, somewhere to the south); but the forty-five-year-old Ernie was equal to this, constructing sheerlegs from spare spars. With this taking most of the weight the task was accomplished and by 16 April, after nine days on the island, *Venture* was ready to go to sea again, almost exactly a month out of Padang. But which way? All were agreed that the boat was no longer sufficiently seaworthy to tackle the remaining 1400 miles to India. A new plan of 'island hopping' was therefore adopted which would keep it within limping distance of land, i.e. parallel to the coast of Sumatra, across the 150 mile gap to the Nicobar Islands, a similar gap to the Andamans, a third to the nearest point of Burma, and if all went well, up the coast to the Indian border around Chittagong.

Venture sailed on with the usual alternate calms and blows. They were feeling the strain. A shrapnel wound in Lofty's side was troublesome; Lissy was coming out in sores; Snowy's malaria was no better; in fact all except Bosun and Tom were in poor shape. On top of which the weather began to deteriorate seriously. Passing Pulau Simaloe on the 18th, under the foresail only, the sea was rising. On the 20th it was estimated at thirty-five feet and wind force six. At 10 am on 21st tragedy came to *Venture*.

In Lofty's words:

As I was the only one with any sailing experience, I took over the
tiller for six hours while the storm was at its height, for the boat
was unwieldly at the best of times and had to be kept running
dead before the seas. The others took what shelter they could
and did their best to save the fresh water and keep the rice
dry. The Lord's Prayer was said more times by all of us then
than during the whole of our lives. The storm was the largest
experienced by any of the party and we all thought that we
would not come through it, for it raged unabated for two days.
Visibility was practically nil and we were continuously drenched
by the rain and flying spray. . . . All at once Bosun stood up
on the deck to reach some coconuts lying on the *tatti* roof and
a sudden wild surge of the boat caused him to lose his balance
and he was thrown overboard before anyone could reach him.
A desperate fight against terrific odds ensued in an endeavour
to pick him up from the raging sea. The sail was lowered as
quickly as our numbed hands and weakened bodies would allow
in order to slow down the boat, but the sea and wind still sped
us on. We got out the oars and endeavoured to bring the head
of the boat round into the wind; but once more the elements
proved too much for our frail craft and she was swamped by the
heavy seas and half filled with water. All hands had to bale to
make the boat seaworthy. Bosun was too far behind and he was
lost in the rolling sea.
  Doc, our mainstay and comforter throughout the whole trip,
said a short prayer for Bosun and we carried on into the unknown.

The bowsprit had carried away in the storm and the boat's hull
had opened up, so that those on watch had to spend the whole
time baling. 'All hands very tired and weak,' noted Dickie. 'The
present diet is insufficient but we do not increase it ($1/_2$lb rice
and two sardines and a pint of tea per day). Sergeant Beaumont
very weak. We still have one tin of milk for him.' Two nights
after Rawson's loss, poor Snowy Beaumont, only 21, died in the
early hours and was buried at sea.
  They kept on, along a chain of islands reckoned to be the
Nicobars, voting to give them a wide berth, even in the present reduced circumstances, as the Japs might well have got
there. Dickie complained to his diary that he could not get their

29. The Author in 1942,
on board the *Anglo-Canadian*

30. Captain Ivan Lyon, MBE,
future leader of commando
operations Jaywick and Rimau (in
which he lost his life) against
Japanese shipping in Singapore
harbour. Recommended for the
VC, he received a DSO

31. The *Krait* "served her purpose magnificently" (p.230)
and is now on permanent display in Sydney Harbour

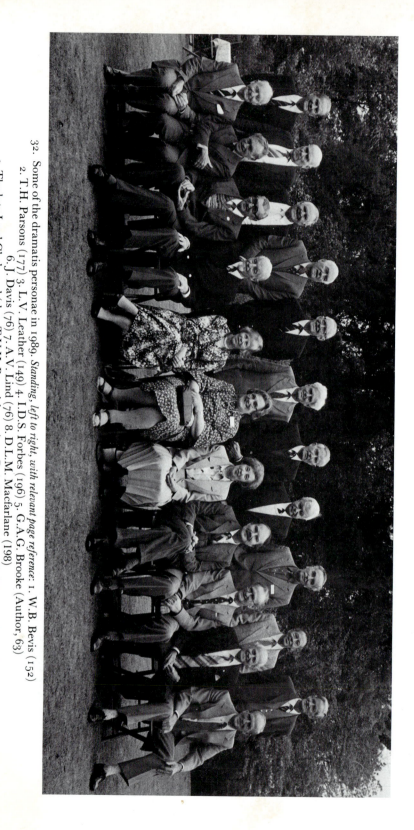

32. Some of the dramatis personae in 1989. *Standing, left to right, with relevant page reference:* 1. W.B. Bevis (152) 2. T.H. Parsons (177) 3. L.V. Leather (149) 4. I.D.S. Forbes (196) 5. G.A.G. Brooke (Author, 63) 6. J. Davis (76) 7. A.V. Lind (76) 8. D.L.M. Macfarlane (198) 9. The late Lord Chelwood (then T.V.H. Beamish, 115) 10. R.A. Fryer (165) 11. P. Whitworth (150)

Sitting: 1. I.W. Stone (205) 2. R.A.W. Pool (205) 3. C.G. Rogers (177) 4. V.C.F. Clarke (208) 5. Mrs. D. Apthorp (100) 6. Mrs. D.S. Lea (née Brown, 136) 7. Mrs. R.M. David (née Ross, 127) 8. C. Lyon (81) 9. J.B. Bradley (237) 10. A.R. North (109) 11. R. Tall (233)

track West of North, noting (he must have known more about sailing than Lofty credited him): 'Need centre-board badly' – meaning that the flat-bottomed boat made too much leeway. 'Dickie's navigation,' commented Gabby, 'was a simple matter but amazingly accurate as we were to find out when next we hit land.'

Lofty again:

> After being cooped up in such a small space we were all getting on one another's nerves and there were plenty of arguments and some near fights. Doc was the peacemaker in all our arguments. Water was continually sloshing up between the floorboards. . . . We had little covering and had to herd together for warmth and when one man turned over everyone had to.

Their morale was now low and this is not surprising. I would not have liked to have tried the trip with a crew of sailors who knew exactly what they were doing; the performance of this oddly assorted party, with an RAF navigator doing wonders, an MO clearly providing 'moral fibre', and all under a WO worth ten, was magnificent. Some of them were seasick and miserable and wished themselves back at Padang, even Singapore! All were weak from insufficient food and the deaths of two of their comrades did not help.

On 27 April one of the Andaman Islands had been left behind but some days after this Dickie was worried that there was no sign of the expected Burmese mainland and all, seriously concerned about the lack of food, agreed that if the northerly course did not bring results within two days, they would steer east and make a landfall anywhere, even if it was in enemy hands. However, the smoke of a convoy was seen on the horizon, followed by a small steamer that passed not far off and finally the water took on a brownish tint. They held a sweepstake on who would see land first. Titch won, discerning mountains in the haze – but on the port side. This did not deter Gabby: 'Three months of wandering were ended – we were safe! Tomorrow would see us with our friends . . . and who knows, in a few days we would be flown to England.' It could not be India but they hoped it might be Burma near Chittagong. The date was 13 May. The rest is sad, like nearly all these stories.

Venture kept along the coast for three days until coming to a village. After local Burmese had told them that they only had to sail 100 miles up the coast, past three towns, to be at Chittagong, they bought a pig, a goat and two chickens, all of which were polished off on the spot. Continuing next day past three villages they turned in at a bay where a large ship was at anchor off a distant town, presumed to be Chittagong. But nearer inshore a small vessel was noted with dismay to be Japanese. They went up a river and learnt from a boatman that it was the Salween and the distant town – Moulmein. As if to show disgust the *Venture* then ran aground and lost her entire rudder. To proceed without it was considered impossible and the party tore up the mainsail to make into food bundles for each man's overland march, it was thought of some few hundred miles. However, they were staggered by another Burman who told them it would take eighteen months as the Indian border was 1500 miles away!

The party was awaiting local guides (arranged by Tiny and Lissy who spoke the language) when these were seen approaching in company with Japanese soldiers. Gabby:

'The river!' said Ernie, 'Come on'. Ernie threw off his clothes. 'I'm off,' he said. 'Who's coming?' I think we all estimated chances in one brief moment, while Ernie hesitated. Then he turned to me. 'Come on, Gabby,' he pleaded. 'You and me.' But I shook my head and then he was gone.

'Put your hands up!' shouted the leading Jap officer, running towards us.

It had been seven and a half weeks and 1500 miles.

*   *   *

Up till now the reader has been bombarded with accounts of heroic endeavour but almost constant failure. So here, for a pleasant change, are three success stories.

'I'm old and tough and dirty and rough, said Barnacle Bill the sailor,' ran a song popular about five years before the war. I don't know about dirty and rough but otherwise it must have fitted that great Australian character, Captain William R. Reynolds, very well. Like Cunyngham-Brown, he turned up wherever he was wanted among the islands, saved 1519 people and got away safely to India at the last moment. Nor was this the end of his personal, lone-handed war against Nippon.

Colonel Dillon met him on the Indragiri:

> There I saw one of the final boatloads arriving in a Japanese fishing boat, owned and captained by an old Aussie in the tin ore-carrying trade in Malaya, and had a crew of two or three Chinese. He was a real old pirate and I had a most amusing talk with him . . . he was going to try and creep and bluff his way by the Malacca Straits to India. He offered me a place. . . . I was sorely tempted, but it could not be done. This old boy, (that is just what he was) had stuck to the rescue work among the islands with nothing to keep him there except his own humanity. Every day reduced his chances of getting away ultimately, as he well knew, practically to zero. I was never more pleased than when I heard the millionth chance came off and that he made it!

Reynolds treated me to a huge plate of nasi goreng in a café at Tembilahan and sent me with one of his crew to borrow the bathroom of a local Chinese. In mid-1943, Mrs C.G. Howell of the Malayan Research Bureau, was compiling records of missing people and narratives of events generally. Captain Reynolds sent her a list of the people he had come across and from that the following account of his doings (somewhat improbably written in the neatest handwriting I have ever seen) is taken.

After a lifetime at sea, Reynolds gravitated to commanding ships based on Hong Kong and so came to know the islands south of Singapore like the back of his hand. He came ashore in 1925, eventually to join up with the Royal Engineers, as an expert in demolition, soon after the Japanese landed. 'Blowing up dredgers, mining machinery, bridges, telephone exchanges,' just ahead of the enemy, he arrived in Singapore on 19 January to report on board the *Laburnum*. He asked to be allowed to put in order some thirty Japanese diesel fishing boats that had been confiscated, but no one wanted to know.

It was obvious on 10 February that Singapore was to be another Dunkirk so I took things into my own hands. Engaging some eight Chinese from a local boarding house, I took them to Telok Ayer, and, choosing the best of the erstwhile fishing boats, we worked day and night reconditioning her, scrounging fuel oil etc and at dusk on 11 February, had her ready for sea. She was a tiny thing, some seventy feet long, and rejoiced in the name of *Kohfuku Maru*. That night I wandered about Singapore buying up odd food stuff and at 10am, on the morning of 12 February, cast off and proceeded towards Blakang Mati, my intention being to take as many of our volunteers as possible, they being billeted at the Straits Trading Company's works. As we neared the strait some twenty Japanese bombers came over and plastered the area with high explosive so we shoved off hurriedly and scooted over close to St John's Island.

After hanging around for some time he sailed for Rhio, only to be placed under arrest by the Dutch. The next morning the place was bombed. Reynolds went ashore to offer his services, gratefully accepted, and left at dusk – it was now the 13th – towing the broken-down vessel *Silver Gull* with a total of 216 women and children (fifty on his own deck). Their destination was Rengat.

On arrival we were met by the Dutch Resident, Mijnheer von Brenkel, his secretary Mr Kaag, and sundry officials, who took charge of our refugees. In conversation we learned that a number of wounded were on the island of Pompong, some 160 miles from Rengat, so without any more ado we commandeered mattresses, blankets and foodstuff, and at 2 am set off downstream to pick them up . . . arriving at Pompong Island at 3 am on 19 February. At dawn we got busy and after a very difficult time took off some seventy-six people of whom nine were dreadfully injured, and full of gangrene. By great good fortune Sister Dowling was among those picked up and was, with the medicaments we had brought along, able to give the badly wounded some measure of comfort, and feed them. We shuffled back into the Indragiri river and so to the tiny piscine port of Tembilahan where there was a small Malay hospital. Here we were again lucky, for Lieutenant-Colonel Albert Coates of the 10th AGA had arrived with Sergeants Glancy and Hughes, their ship too having been bombed and sunk. As it was low water when we arrived we had a strenuous time getting our wounded on to the decking of the spidery jetty. That night, Coates did seven major operations alone, Sergeant Glancy acting as his anaesthetist, Sister Dowling being 'all in'. Two very stout lasses at this period were Sisters Brenda Lee (Mrs McDuff) and Patsy Brennan (Mrs Clark), both formerly of Batu Gajoh Hospital. . . . Immediately after we got rid of our people, we cast off and once more returned to Pompong. On this trip we picked up ninety-six people. . . .

Thereafter we shuffled back and forth to the islands of the outlying archipelago – the first eight days and nights we did not stop. In turn we visited Moro (Monkey) Island, Benku, Singkep, Pompong and Lingga, the Malay fishermen, by arrangement, bringing stragglers to those rendezvous where we picked them up. On 6 March we undertook an espionage trip, at the instance of the Dutch Resident, visiting in turn Tanjong Pinang, Tanjong Bali and Tanjong Batu. At the former we fought an action with a Japanese patrol vessel, finally chasing her into a small strait south of Rhio. Other than a peppering from their automatic arms we suffered no harm, and gave more than we received. We returned via the north part of the island of Singkep, it being too dangerous to go into Dabo. . . . Reluctantly we steamed away and returned to Rengat, gathering a number of men in small craft en route. On this passage my Chinese crew deserted at Tanjong Batu where there is a big Chinese community, leaving Messrs Alex A. Elliott and George Papworth, who had been with us from Singapore, together with myself to handle the ship. On arrival at Rengat we were given instructions to proceed to sea, lest we be captured, the Japanese then being some ten miles away, and coming from Djambi. After a sleep which we badly needed, we cast off, our objective this time being India. By dint of steaming by night, and hiding in creeks masked by mangroves, and fish traps by day, we slowly made our way westward through the Malacca Straits, visiting the ports of Bengkalis and Bagansiapiapi, en route.

On this stage of the journey we had picked up Madam Looi Pek Sye, a twenty-five-year-old Cantonese girl, with her three-year-old daughter Looi Laur Kwai (twin seasons) and a seventeen-year-old Malay boy, Saitaan bin Abdulhamid of Kuala Lumpur. The *nonya* cooked food when she was not too seasick, took the wheel whilst I got snatches of sleep, and was as good as two men. Her story is an epic of courage and fortitude from Ipoh to India via Sumatra and would make a best seller in any country. On 26 March we were off Diamond Point and from there shaped a course northward of the Nicobar Islands, and on reaching this point hauled away westward in the long run across the Bay of Bengal. At 3pm in the afternoon of 31 March we reached the land and shortly afterwards anchored in the roadstead of Negapatan – Madras Presidency – six miles south of the port, and twenty miles ahead of the reckoning. A pretty good feat considering we had no charts or instruments – a compass and a gigantic ego being their substitutes. Verily, we rested in the Shadow of Allah! From here on I suffered enough vicissitudes to drive me crazy, but they form no part of this story. Suffice is to say that I answered about a million questions, went hungry for two months, and finally took my vessel (now rejoicing in the name of *Suey Sin Fah* (Lotus Bloom) to Bombay and thence, pick-a-back on another vessel, to Australia.

Ivan Lyon had met Bill Reynolds up and down the Indragiri and the latter's epic escape to India was no doubt common knowledge when Ivan arrived in *Djohanis*. So it was a natural step to enlist the 'pirate' and his highly suitable Japanese fishing vessel for the projected raid on Singapore (see page 81). Reynolds set out for Australia but had to put back with engine trouble and was eventually transported there on the deck of a merchant ship. Re-engined, and re-named for the second time, the *Krait* served her purpose magnificently, but Ivan had decided to replace Bill Reynolds. Apparently he blamed him for much of the engine trouble. It was a hard decision to have to make after all Reynolds had proved himself capable of and the latter must have been bitterly disappointed. No doubt his age was against him too – he must have been in his sixties. Regrettably, it has to be recorded that this very brave old man did not survive his next exploit.

The surgeon, by then Sir Albert Coates, wrote after the war:

When Reynolds reached Australia, he called on my wife and informed her of my doings on the east coast of Sumatra. He became a member of the American Intelligence and Economic Services and was taken by submarine to Borneo, with the intention of contacting some Chinese agents on the island. Unfortunately he was captured and imprisoned in Santosa prison, Balikpapan, Borneo. He left scratches on the door of his cell until 10 February, 1944, when he indicated by printing on the door that he was being taken to Sourabaya, Java. He was a brave man who loved adventure and made the supreme sacrifice. I treasure his own short note to me and look back on his rescue work as a highlight in an otherwise depressing picture.

As a memorial to Bill Reynolds and all the brave men and women he was concerned with, *Krait* is now on permanent display in Sydney Harbour – see figure 31. He was awarded the MBE for his rescue work among the islands; not adequate, one might think.

*   *   *

Petty Officer G. L. White of the *Grasshopper* will be remembered for delivering two babies on Posik Island. When the assorted survivors left Singkep for Sumatra – most to be taken prisoner – he and two others elected to remain behind in the hopes of sailing a lone furrow, to 'marinize' a metaphor. One of these was Lieutenant (E.) Thompson RNVR of the *Kung Wo*, last heard of setting off from Benku Island – having given me his .22 rifle – with Cunyngham-Brown, hopefully to repair a motor boat (see page 56). The other was A. B. Leee. PO White's account of their doings is a gem of pen-pictures and humour.

The enemy were beginning to occupy all the islands and the Controleur of Dabo, always such a tower of strength, sent the trio, with RSM Lamport and Gunner Fixter who had joined them, to the out-of-the-way village of Penuba on Selajan Island. 'The women there were bare-breasted and pleasant to look upon, but all our thoughts were directed to our chances of survival.' These received an unexpected, lucky break in that natives from another island chose to raid Penuba and were beaten off with the help of the five Europeans; in return a Chinese dignitary gave them a boat twenty feet by eight feet. It had lain unused, the engine covered with rust, for a long time, but Thompson managed to get it working. In the course of this they were surprised by a Japanese officer and platoon who were touring the islands in a motor boat. He told them to stay put until he returned, at which they redoubled their efforts and, having been given five drums of diesel oil and sundry provisions, after heartfelt goodbyes were off. White, who was surprised that no one laughed at their proclaimed destination – India – wrote in his log '11 April, 1942

(nearly two months after the fall of Singapore): Weather good.
left Penuba. God be with us.' The first alarm was next morning
when a Jap plane buzzed them, flew away, returned and then
left for good, leaving their hearts working overtime. A patch on
the bows then began to leak, Lee broke out in boils and Gunner
Fixter announced that he wanted to be put ashore. No amount
of reasoning could dissuade him, so they ran up a small creek,
gave him a rifle and his proportion of the stores and watched him
disappear into the swampy jungle (to be taken prisoner and die
fifteen months later of beri beri).

Potential disaster then struck. 'As Thompson started the
engine he let loose a stream of words that would have turned
a Chief Stoker green with envy. A piece of the engine's control
gear had broken off, and it would now have to run continuously
night and day. No more stopping and starting.'

So they just ploughed on and on. It began to rain hard; no
bad thing as they topped up the water tank and, when two Jap
troopships appeared at anchor ahead, were able to slip by unseen.
A reconnaissance bomber then came down and inspected them
closely. 'I thanked God for our big straw hats as my bald head
was not sunburnt and would have shown up like a full moon,'
wrote White. The Sumatra coast faded away the next day, so
he altered course to the north-west. They were all very cheered
at being at last in the Indian Ocean 'with our bows pointed
directly (I hoped) at Madras'. Lee's boils were painful but he
only complained with a few choice words when they doctored
him. He and Thompson kept the engine running. Lamport and
White took turns at steering, by the sun during the day, by stars
at night. When neither were visible, 'I kept the sea running in
the same relative direction and hoped for the best.'

Sunday came round for the second time and White held 'hands
to prayers' and they sang 'For those in peril on the sea' – 'that
meant us'. Although they had little food the calls of nature still
had to be obeyed, over the stern – 'I always had the fear that
a shark or something would make a sudden snatch at what it
thought was dangling bait!' The sky became overcast, a fair
breeze blew and it became 'a bit rough'. They reckoned they

were safe from aircraft by now, though knew nothing of course of Admiral Nagamo and his carriers, which at that time were making hay in the area.

More worries loomed up, in four hours this time. Thompson fell ill with malaria and all they could do was make him lie down and keep warm. On the 13th day they suddenly saw a huge, half-submerged mass keeping pace with the boat off the port bow. A whale? A huge ray? With relief they watched it slowly disappear. Fuel was now low in the last drum and all the time White was privately worrying whether, without any sun, he was going round in a circle and heading back to Sumatra, or perhaps had missed India altogether.

Then at last they saw land. Nearer and nearer it came, Lee saying he'd kiss the little engine if it wasn't so hot. Surf broke on a beach where there were natives. It became very rough and as the boat turned over, they grabbed Thompson and struggled ashore. Surrounded by helping hands, all jabbering at once, they found one who could speak English and he sent a runner to the nearby Pulicat lighthouse. An Englishman picked them up in his car, took them to his house and in no time they were bathing, eating and then nestling contentedly between clean sheets. The Naval authorities were contacted and the adventure was over.

The target, Madras, was only twenty-six miles away after seventeen days, 2680 miles and not even a compass. A triumph of leadership against the odds.

*   *   *

A category of escapes which has not received any detailed treatment here is that of soldiers cut off in the retreat to Singapore Island who made their way directly to Sumatra around the time the city fell. Colonel Cumming vc and his Indians of the Frontier Force Regiment, Sergeant Gibson and other Argylls already referred to, and a Signalman Ball were among those who did this, as was Corporal Bob Tall of 287 Field Company RE, whose story is as outstanding a one of coolness, bravery and resource as one could wish for.

During the fighting near Batu Pahat in South Johore, in which the composite 'British Battalion' of the 18th Division were under heavy pressure from a division of the Japanese Imperial Guards, his unit was cut off and surrounded in the village of Sanggarang. After men from 2nd Battalion, the Cambridgeshires, had made many attacks on a strongly held road block without avail, the order was given 'every man for himself' – the Army's 'Abandon ship'. Trucks and equipment were rendered unserviceable and the remaining officers and men took to the jungle that fringed the road. Heading north-east, Tall, who had a compass, and three men joined up with a friend, Sergeant Large and a few others; taking it in turns to hack at the undergrowth, they made a wide detour – during which Tall collected the 'dog tags' (identity discs) of many British dead – aiming to strike the road again south of the enemy. Back on the road near Benut, moving along with groups on alternate sides, they rounded a corner to be confronted by another road block in the form of a felled tree. A large number of troops in full marching order were resting beside it, a machine gun covered the approach and there was an outlying sentry. It was hoped they were Indians – known to be in the vicinity – and telling the rest to give them covering fire if need be and taking a man who could speak Urdu, Tall and Large approached the sentry down the middle of the road. To their horror he turned out to be Japanese, but unabashed, Tall coolly gave him the Nazi salute and said something in German. Brought up as a keen wildfowler and small boat man in the Fens of East Anglia, he had been in the habit, as a boy, of shooting matchboxes from the hip with an air gun; he now had his rifle slung behind his shoulder, barrel down with a bullet 'up the spout' and the safety catch off. At this point there was shooting to one side and more Japanese poured out of two bungalows.

The sentry beckoned to him and turned towards the road block at which Tall, all in one movement, swung the rifle forward and fired, hitting him. The machine-gun opened up and blasted the pack off Tall's back. The gunner probably thought he had hit his target because he stopped firing, at which Tall, who had been knocked over but not hurt, shot him between the eyes. The gun started up again as the man slumped over it, whereat the Number 2 made to push the body off, but was shot as well for his pains.

Tall then pulled out three grenades and tossed them into the thoroughly aroused soldiers. Presumably most of them took cover for the few seconds before the explosions and Tall hurled himself into the thick jungle on the other side. As he did so a grenade was thrown at him – possibly one of his own – and he was hit in the leg by splinters. He also received a bayonet thrust in the hip, but by chance the point caught in a buckle of his equipment and so did not go deep. He hit the bayonet wielder in the eye with his rifle and also 'gave him the butt' for good measure. The Japs then came after him as one, but cleverly he had doubled back to hide in a mudhole just off the road. He lay still. Sometimes their boots nearly touched him, but he was not discovered. Sentries were posted along the road, but when darkness fell they were withdrawn and he was able to crawl, slowly and painfully, deep into the for once welcome jungle.

There had been no reaction from the rest of his party, who had also dived into the jungle (being captured later). Having seen Tall's pack disintegrate they thought he must be dead and reported the fact to the subsequent POW organisation, for him eventually to be listed as 'missing, presumed killed'. Encountering one of them after the war, the first thing he said was, 'Why the . . . didn't you give me covering fire?'

There ensued a five-day, eleven-mile trek to the coast, mostly crawling on account of his leg, during which he had nothing to eat or drink.

Once, on all fours, he almost ran into a black panther, when another early experience came to his aid; he remembered when working with a trainer of circus animals being similarly confronted by a lion. 'Stay still!' the trainer had yelled, and he froze now, the panther moving off without further ado.

Eventually he came to a creek where a small sampan was high and dry, but was too weak to launch it and lay down alongside in the mud to await the tide. A steamboat came past and he watched it towing boats full of enemy troops further up. Then to his horror two four-foot iguana lizards (which are carniverous, they will in fact eat anything) came to investigate, crawling over his back. I asked what it felt like. 'They were very cold,' he said. To add insult to injury, he was not only in a bad way, but had contracted malaria. The first tide did not come in far enough, though Tall tried putting stakes under the boat; however, he was successful at the next one and had the pleasure of washing himself clean of accumulated filth. Having made a sail from his shirt and shorts, he steered with the one oar and made fair progress along the coast towards Singapore, keeping about two miles offshore.

By now Tall was only conscious in fits and starts. He had two grenades left and threw them into the water to stun fish, but the only result was damage to the sampan. Sheltering under a thwart from the burning sun, he sailed on for about five days, now over eleven without food and five without drink (there had been brackish water in the bottom of the sampan when first found).

Then, as if in a dream, he was aware of an odd noise. The sampan had grated alongside a pagar. It was inhabited by two Chinese fishermen and, after winching him up onto its platform in a fish basket, they laid him down in the attap hut and, starting with sips of water, looked after him well for several days until he was partly recovered. By this time Singapore had fallen. A junk arrived to collect the fish. It was bound for Sampajan on a large Sumatran island about level with Singapore and they took him off, dressed in Chinese clothes and lying on the mound of fish into which he burrowed whenever a hostile plane came over. The trip took another three or four days and he was about the same time in Sampajan, where the Controleur was expecting the Japanese any moment and Tall's wounds were dressed at a native hospital. He said goodbye to his Chinese saviours – not a word of English had passed between them! – and was fortuitously enlisted by the local Chief of Police as an escort for some rich Chinese going to Benkarlis, up the coast. There he got to Pakanbaru – on a river north of the Indragiri – to fall in with two tough and 'trigger-happy' Australians. They couldn't drive, so when they stole a lorry, Tall drove them to Fort de Kock and then on to Padang, arriving just in time to embark in the destroyer *Encounter* as deck cargo for Batavia. By this time he had joined a party under Captain Sibley of his unit, 287 Field Company, which got to Bandoeng, then by lorry and train to Tjilatjap, whence they sailed for Colombo in the *Wu Chang*. As we know she had three torpedoes pass underneath her before arriving safely.

Thus, traumatic to the end, Bob Tall's solo escape ended as he was determined it should and as he so richly deserved.

*　　*　　*

This being a book about Singapore's Dunkirk, subsequent escapes are, strictly, outside its scope. But I feel it would not be right to omit any mention of the very brave escapes from prison camps. Very brave because to be recaptured, and the chances of success were minimal, invariably meant execution. I have come across three escapes (of six, ten and two individuals respectively) from Thailand/Burma railway camps, two from Singapore (of four and seventeen individuals), one from Rangoon (of one man) and one from Java (of four). There may well have been others. Of these forty-four, only four individuals were successful, one of whom was in fact recaptured after months free and another's escape took place almost at the end of the war.

Considering railway camps: six prisoners who got away from one in Thailand were summarily executed on recapture. On another occasion ten escapees from Sonkurai (also in Thailand) hacked their way through dense jungle for nearly six weeks, during which five of their number died. On reaching comparative civilisation the survivors had had nothing to eat for twenty-one days. They were then sold to the enemy by a Burman and sentenced to death. One of them, Lieutenant J. M. Bradley RE, has told how they were only spared by the intercessions of senior British officers – including Colonel Dillon – summoned to witness their execution, and by the fluent Japanese of Captain Cyril Wild, who reduced a certain Colonel Banno to tears by his eloquence. Though spared, the five were sent to Outram Road gaol, Singapore, where they were brutally tortured by the Kempeitai.

Corporal R. A. S. Pagani MM of the East Surreys, taken at

Padang, escaped from a Burma Railway camp near Thanbuyazat and, passing as an Indian, managed to join the legendary Major Seagrim and his Karen guerrillas. He operated successfully with these for four months, only to be betrayed, badly wounded after a skirmish. He pretended to be a shot-down pilot and got away with it, though also appallingly treated by the Kempeitai. Sergeant Denis Gavin of the *Venture* escaped from a column on the march in Burma, reporting to the advancing British Army near Pegu.

When one man escaped from Rangoon gaol (it is not known whether he was successful) the Japanese executed twenty prisoners in reprisal. Four men, including Colonel Dalley (of 'Dalforce', Malaya) and Leading Seaman T. H. Parsons of the *Li Wo*, escaped from Muntok (Banka Island). Betrayed in Java, they were returned unrecognised to a camp there, or would certainly have been executed. At Singapore, senior British officers were forced to witness the brutal execution of four recaptured escapees – two British and two Australian – from Bukit Timah camp. Also at Singapore, seventeen men escaped from Pasir Panjang, led by Flight Sergeant C. McCormac. Two were killed initially by guards, seven by a patrol unfortunately encountered and a further four by air attack on their boat next day. The remaining four were miraculously picked up by a Dutch flying boat and left in Sumatra, where one died and another married a native girl. The two left – McCormac and an Australian civilian called Donaldson – took six months of all too exciting adventures to contact an Allied underground organization in Java, whence they were picked up by an aircraft from Darwin.

When McCormac's erstwhile gaoler, who had enjoyed slashing his face with his sword point, was sentenced to death after the war, the sword was obtained through Admiral Mountbatten. It is thought relevant to end this particular list of escapes – if not others – with the last words of the (eventual) Squadron-Leader's account:

'The sword is locked away in a cupboard now, safe from the inquisitive fingers of our three children; but sometimes when I am alone I will take it out and think of things that cannot easily be forgotten.'

IX

Reflections

To round off, some random thoughts, prompted by the foregoing, may be in order.

Lazing on our tropical island was sometimes delightful; Vivian Bulwinkel remarked similarly on hers; Colonel Dillon would have liked to do the prauw trip again in peaceful circumstances, and Sergeant North was enraptured by the scenery gliding past the junk *Hiap Hin*. Even now I do not have to close my eyes to recall the feeling of unreality engendered by this unholy alliance of danger and beauty that was so often with us.

The enterprise, initiative and pure guts of the soldiers and airmen who literally launched themselves into the blue in boats of all sorts – there were sailors too but we were hardly stepping into the unknown – are enormously to be applauded. My only reservation is that some of them took 'where ignorance is bliss' unnecessarily far. Colonel Warren funded, I believe, eight small prauw or sailing kolek attempts; all failed for lack of nautical know-how of which there was plenty at hand; if only one or two of the regular sailors languishing at the Malay school had been invited each time, some unnecessary pitfalls might have been avoided.

I am conscious, with sadness – because of happy memories of Australia when based there at the end of the war – that Australian soldiers do not come too well out of the foregoing. But one must try and be factual when writing what is, after all, history. Sometimes they did so well in the campaign (also, by all accounts, in captivity) and sometimes so badly.

239

Perhaps incidents at Singapore, in one of which I was personally concerned, and another, of an unbelievably disgraceful character, that much affected me, have coloured my outlook. Against
these should be set a statement by one of my heroes, Brigadier
Iain Stewart: 'The 93rd* had met this fine unit before and in
the undignified "pot calling the kettle black" recriminations that
have at times occurred over Singapore, it is well to say that if
the 93rd had to choose a unit with which they would like to go
into battle, they would not look beyond the 2/29th Australians.'
And Field-Marshal Slim wrote, 'Some of us may forget that of all
the Allies it was Australian soldiers who first broke the spell of
the invincibility of the Japanese Army; those of us who were in
Burma have cause to remember.' In truth the Australians were
basically tough, brave and self-reliant; what a pity it was that
on certain occasions these qualities went to waste.

It was said in the introduction that this was not just a story of
horrors but of heroism and self-sacrifice, on the part of doctors
and nurses as much as anyone else. All the latter – mostly
Australian – were heroines as far as I can see. Further, it has
cropped up several times here that the experiences related were
nothing to what followed in the prison camps. These caused some
mental breakdowns, but it seems comparatively few, physical
tolls being the killers. The vast majority who came through
have proved remarkably resilient, the more surprising because
not many had any experience – previous to Singapore – of
modern war. They stood up to the sudden and continuing horror remarkably well and I fear there is a moral in this for us
today.

A correspondent to a local paper wrote recently:

I learn that of the servicemen involved in the Falkland Islands
campaign, one in eight suffered trauma and mental illness. This
campaign lasted only twelve weeks. As a veteran of XIV Army
in Burma from the siege of Imphal to Rangoon, including the
bitter fighting at Meiktila, I find this puzzling. I was aware of no

---

* Argyll and Sutherland Highlanders.

colleagues suffering from the effects described after a campaign lasting nearly four years.

We felt privileged under (then) General Sir William Slim to help defeat the Japanese armies that had taken Malaya and Singapore. Is training at fault or are we a different people?

This letter generated a spate of indignant replies, all outraged at such a viewpoint, from which one can only conclude that indeed we are a different people. The media are somewhat to blame; forty-five years of peace, except for comparatively minor campaigns, having inevitably bred journalists and broadcasters of breathtaking ignorance (anyone who has fired a shot in anger is a veteran and casualties are horrendous if they reach double figures). I have no wish to belittle our men of all three services who did supremely well in the South Atlantic, but total British casualties in the 3-month campaign were only 257 and if one in eight do have psychological problems it would seem that the outlook for any future conventional conflict is not good, as I doubt whether our likely enemies suffer from similar softness.

I am no 'Bible-thumper' but wonder whether the lack of any spiritual strength to fall back on, following the rejection of religion that is prevalent nowadays, has a bearing on the matter. There are several references to praying for help in these pages; even if it makes one smile, Petty Officer White holding 'church' in the middle of the Indian Ocean must have given his comrades a boost and the heartfelt plea of Jennings and Hall was certainly answered dramatically! It seems a pity that many a modern youth has denied himself, or been denied, this useful standby.

It is extraordinary how the human spirit can come up with an antidote to impending disaster, as if it were shielding the outer man from the full effects. Personally I never really came that close to disaster, but did experience a sort of mental blackout regarding thoughts of surrender at Singapore and, when stuck on our desert island, never lost the belief that all would be well in the end. Sjovald Cunyngham-Brown, when taken prisoner and told he would be shot, experienced a peaceful numbing of the senses and general relief that there would be no more struggle for weary body and mind. Similarly, Dickie Pool, lined up at the guardrail of ML 311 actually facing a Japanese firing squad, has told of 'a sort of mental and physical sickness (that) stifled all thought, except that in the next second everything would be over. The feeling of helplessness was so great that there was no question of fear'. It seems that conditions have to be pretty bad for this phenomenon to develop, happily not often in peacetime.

There is another and much pleasanter outcome of war which most of those concerned have enjoyed and that is the sense of comradeship that lasts. Lord Harewood – captured in Italy – once said, 'You never really know a man until you have been a prisoner with him,' and, if it is not presumptuous of me, who avoided capture by the greatest good fortune, to comment on those not so lucky, the point was well made by Sister Jessie Simons of the *Vyner Brooke*, in her book *While History Passed* – 'Looking back over those years I find that in many ways I do not regret the experience. I learnt the meaning of comradeship. There is an indefinable bond among those who have lived and suffered together.' Perhaps it is not surprising that FEPOWs are still a close-knit brother- and sisterhood after more than forty years.

The lack of bitterness against the Japanese on the part of the majority of FEPOWs has always seemed to me a remarkably Christian attitude. On 'VJ' day, my ship, the carrier *Formidable*, was about 250 miles off Tokyo and we were soon repatriating Australian ex-prisoners. Most were skeletons and many were very ill with up to three deficiency-originated diseases, but we were all surprised and somewhat uplifted to note the 'Forgive them for they knew not what they did' attitude on the part of most; and when the War Crime trials got under way the investigators in many cases found it difficult to get FEPOWs to make positive complaints against the Japanese ('often they made excuses for their captors' according to Captain Dick Storry). Those I have spoken to since usually say they were and are only too happy to forget the Japanese and all their works, the common attitude being one of contempt rather than anything else. In spite of all this I do feel that, though many perpetrators of atrocities paid due penalty after the war, the Japanese nation as a whole was not made sufficiently aware of the enormity of the crimes of its soldiers.

'Soldiers' is intentional because the Japanese Navy did invariably behave well. They were of course trained originally by the Royal Navy (the Japanese Army was trained by the Germans) and kept the connection going until the early thirties, being anxious to and apparently successful in fostering the traditions of the Silent Service. Margot Turner's doctor, the officers of the *Asigara* and of the tanker that captured the prauw *Setia Berganti*, others (not recorded) who picked up Sjovald Cunyngham-Brown after the loss of the *Van de Warveijk*, and forbearance in dealing with the *Mata Hari* and *Giang Bee*, are examples.

I myself have found the Japanese a complete enigma, compounded by the fact that, having been sunk twice by them and otherwise incommoded, I was sent to Japan (during the Korean War) for eighteen months, expecting to hate their guts; in fact I was won over and came to like them, if not unreservedly, very much. Of course at the time butter wouldn't melt in their mouths – Japan being still under occupation – but I had forty working for me, from junior ex-officers to peasants, with good opportunities to get to know them in the time available. However, it is said that no Westerner can hope to fully understand the Japanese with less than a life-time's study, since Western logic and ethics are irrelevant to the matter. A telling reply was given by a French woman married to an aristocratic Japanese when asked if she really understood him. 'We get on extremely well,' she said, 'except that every now and then his mind slips back a thousand years.' In 1942 the Japanese were only eighty-seven years out of the Middle Ages, and perhaps it is understandable that in that time they could learn to make aeroplanes, tanks and torpedoes (the latter far better than anyone else's!) but not to make themselves into humane people. Of course one must not give the impression that every Japanese soldier was a devil, but it is a fact that most were intrinsically sadistic. To such mentalities it was perhaps inevitable that they should torture prisoners in order to extract information, but when someone was lying waiting for a dressing, and a Japanese soldier came up and 'ground his heel into the man's wound' one wonders what sort of animal could do such a thing. The Kempeitai, the Japanese secret police, were unspeakable and apparently answerable to no one; it was right that many paid for it with their lives after the war.

The recent disagreements about sending Prince Philip to represent the Queen at Emperor Hirohito's funeral seem to have been clearly divided between those who had been his wartime guests and those who had not. Possibly the latter, even though a huge majority, should have deferred to the former.

The relevance of this today is 'Have they changed?' I had organized a cricket match between two of our Korean War ships and the spectators were joined by three little Jap cherubs of about five with their shiny round heads and large black eyes. 'Aren't they sweet?' said someone. 'Don't you believe it,' rejoined a hoary old Chief Petty Officer, 'the little buggers'll be cuttin' our heads off in twenty years time!' They may not be cutting our heads off but they are successfully cutting our economic throats. Friends who deal intimately with the Japanese say that, though basically honest, they are still inscrutable and curiously emotional in unexpected ways (in the tradition, presumably of Jim Bradley's Colonel Banno, who was reduced to tears.) It is a strange world. They are now being encouraged to rearm in defence of the Pacific area. On the credit side, they are certainly magnificent fighters and it is nice to think they should be on our side next time.

It must be admitted that the Malays were occasionally doubtful in their loyalty, by which is meant that most were loyal but some not, usually depending on the proximity of the enemy, whereas the Chinese were invariably on our side. Of course their homeland had been suffering the ravages of a Japanese invasion for several years and to them war in Malaya and the Dutch East Indies (Indonesia) was but an extension of the struggle. Many Chinese risked and some lost their lives to help Europeans, particularly soldiers cut off in Malaya and one wonders whether they were properly rewarded after the war. The attitude of Javanese and Sumatran natives was much more often hostile (except, it seems, fishermen on offshore islands).

The Dutch had in fact been experiencing considerable political unrest, exploited to advantage by the Japanese until their ruthless behaviour proved counter-productive. Considering that the Dutch had integrated much more closely than the British with the local population, often for instance, intermarrying, it is surprising that the latter were so hostile. Presumably the British 'loose-rein' style of colonial rule was more successful than the Hollanders' tighter control.

In this connection I think the lie – so often appearing in books written soon after the war by unfortunates who had only been in Malaya a short time – about 'whisky-swilling planters' who continued to dance at Raffles Hotel has long been nailed. I described in an early chapter the difficulties of the civil administration in the face of the enemy's high-speed advance, in particular the necessity to maintain *sang froid* in front of Asiatics. Some civilians may well have danced (as their counterparts did in London) but only when off duty from the voluntary jobs that virtually all took on. A relevant parallel is that the officers of at least one destroyer changed into mess kit every evening of their non-stop week in and out of Boulogne, a lesser known but equally dramatic evacuation as Dunkirk. A colonel rescued by them said that a glance at their bow ties did more for him than anything else!

Another silly legend that dies hard is that all the big guns at Singapore were facing seawards and would not fire inland. The necessity had not been anticipated but most could and did fire inland, though some of their ammunition, being naval armour-piercing, buried itself very deep before exploding. Several accounts in this book tell of the shells flying over the harbour and there is at the Imperial War Museum an interesting article by the CO 9th Heavy Regiment, RA – Colonel H. D. St G. Cardew – who, after detailing the guns' many targets, says, 'I saw one of the 9.2 inch batteries a short time after the capitulation and I noticed that the bores were almost smooth from incessant landwards firing and their detachments exhausted.'

I have never understood why all concerned talked about 'Fortress Singapore'. In another book I described how, on the first day ashore from HMS *Prince of Wales*, some of us from the Gunroom took a taxi down the length of the island to the city and were astonished to see not one single sign of any fortifications. Even then of course there was time to build some defences, but that was one of the unfortunate General Percival's two main omissions and another story. Churchill, for some unknown reason, was under the impression that Singapore was an impregnable fortress; Percival in his book *The War in Malaya* repeatedly alludes to 'The Fortress' and even in 1976 Cyril Connolly in the *Sunday Times* was comparing Fortress Singapore with the Maginot Line. If it was an agreed ploy at the time to hoodwink the Japanese, our Intelligence must have been even worse than it was revealed to be. The future enemy had spies all over Malaya, many being serving officers and General Yamashita knew everything, even to the extent of declining the fourth division that was offered him, as not being necessary.

The whole, bad business, the climax of which was the greatest disaster ever to befall British arms, and even greater in its blow to British influence in the Far East, had its foundations in successive governments failing to provide for the adequate defence of Singapore. This they dared not do in the face of a pacifist peacetime electorate. The motto of the Royal Naval Gunnery School 'Si vis pacem para bellum' (If you want peace prepare for war) was to the latter but a collection of dirty words and so all the trials, tribulations and deaths that made up Singapore's Dunkirk followed as night follows day.

Colonel Cardew, who was taken prisoner, ended his article with an impassioned plea that should be framed on every MP's desk and posted to CND supporters and other 'pacifist at any price' gentry once a month. 'In future,' he wrote 'let us hope that we shall remain strong enough . . . to ensure that these things will not happen again. Let us have the right weapons in the right place, at the right time, and above all, let us not underestimate the power and strength of the enemy.'

Amen.

Bibliography

The following books have been quoted from:

Apthorpe, D., *British Sumatra Battalion*, The Book Guild
Gavin, D., *Quiet Jungle, Angry Sea*, Lennard Publishing
Brooke, G., *Alarm Starboard!*, Patrick Stephens
Coates, A. and Rosenthal N., *The Albert Coates Story*, Hyland House (Australia)
Gibson, W., *The Boat*, W. H. Allen & Co
Gilmour, O., *Singapore to Freedom*, Burrow
Jeffrey, B., *White Coolies*, Angus and Robertson (Australia)
Jennings, M., *An Ocean without Shores*, Hodder and Stoughton
Larkins, J., *A Tribute to Australian Women*, Rigby (Australia)
McCormack, C., *You'll die in Singapore*, Morley Books
Percival, A., *The War in Malaya*, Eyre and Spottiswoode
Rivett, R., *Behind Bamboo*, Mrs J. Rivett
Smythe, J., *The Will to Live*, Lady Smythe
Varley, E., *The Judy Story*, Souvenir Press

Others of much assistance were:

Barber, N., *Sinister Twilight*, Collins
Bradley, J., *Towards the Setting Sun*, Privately
Cunyngham-Brown, H., *Crowded Hour*, Mackay
Gordon, E., *Miracle on the River Kwai*, Collins
Hartley, P., *Escape to Captivity*, Dent
Hamond, R., *The Flame of Freedom*, Leo Cooper
Holmes, R. and Kemp, A., *The Bitter End*, Bird
Hough, R., *Escape from Singapore*, Kimber
Jeffrey, B., *While History Passed*, Heinemann
Lim, J., *Sold for Silver*, Collins
McKie, R., *The Heroes* Angus and Robertson (Australia)
Montgomery, B., *Shenton of Singapore*, Leo Cooper

Nelson, D., *The Story of Changi*, Changi (Australia)
Pool, R., *Course for Disaster*, Leo Cooper
Rose, A., *Who Dies Fighting*, Cape
Saunders, H., *Valiant Voyaging*, Faber
Simons, J., *While History Passed*, Heinemann, London
Simson, I., *Singapore, Too Little Too Late*, Leo Cooper
Skidmore, I., *Marines Don't Hold their Horses*, Allen
Stewart, A., *Let's Get Cracking*, Johnson (Sydney)
Stewart, I., *History of the 2nd Battalion Argyll & Sutherland Highlanders*,
    Nelson
Storry, E., *Second Country*, P. Norbury Pubns
Woodburn-Kirby, S., *Singapore: the Chain of Disaster*, Cassell

Index

249